Marriages and Other Dilemmas

Collected Stories and a Memoir

Kitty Beer

Plain View Press
1101 W. 34th Street, STE 404

http://plainviewpress.net
Austin, TX 78705

Copyright © Kitty Beer, 2022. All rights reserved under International and Pan-American Copyright Conventions. No part of this book may be reproduced or distributed in any form or by any means, or stored in a database or retrieval system, without written permission from the author. All rights, including electronic, are reserved by the author and publisher.

ISBN: 978-1-63210-096-2
Library of Congress Control Number: 2021922458

Cover art: Woman in All Her Glory by Chris Neiman, Neiman Art, https://neimanart.com
Cover design by Pam Knight

We Find Healing In Existing Reality
Plain View Press is a 45-year-old issue-based literary publishing house. Our books result from artistic collaboration between writers, artists, and editors. Over the years we have become a far-flung community of activists whose energies bring humanitarian enlightenment and hope to individuals and communities grappling with the major issues of our time—peace, justice, the environment, education and gender. This is a humane and highly creative group of people committed to art and social change. The poems, stories, essays, non-fiction explorations of major issues are significant evidence that despite the relentless violence of our time, there is hope and there is art to show the human face of it.

*to my sister Frances,
whose warm heart and brilliant mind
have guided me through the years*

Contents

The Old Lies Are the Truth	7
Family Values	17
Amy's Arm	25
What's Going On?	35
Mrs. Professor Bostwick	43
One Two Three Cry	51
I'm Dolores	61
Imagining	65
If Fish Could Cry	73
Sally Lawton	81
The Difference	91
Snapshots	99
The Voyage	103
Choices	113
Dark Matter Mansion	123
Crescendo	135
All of It: Memoir	**175**
Foreword	177
1 Childhood	179
2 Sixteen	189
3 Harvard	195
4 New York	201
5 Montreal	205
6 Munich	207
7 Geneva, New York	211
8 Ithaca, New York	215
9 New World	223
10 Haskell Street	225
About the Author	**227**

The Old Lies Are the Truth

She hadn't reckoned on Gemma.

It was so smooth and sweet for Grace, the years mistressing Harry, then when his wife finally had to go to a nursing home, their coming together easily, the long-deserved reward. She figured her struggles were over. But she hadn't reckoned on Gemma.

Gemma was Harry's middle-aged daughter, a big boned, big lipped, hearty voiced woman who could be called handsome if your taste ran that way. It's important to note that Grace was sixty-eight when the affair started, Harry three years older, so they were no spring chickens and they had paid their dues plenty in many ways before the day they even met. Well, met for the second time, that is, because they'd known each other in college, briefly, dating other people. Harry remembered the color of Grace's hair, "autumn gold," he called it. No, she hadn't let it go grey, but by then it looked more like bleached blonde (which it was).

Oh it was lovely that evening they met again, at an alumni event. Harry's wife Tessie was already pretty badly off. She was in a wheelchair and not too aware of her surroundings. Harry and Grace were very solicitous, bringing her goodies she hardly touched, and re-filling her glass of ginger ale. And in the meantime they danced, oh yes, to old tunes they both loved, getting out of breath and laughing, and snuggling a little even at that early date. She'd been a widow for five years already, and knew she still liked sex. Harry turned her on, and she told him so.

He was in her bedroom three days later. He and Tessie only lived a dozen miles away, in the next town. It was a perfect setup. They were both retired, of course, with flexible time. Harry got so he liked to drop by a couple of times a week in the afternoon around four. They called it their Tea Time, but they spent a lot of it in bed, at least at first. Luckily he was able to take Viagra, so that was great, but sometimes they just skipped it and invented new substitutes. Not to get too graphic, one was called "submarine."

Harry took good care of Tessie. He didn't move her to the nursing home until her doctor insisted on it. Up to then, he fed and bathed her himself, with the help of a healthcare aide who came in every day. Harry was a retired executive, so money was no problem. In short, he and Grace never felt guilty about Tessie; she had no idea her husband had a girlfriend and possibly wouldn't have cared if she did. And Grace made him so happy he was a better partner for her, returning home all aglow and affectionate.

So that went on for a couple of years. Then after Tessie had to go to the nursing home, Harry started staying overnight, and pretty soon they were practically living together. They decided on Grace's little condo in mid-Cambridge, near public transportation and easy shopping. He was gradually moving out of his big Arlington house and had just put it on the market, when Gemma turned up.

Harry and Grace were making one of their frequent trips to his house to choose stuff they wanted to keep. It was a lovely October day, sparkling with sun and just crisp enough for sweaters. The maples in his front yard were loud red. Grace stooped to pick up a pot of marigolds, exclaiming, "Let's keep this!" when the door opened before they got up the steps.

"Hello, Dad."

They were the most ominous words Grace had ever heard. The tone was flat and the words bespoke total possession.

"Baby!" cried Harry, all thrilled and throwing his arms around the woman.

Why was this child turning up now, Grace wondered. Gemma lived in Germany though long divorced from her German husband. Grace had heard many stories about her as a darling little girl and vivacious teenager, but she'd frankly never imagined having to deal with an adult version. Still, she tried to be welcoming and gracious—not that either of them noticed, they were so wrapped up in each other. They left Grace on the steps and went into the house jabbering together.

Grace kept standing there, unconsciously holding that pot of flowers, tears threatening, until Harry came rushing back all apology, and dragged her in, yelling, "Gemma sweetie pie, come meet my best friend, you're going to just love each other," and there she was face to face with this big boned beauty smiling only with her huge red mouth, her eyes ice. Grace was immediately and acutely aware that to the child this was her mother's house, and this man her mother's husband. All of which was only too true.

The living room felt different and Grace soon figured out that Gemma had moved everything back to where it was originally. For example, Grace had moved the small lamp to the sofa and replaced the coffee table with foot cushions, just to make it more cozy on the few occasions she and Harry spent time there. There were new smells, a waft of fresh gingerbread. A vase of flowers glowed on the reinstated coffee table. Gemma did not have to announce that she'd moved in. Harry was so happy he asked only one question, "Why didn't you tell us you were coming?"

Gemma didn't wince at the "us." But she pretty much ignored Grace except to emphasize her visitor status by elaborately offering coffee.

"No, no Dad," Gemma breathed, "because I didn't want you to bother with anything. I came as quick as I could, to help you out. How's Mom?"

"She's great, she's doing real well. She's made some friends, she loves the doctor. They give her exercises every day, they give her puzzles to help with her memory, and boy do they feed her, feed her very well."

Grace could tell Harry was falling all over himself to convey his concern. She knew very well that he'd been mostly relieved not to have to deal with nearly comatose Tessie all day long. Listening to the two of them, Grace felt an outsider, miles away, an observer from a different realm where she wasn't welcome or even recognized as the same species. She had put the marigolds on a side table, but Gemma didn't take long to remove them, out of sight somewhere.

They all sat drinking coffee and nibbling on gingerbread. Harry did not tell Gemma he was putting the house on the market, and Grace kissed that project goodbye. She was in a state of shock. She'd been so thoroughly supplanted she no longer knew who she was. Harry hardly referred at all to his life with her, and she began to even doubt they'd be going to Bermuda for Christmas as they'd so joyfully planned.

"I'm going to make your favorite dinner tonight, Dad. Lamb chops and…"

"Don't tell me," cried Harry excitedly, "and mashed potatoes with applesauce. Lamb chops and…"

"Mashed potatoes with applesauce."

Father and daughter fell back in their seats in spasms of intimate laughter.

When Harry was finally driving Grace home, she waited through his delighted exclamations until he calmed down. Then she said very quietly, "I take it we won't be having dinner together tonight."

2

As soon as she learned her mother had to go to the nursing home, Gemma knew Grace would be trouble. First of all, her father informed her by email instead of calling. Matter of fact, he hadn't called for weeks. He rarely mentioned Grace, but that didn't keep Gemma from filling in the blanks and building up a crisis. Clearly, with her poor mother stashed away out of sight, this pushy, wily woman was taking over her father's life

Two things kept her from getting on a plane. One was her job, her toady secretary service to the chairman of the English Department at Munich's university. The Herr Professor Doktor vastly needed her language expertise, but he never acknowledged it. She wasn't even paid well. But when she'd taken the job eight years earlier in the throes of newly single fears, she'd been glowingly grateful. So, even though she felt safer now in the world, somehow she simply stayed. She liked her colleagues and the view from her desk of Schwabing's cafés and tree-lined boulevard.

The other factor keeping her from rushing to save her parents was her son, Stefan. Though twenty-five and teaching at the Technische Hochschule, he still lived at home and depended on her for meals and laundry. This was ok with Gemma. She adored him and liked the company. She also was gratified that he hadn't moved to Berlin to be near his renegade father. It was a small but gratifyingly galling victory in the sea of her previous humiliations at the hands of her former husband.

But with the autumn mists came an implacable nostalgia for Cambridge, its sudden sharp ocean smell, violent fall colors and navy blue sky, brick sidewalks, bookstores on every corner. She hadn't been home for years, she hadn't called it home for years. At the same time, the Herr Professor Doktor had to go to London for a conference, so she was able to persuade him to simply close the office for a week. Stefan hardly heard her when she announced her plans; he had a new girlfriend who was giving him ultimatums of some kind. Gemma worried that he'd eat only *wurst* and *sauerkraut* but she stocked up on vegetables and fruits and hoped he'd be tempted.

On the plane, Gemma began to feel empowered. First of all, she was pleased that the night before she had allowed her boyfriend to have sex with her on the kitchen table. He was always pestering her for ridiculous, embarrassing venues like that and she was always refusing, so this concession made him drivel with gratitude. Franz was getting more and more difficult to please; they'd been dating for three years now, and she figured his infatuation was fading. But she had a few tricks still up her sleeve. She liked Franz. He was far too good looking and far too attentive to other women, but she enjoyed the way he kissed her all over. He was a good lover.

In addition, Stefan actually thanked her for the healthy food she'd left for him. He noticed what she had done, appreciated it, and told her so. All of which was novelty. He was growing up at last! And best of all, she was going to rescue her father, without giving him the opportunity to prepare any defenses. She would re-instate her mother in her rightful place, if not in her own home, at least in Harry's heart.

Gemma knew she looked good in her new violet wool suit with the pearl buttons, a color that flattered her dark hair and olive complexion. She'd carefully chosen a lipstick just a shade lighter—she always made a point of emphasizing her generous mouth. She'd long since learned what a draw it was for men, and rather dazzled women as well. Her smile had got her out of more scrapes that she could count.

Gemma had hardly been home for ten hours, mostly spent asleep conquering jet lag, when she heard the car in the driveway and knew the time had come. The first confrontation went very well. Thank goodness she'd already put gingerbread in the oven. Over coffee she frankly examined the competition and felt fairly secure in her goal. The woman was pretty for an old lady, although the blond hair was a bit much, but she was lumpy in the waist, rounded in the shoulders, and droopy in the chin. She was awfully quiet too, lacking the cheery energy that had been typical of Tessie. Of course, Gemma hadn't seen her mother for years, and on the phone the last time they talked she was barely articulate, so she knew old age was taking its toll. She broached going to visit Mom almost at once.

"Sure, baby," her father readily agreed. "We'll go over there tomorrow. I visit every week."

Once a week! The institution was only two hours drive away. This Grace person really had her talons into the man. Gemma tried hard to seem friendly to her, but the woman was clearly not convinced. Grace positively trembled, when she wasn't on the verge of tears. She kept looking at Harry, as if he'd back her up, but of course he never did. He was in his little girl's thrall, well and good.

"You'll have to be prepared, though," Harry was telling her gently. "She might not recognize you right away."

"You mean I've changed that much?"

"Oh, no, baby, you're as adorable as ever. You don't look a day over thirty. I mean, her mind wanders. She lives in the past a lot."

"Why won't they let you bring her home?"

"Oh, baby, believe me, I tried to convince them. But she needs twenty-four hour care. She can't be left alone for a minute."

"Maybe we could bring her home for a little visit while I'm here," suggested Gemma cozily. "Wouldn't that be lovely?"

She noticed with satisfaction the clattering of coffee cup on saucer as Grace's hand shook in response to this salvo.

When Franz called Gemma, she obliged him by recounting every detail of their kitchen coupling. He was already talking about what they would do when she got home the following Sunday. He seemed to have in mind some absurd plan for the bathtub. But Gemma's mind was elsewhere, plotting a final coup.

3

Grace spent a lonely evening. Before she fell in love with Harry, she'd usually enjoyed her evenings home alone, cooking a simple dinner, watching a bit of TV, calling a friend, reading a favorite book. Her little living room exactly suited her, old furniture accumulated over the years, nostalgic and comfortable. A sweet view onto her quiet street, the weeping willow in her front yard dangling yellow tresses over the last of her autumn daisies. On the mantelpiece were lined up recent birthday cards from her children and her brother in Michigan, and photos of her and Harry on their last excursion to

Cape Cod. Harry was wearing a Red Sox cap, grinning like a kid, both his arms around her.

He didn't even call. Everything seemed so empty without him. She began to feel he was lost to her, and that her heart would break.

Grace's friend Lydia said she should give him an ultimatum. That sounded too drastic, especially since it had a good chance of backfiring. But after going out to the movies with Lydia the next evening she felt better, and decided to step up her volunteer work at the nearby grade school. It all was a bit like the mourning she'd gone through when her husband died, the stages of grief you might say. Lydia forbade her to call Harry, and that she was able to do. She even stopped staring longingly at the phone.

What had she been doing in April that year when they met? As far as she remembered, she'd been perfectly content. Why couldn't she just go back to that life? But her heart ached so, and she couldn't get his image out of her head, and she kept re-imagining his touch and his laugh and his quirky endearing habits like pouring milk in the bowl before his cereal. She gave up trying to explain her pain to Lydia. It was an old acquaintance she ran into in Harvard Square who gave her the best advice.

"Don't try to compete with his child," the woman said. "I had a boyfriend once who got divorced and had to give up his kids. He was a mess. Work with the girl. Make it work."

Grace stood there on the corner looking after her, mouth open. Of course. If she wanted her man back, she'd have to embrace the daughter he loved. Could she do it? Gemma was formidable and hated her guts. Nevertheless, this was an idea that had a glow of hope to it.

Grace would probably have got up the courage to call and invite them both to dinner, but fortunately she didn't have to face that ordeal. When she got home, Harry was sitting in her living room.

He gave her a hug and a kiss before either of them said anything. "It's been four days," he whispered in her ear.

"I missed you."

"Is it Tea Time?"

"It could be."

"Forgive me?"

"I love you."

"I don't know what to do."

"We'll make it work," she promised.

4

After Harry and Gemma went to visit Tessie, Gemma broke down.

"Oh my God, Dad, Mom's a wreck, why didn't you tell me? She doesn't know who I am, she can't put two sentences together, she asks the same questions over and over. She's like an idiot. What happened to her?"

Harry patiently explained, throughout the rest of the day and the next, everything he knew. He had a hard time convincing his daughter that he and Grace didn't have something to do with it.

Gemma refused calls from Franz and even forgot to put on lipstick. She insisted on keeping the drapes and shades pulled, shutting out brilliant fall sunshine. Harry went outside to rake leaves, but it didn't make him feel much better. The place was like a funeral home, all about sickness and loss and sorrow. Worst of all, he felt that somehow this tragedy was all his fault. It was unforgiveable that he'd been having such a happy time when the rest of his family was so miserable. He kept apologizing. But at least Gemma dropped her proposal to bring Mom home.

Gemma was due to leave for Munich Saturday night, but she called her office and got an extension. She didn't tell her father that she could lose her job as a consequence. She didn't care. When she called Stefan, she could tell that his girlfriend was living there with him, and she didn't care about that either. All she wanted was to make her father as miserable as she imagined her mother was. It was only fair.

The three of them finally had dinner together on Friday. Gemma had had a fit when she learned Harry went to visit Grace. She even got an inkling that they may have been having sex, which absolutely outraged her. She barely resisted phoning the wanton and giving her a piece of her mind. Instead, she went with Harry to Grace's house.

Dusk was falling at six o'clock, but the air was clear and warm. The weeping willow in Grace's yard was still yellow with leaves, still caressing the white daisies drooping a bit from morning rain. On Grace's front porch stood two comfortable looking lawn chairs, close together. Gemma came prepared to suffer, and she did.

Grace's house was everything her mother's wasn't—shabby, colorful, intimate, and undignified. None of the pictures on the walls were by famous people. Lots of shoddy watercolors by friends of hers instead. Photos of her relatives and of Harry everywhere. Gemma was infuriated at Grace's efforts to be nice. The woman was falling all over herself pretending kindness and concern. To boot, she was wearing a silly frilly apron with red lace trim. Imagine! An old lady trying to be cute!

Halfway through hors d'oeuvres, Gemma's throat closed with gall so bitter she could hardly swallow. They were talking about her childhood and Harry was recounting a favorite tale of his about how he taught her to ride a two-wheeler. He was beginning to relax and enjoy himself, two glasses of wine already under his belt and obviously relishing the stuffed mushrooms. Grace, sitting opposite him but adoringly leaning into his space, was smiling encouragement and pride. Did they know, Gemma asked herself, what fools they were making of themselves?

All at once, Gemma found herself exclaiming, "No, no it wasn't like that at all. That's what you always say, and it's not true. Mom made you come out and help me up when I fell. Nobody showed me how to ride my new bike, I did it all myself. And you weren't there the day I won the swim match either, nor when I was in the Christmas play, nor when I went trick or treating, nor when everybody's parents came to the school fair except you. And I won first prize for sixth grade geography, but you weren't there and you didn't even notice!"

Harry got up half way through this diatribe, stood stock still arms hanging, staring at her. She went on and on about the sixth grade prize, listening to her own choked voice with humiliation and amazement. She hadn't even known that she remembered these agonizing slights on the part of her father, but it all came back in a storm of pain. She could taste the decades-old rejections in her acrid tears.

Harry tried to speak, finally just left his mouth open. Grace rushed to stand behind him, clutching the back of his chair with both hands. Gemma was in the middle of the room, yelling. She was horrified but at the same time wild with freedom.

"You were a terrible father," Gemma screamed joyfully, "you were a terrible husband too. You were never home and always in a bad mood when you were. We were happier when you were gone, Mama and me. Mama and me. You bastard, you devil, *was für ein Mann bist Du?* You call yourself a man?"

Harry's face was getting redder and redder.

"That's right," she yelled, "have a heart attack. Have a heart attack. If you have a heart at all."

"Gemma," Grace pleaded, "stop it. Leave him alone."

Harry finally said hoarsely, "I'm going to tell you something I swore I never would. Your father was the goddamn milkman."

Gemma gasped, "Nice try," in total denial. Then a monstrous dawn spread across her face. "Mom wouldn't."

"Didn't you always wonder about the color of your goddamn skin, girl?"

Gemma vaguely remembered a charming Spanish-looking man bringing in milk bottles, putting them in the fridge. Very nice, helpful behavior on the part of a milkman. Both of her parents had pink Irish skin and freckles. She dropped onto the sofa, collapsed like a rag doll.

Grace moved to stand beside Harry, her hand on his arm. "Don't."

But he repeated viciously, "Your father was the goddamn milkman."

While Gemma began to writhe, muttering, he went on. "What did you expect me to do? I still loved your mother. I tried to love you. I busted my butt to be a good father to you, damn it. I did everything I was supposed to do. Your mother made it up to me, she was an angel after that. I convinced myself we were a happy family. Well, we were, we were. Don't you remember any of the good times?"

"Dad…Dad," Gemma stuttered, shuddering. "I don't have a dad?"

"So cut out the whining, and start thanking me, girl."

"It was all lies, all my life."

"I did my best." Harry's voice was clear now, tinged with pity. "I did my goddamn best."

Gemma rubbed her arms briskly, then tenderly, as she conjured up Franz, his eager lips. She imagined getting on the plane, arriving at her house, hugging Stefan. She saw with terrible clarity why she'd moved so far away from home in the first place. She had always in her bones known the degrading truth.

Family Values

Kirk and Wendy followed them into the woods, keeping well behind, out of sight. He knew where they were headed.

"Bruce has an old trailer a ways out behind his cottage," Kirk had explained. "He's kept it there for years, for his trysts. Different women."

"A fuck truck," Wendy said slyly.

Bruce chortled. "Put bluntly, yes."

"But why not just use the cottage? His family's back in Boston."

"I don't know. It's sexier. It has lots of comfy bedding. The cottage is too prosaic?"

"Reminds him of his wife I'll bet."

"Whatever."

Kirk was short with Wendy when she touched on the subject of wives. He had one himself, a bitch named Nancy who quibbled at his every move. "She shadows me like a bat," he liked to say.

Bruce and Charlene had come to the small clearing where the white and rust trailer, style 1970s, crouched expectantly. Wendy knew Charlene. She was the new mail girl, probably about twenty-five, plump and sweaty, jolly and sad. Bottom of the totem pole at the office, where Bruce ruled jocular as head honcho.

It was dark now, at eight o'clock on a mild October night. The half moon was so bright it cast shadows among the pines like imitation sunshine. Lights went on in the trailer as Kirk and Wendy crept closer. He had hold of her arm, slowing her to caution. She could feel her fear and excitement building. What if they got caught? Bruce could fire them both. But what he was doing in there with Charlene mesmerized her. She prayed they would not turn off the lights. But damn, they did. So the trailer was in darkness and sounds began, muffled but sharp, that could have been pain but were no doubt pleasure. The trailer began to rock gently. Just barely, by milky moonlight, Wendy through the little window made out the undulating shape of buttocks—could that really be her boss? It was so awful and thrilling that she groped at Kirk, who in turn was breathing fast on her neck.

It was all over much too soon. Kirk and Wendy crept away as fast as they could.

"But what if they do it again?" Wendy objected.

"Never mind, we can't risk it," Kirk reasoned.

They reached his car, parked at the side of the dirt road, and drove straight to the motel in Eastham where they made furious love in the pasty light of the television screen.

Wendy was a good girl, as they say. Kirk had had a terrible time convincing her to sleep with him. Her mother had very strong opinions about being "the other woman," which Wendy repeated tearfully all too frequently. But when she shook her little head, those blond curls and the eyelashes going, and clasped her hands over that gorgeous bosom, Kirk found eloquence for his pleas. It turned out that tales of Nancy's cruelty to him worked best, so he came up with some doozies. For example, one night Nancy poured hot chili all over his head and beat him with a broom. Not quite, but it got a sweet embrace from horrified Wendy.

This was not the first time he'd secretly brought his lady friends to Bruce's hideout, but Wendy was the first one to be so turned on. He'd been right: underneath all that demure demeanor was a red hot number. That wild night in Eastham he even told her he loved her—without being asked.

So the affair progressed as they usually do: thrill, then comfort, then a hint of stagnation. Kirk knew the syndrome well. It was April before the first signs appeared, so Wendy had kept up his interest all winter long. But one day he noted that the legs of the new girl in Accounting were superior to Wendy's, which were a bit too heavy. Then, when he was late for their next rendezvous, he yelled at her accusing whines. Oh boy, this was too much like marriage. He began to make plans to pull back, carefully. They'd have to continue working together and he did not want trouble with Bruce above all. He was up for a significant raise and Nancy wanted a Subaru.

Bruce was fairly circumspect, but nevertheless everyone in the office knew who he was after. He dropped Charlene around Christmas and they waited to see who was next. To Wendy's irritation, Charlene didn't look dejected or ashamed but on the contrary seemed to consider her fling with the boss a badge of something. When Wendy first realized that she herself was Bruce's new interest, she was almost insulted. Following in the path of stupid fat Charlene? No way. Plus, she could not get that image of her boss's rear end out of her mind. It made him ridiculous, or at least too human. But she was flattered, too. Bruce was not bad looking, sturdy and athletic, with thin expressive lips and nice eyes. And besides, he had power, which was always a turn on. He had big-time power over Wendy—she could be unemployed tomorrow pretty much at his whim.

Bruce made his first move one Friday afternoon when he stopped by Wendy's cubicle.

"Hey there, beautiful," he crooned. "Plans for this weekend?"

This was not unusual. Bruce was always courtly with his female employees. But he was leaning so close over her, she could smell his muscle. She turned her head to look up straight into his eyes.

"Oh, I'm always busy weekends," she crooned back.

In fact, Kirk had promised to try to get away to take her to the movies on Sunday. But she was fairly sure Bruce knew nothing about her liaison with Kirk.

"How about a drink right now? You deserve it."

"Have I worked that hard?" she laughed.

Bruce laughed too, and as they laughed together, Wendy knew she would go for it. Just to watch how he operated, as she put it to herself. But she was shocked at how excited she was on her way to the bar he'd mentioned. It was about eight blocks west of Tremont Street, naturally not one the staff frequented. The April evening was soft and sweet, the sun still scintillating at six o'clock.

Bruce was already there—smart move—in a booth and he got up to help her off with her jacket. Doing so, he was careful to brush his hands against her arms. He was good. Everything he did was predictable and flattering. He only brought up his wife briefly, to lament her loss of interest in sex or anything else.

"She's so depressed all the time, poor thing. It's hard for her."

"Hard for you, too," Wendy said, obedient to the cue.

"You bet. Have another glass of wine?"

"Oh, no, thanks, Bruce. You're so kind. I have to get going."

"Where to? Can I drop you off?"

"I'm having dinner at my mom's." Which happened to be true. "I'll just take the bus."

"Can we do this again?"

Wendy knew it was her chance to cut this fling in the bud. But she said, "Sure, I'd love to, Bruce. I enjoy talking with you."

Yikes! Wendy was surprised at herself. Her passionate performances with Kirk had given her a sexual confidence that emboldened her. She'd learned what lust was, and she liked it. She frankly admitted to herself that she felt lust for her employer. Would he try to take her to the trailer in the woods? The thought made her breathless.

But there was a hitch. As soon as he realized his boss was after his mistress, Kirk was furious. He confronted Wendy at their very next tryst on Saturday morning, as soon as he walked in her door.

"You had drinks with him! Everybody's talking about it. What were you thinking? You're my girl."

"I am not."

Wendy stood proudly in her dining room, where she'd laid out a nice brunch for them, cloth napkins and all, wearing a saucy low cut red number he liked. She was acutely aware of how sexy she looked, as she shook her blond curls at him with gusto.

"Wendy baby." Kirk was pathetic.

That morning Wendy gave Kirk the best of her trailer-awakened passion, heated by his desperation and by Bruce's desire. It was excellent sex, and Wendy reveled in her prowess and success. She looked forward to prancing around the office to everyone's admiration, now that she had two men after her. But instead, the whole scenario changed the next day, when she visited her mother for Sunday dinner.

"Do you mean," cried Mom, "that your married boss is trying to seduce you?"

"Well, put that way. Yes, I think so." Wendy had never mentioned Kirk, but she wanted to get her mother's take on the boss situation, without confessing in any way her own complicity, and certainly not her temptation to capitulate. "Naturally, I don't encourage it."

"Naturally."

Her mother was sitting on the other side of the kitchen table, looking younger than her fifty years, in spite of the well worn apron. They were snipping the ends off string beans. Roasting chicken smells came wafting deliciously from the oven.

Wendy said, "I just don't want to make him mad, you know. It's a problem."

"So ask for a promotion."

"What! How does that have anything to do with it?"

"You've been Office Coordinator for three years now, Wendy honey. Isn't there an opening in Admin? I thought you said Mr. Thorpe was leaving. What's his title?"

"Mom, Thorpe is Marketing Associate!"

"So? Why can't you be Marketing Associate?"

"He makes three times as much money as I do."

"Good. Your Ford is five years old. You need a new car."

Wendy threw her last bean into the pot and jumped up from the table. Her head was spinning because in spite of herself she'd actually started to imagine being in that exalted position. But she couldn't envisage such a discussion with Bruce. It just seemed so, well, impudent.

"Honey pie." Her mother was watching her struggle with loving amusement in her eyes. "You can do it. For God's sake, if he can propose to bed you, he can promote you. Right?"

"Mom, it doesn't work like that. And you know it."

"You've done public relations in other jobs," her mother urged, "you've contacted media, even interviewed that critic for the *Globe*, remember?"

"Yes, but I was just a secretary then. It doesn't count."

"It counts. Don't make my mistake. I never moved beyond teaching elementary school. I should have applied for Principal."

"Mom, this is all fantasy."

Her mother got up, ran water in the pan of beans and put it on the stove. She donned an oven mitt and checked the chicken.

Then she turned with a smile and replied, "Not to me. Come on, Wendy child. Wake up. You've got the experience, the smarts, and the clout. Go for it."

On Monday, Wendy arrived at the office in a state of nerves, but carefully conservatively dressed and made up, like the women executives she'd seen on television. Through his secretary, she made an official appointment to meet with Bruce right after lunch. The secretary leered but Wendy gave her no satisfaction.

Wendy spent the morning obsessively busy, accomplishing little. When Kirk stopped by her cubicle, she told him she had a sore throat so couldn't make any plans. At one o'clock sharp she walked into Bruce's office, and shut the door.

He was clearly expecting some form of capitulation. He glowed with self-confidence and goodwill.

"Wendy," he purred, "don't you look spectacular. Good enough to eat."

His suggestive laugh was not the least bit thrilling, but instead conjured up chunky Charlene, the trailer in the woods, and especially the butt by the light of the moon. The image reduced him to a frantic, silly boy. She sat down with great dignity, not smiling.

"Bruce," she said in her mother's voice, "I've been with the company three years now. All my performance reviews have been tops. I feel I'm due for a promotion."

Bruce started to grin, then stopped. "What do you have in mind?"

"Thorpe is leaving at the end of this month. So I thought Marketing Associate would be a good fit for me."

Bruce's deepening frown and her own bluntness combined to make her shaky. She clung desperately to the moonlit scene, playing it over and over like a prayer. But it was a losing battle.

"Wendy, I'm afraid you're overstepping yourself, my dear. You are not qualified for that position. Besides, Jerry's up for it."

"Jerry!" Wendy's scorn ripped through her intimidation. "He's been Assistant Personnel Officer for a hundred years. He didn't even go to college. You can't be serious."

Bruce sighed. "Look, you are not qualified, period."

"I am. I'm more qualified than Jerry, for sure. I'll be a terrific Marketing Associate. I have media contacts and media smarts. I'll email you my resume this afternoon."

"Look, Wendy." Bruce got up from his chair and came around the desk to stand over her. "I think you got the wrong idea when we went out for drinks. You're a beautiful woman. Frankly, I want to get to know you better. And how. But that has nothing to do with a promotion."

"The hell it doesn't."

Wendy stood up and looked Bruce straight in the eye. "For your information, I don't sleep around, certainly not with married men. I'm ambitious, just like you. I know my own value, and I demand respect for it."

"Wow." Bruce took a step backwards. "What a dynamo."

Wendy heard her own words, tasted them, memorized them, treasured them. Heard herself repeat them to her proud mother. Hardly heard Bruce's breathy final comment, "Whoever would've thought. I'll be damned. Don't go anywhere, Wendy, this company just might find a place at the top for a woman like you."

Amy's Arm

The gospel according to Diane was that Amy always won. Not so much games and contests, but the goodwill and affection of their parents. For example, at age nine, when Amy was twelve, Diane was awarded a piano prize at school. That very same day Amy learned that she was cast as Mary in their church's Christmas pageant. Which announcement do you think got all the breathless hugs and brags? Amy as Mary was the highest honor imaginable. A paltry piano prize? Even though it included playing Mozart from memory? Hardly a gasp.

Amy was better looking too. Her hair was corn silk blond, while Diane's was darker, with enough red highlights to give her freckles. Amy was petite, while Diane's heavier build made her a klutz at dancing. The two girls fought like cats all through childhood, though when they reached teen age, their rivalry became more subtle. When Amy started dating, she pretty much lost interest in hostilities with Diane, and even seemed to forget that they'd been enemies. Diane never forgot, though, and even resented Amy's newfound warmth as if it were a ruse to catch her off guard.

Their parents, Carol and Jimmy Gavin, came from humble origins, growing up on the wrong side of Huron Avenue in Cambridge. Jimmy's grandfather had managed a grocery store, a terrific step up from his Irish immigrant father who drove a bread truck. Jimmy's father grew the grocery business to eventually include a chain of stores. By the time Diane was five, the family was affluent enough to move to a big old Victorian house on the right side of Huron Avenue. Carol and Jimmy were ecstatic over their new abode, symbolizing to them fulfillment of the American Dream. They were a happy couple, simple in their tastes if not in their ambitions, and they didn't have a clue to Diane's heart.

Jim Gavin worked hard running his growing grocery empire. He liked working hard. But what he talked about when in his cups was his stint in the army, the action he saw in the Gulf War. He loved to entertain his family with stories of Arabs and camels and harems and sheiks, sometimes bringing in thrilling references to bombings and hand grenades and corpses. He liked to display and explain his Bronze Star, which he'd won chasing Kurds.

One day when Diane was seventeen, she brought home her first serious boyfriend, Luke Sanders. He was a big hit with her father because he knew all about the terrorists in the Middle East, and enthralled her thirteen-year-old brother Jamie with his football prowess. Luke even charmed her mother with his skill at Scrabble, which they all played together that rainy Sunday afternoon in April. The scene was seared in Diane's memory—the clock ticking on the mantel piece beside her mother's porcelain shepherdesses; the heavily curtained bay windows spotted with driving rain drops; the slightly musty odor overrun by baking cookies; lamplight shimmering Luke's dark hair curling over his collar, his dancing blue-green eyes sparkling at her—because just at the wrong moment, Amy showed up.

Amy was a freshman at Lesley University, not doing very well by all accounts, losing interest in her major, marketing. She lived in a dorm but had been coming home more and more often, to chill out as she put it, just walking in the door, always to a joyful chorus of welcome, of course. So in she struts, straight into Diane's glowing, triumphant reign, turning paradise to dust.

The Scrabble game was abruptly abandoned. Carol made her elder daughter a cup of tea, Jimmy regaled her with anecdotes from a recent advertisers meeting (he was convinced she was headed for corporate big time), and Jamie shouted about his A in social studies. Diane said nothing, watching Luke fall prey to Amy's charms like the rest of them. Amy was looking tired, but also somehow more beautiful than ever, her blonde hair longer and silkier, curling round her face from the damp, her sloppily unzipped jacket only emphasizing her lithe little form. After beating out the competition at her high school, literally pushing aside rapacious cheerleaders and even the homecoming queen, Diane was losing her hard-fought conquest to slimy Amy. It was too much.

Diane had finalized ownership of Luke by letting him sleep with her just the week before, her first time. It had been a bit uncomfortable for her, in the back seat of his parents' car, but worth it because Luke thereby became submissive. All she had to do when she wanted something was promise sex, or better, just reach for his crotch. It was so easy. She no longer wondered why girls gave in to boys—it was a power trip to end all power trips!

"Oh," Amy was simpering, "I've heard about the team's good work this season. Do you know Lucy Grimes, she's a senior? She keeps me up to date."

"I'm a senior too, sure I know Lucy. Great kid. Who was your favorite teacher?"

"Oh, I really liked Mr. Graham, the art teacher. He was so cool. What about you?"

Diane wanted to scream at this inane conversation. She and Luke talked about music, about her plans to apply to Julliard, and his to form his own rock band. He understood Mozart. Why was he being such an asshole?

But Luke and Amy sat there together in the bow-window seat, on the gold colored velvet cushions Mrs. Grimes had specially made to fit the space, among the colorful pillows Diane had helped pick out, in the fading spring light, heads too close, one blond one dark, the chemistry between them screaming. With horror, Diane realized that all women had that power, neutralizing her ammunition.

Perhaps Diane gave in too easily. She felt defeated in the first minutes. She didn't urge Luke to stay for dinner, and when he tried to get her into the car as they were saying good bye, she quickly pulled away as if he'd insulted her. She sulked at him in school, and was not surprised when he stopped seeking her out. It was no surprise either when one heartbreakingly gorgeous June afternoon she saw Luke and Amy downtown, holding hands.

Shortly thereafter, Amy moved back home into her old room for the summer. She'd finished poorly at Lesley, and confided in Diane one evening that she was dropping out. The sisters had resumed their dinnertime girl talks, in the brief respite between helping to cook and being called to the table. Amy, apologizing, had confessed to dating Luke, and Diane had sworn forgiveness, secretly crossing her fingers as she said it, seething with anger. She did have a new boyfriend, but a poor substitute. She still endured tormented daydreams picturing Amy and Luke having sex.

One evening when they were all sitting around the dining room table finishing dessert, chocolate pudding with whipped cream, Amy announced, "I have big news."

Amy had already landed a summer internship in a small business office, with a lot of help from Jim's connections. So he asked her what more could possibly be big news.

"Well, Dad," Amy breathed. "Guess."

"You're getting married," cried her mother.

"No way."

"You're cutting all your hair off," sneered Diane, laughing to show she was just joking.

"You're going to Timbuktu," shouted Jamie, who was very good at geography.

"Sort of, Jamie. You're warmer than the rest of them." Then after the family was reduced to breathless silence, Amy added, "I joined the army."

The fuss that followed was dominated by Jim yelling, "What, what!" while Carol brought herself to tears deducing that her daughter would immediately be killed. Jamie was wholeheartedly enthusiastic, bragging that such was his very own ambition, he was "going to show those Muslims who was who" as soon as he could carry a gun. Diane sat quietly exulting, working on a serious expression. What a perfect way to get rid of her bane. Amy would have to go far away, wouldn't she? But what if she were covered in glory or something? Never mind, that had to be far enough down the road and iffy enough to leave most of Diane's reaction unadulterated relish.

The big surprise was Jim's chagrin. It was clear that Amy as well as everyone else expected him to be proud and happy. He was not. He drooped and moaned as if he had a stomach ache.

"You have no idea what it's like," he said.

"Yes, I do, Dad," Amy protested. "You've told us all about it."

"No, I haven't, no I haven't. I don't want you to do this. I don't want you to do this, honey."

"Too late, Dad. I'm inducted. I'm starting training in two weeks."

"What about your new job?"

"Sorry, Dad. I thought you'd agree that this is more important. I want to serve my country, like you did."

Carol was over behind Jimmy, draped around his neck weeping, Jimmy was patting her hand like someone had died. Jamie wanted to know if Amy would wear a helmet. Diane asked where she'd be training. Amy didn't respond to anything except her father's woe. She kept assuring him that she knew all about war, that she had thought a long time about her decision, and that she was hoping to go to Afghanistan.

"I'll send you a postcard," she joked, but nobody laughed.

That fall was wonderful for Diane. She was a senior, grades good enough to apply to Julliard and Berklee. She acquired a new boyfriend, Zack Murphy, captain of the basketball team and devoted to her. He had access to a friend's apartment and taught her some sexual moves that brought her to orgasm for the first time. They both loved folk rock, and bonded ecstatically at concerts. To the Christmas prom she wore a glorious emerald-green silk affair that showed off her sizeable breasts, and with Zack holding her so close, she did not need to know how to dance. Other guys kept trying to cut in. She was a hit.

She was a big wheel at home, too. While Jamie was staging outrageous teenage rebellions, scoffing at curfew and mocking warnings about health and safety, the parents rested secure in the knowledge that Diane would do them proud. Word came from Amy regularly, and they all gathered to see her on Zoom the day before she shipped off to Kabul. She looked a bit ridiculous in khakis, the soldier's cap too big for her, the gun an unwieldy toy. Her hair was all chopped off and limp. She smiled a lot but it was not convincing. Gazing at her, Diane felt an unfamiliar kinship, a discomfiting sympathy. While she still profoundly hoped that Amy would stay away for a long time, she recognized an emotional tie, a new meaning for the word sister. She sincerely hoped that Amy would not get herself killed.

The news came in February. It was one of those balmy days that break winter's grip, melting snow banks, running cheery little brooks along the curbs. People put on their spring rain boots and took off their heavy parkas. The sun was gloriously warm, and at four in the afternoon still shining bright. Zack dropped Diane off—he always drove her home in his funky old Honda—and she ran up the steps and threw her backpack on the hall floor as always. She had a lot of homework to do for her advanced class in European history, and a difficult piece to practice for an upcoming concert.

But Carol was not in the kitchen. She and Jim were in the living room sitting side by side in silence.

"Amy's been wounded," Jim said like a zombie.

The brilliant sun slanting in across the old room suddenly seemed an insult. Diane sat down heavily, shocked as much by her parents' ponderous grief as by her sister's ordeal. She felt guiltily healthy and secure. She felt as she sometimes did when looking at Christ on the cross: how could she think about anything selfish when the most holy had suffered so much?

Carol stated in a horribly cold voice, from a tomb, "She got blown up."

"Roadside bomb," Jim added, stony-faced.

Diane wanted them to scream and cry. In the end she made enough noise for all of them, storming around the house in a furious tornado, knocking over chairs and ripping up newspapers. Then she collapsed exhausted. But she did not get the attention this warranted. No, Jim and Carol still just sat there, more silent and paralyzed than ever. So it was she who answered the phone, fixed dinner, told everyone Amy was going to be fine, made her parents drink some whiskey, ordered Jamie to finish his homework and brush his teeth. It was she who doggedly pursued developments to come up with a date Amy would be able to come home after her rehabilitation in Frankfurt, Germany.

Amy arrived on a misty May evening, after heavy rains. The trees in fresh bloom dripped noisily into sodden puddles. She pulled up in an army jeep, in uniform and accompanied by a medic with a red cross on his sleeve. Everyone could see at once that, although she could walk just fine, Amy only had one arm.

The house was like a funeral parlor for days. Friends who came by to visit, bringing casseroles, fruit, soups, sat grimly in the darkened parlor, whispering. Jamie was forbidden to bring pals over, and Diane had to tiptoe everywhere to avoid accusatory stares. Meanwhile, Amy sat in bed, with that useless lump hanging from her shoulder, crying and sleeping and eating—lots of all three. She said she wanted to die. Then Carol came down with some flu, she was so distraught, and spent a whole week with a fever. Jim took as much time off from work as he could, but this was not acceptable in the family's culture, so poor Diane curtailed her academic efforts to keep the household running.

She didn't really mind. She knew how important she'd become to everyone, and adjusted to the role of boss with agility. But this whole lugubrious reign of Queen Diane came to a sorry end in one day. It was the first of June, a Saturday, so Diane was home when the mail came. She had been on Julliard's waiting list; now she was rejected. Tears and sobs, a lot of crashing around the house, curses to make a pro blush, then slamming of her door as she barricaded herself in her bedroom.

Carol dragged herself off the couch where she'd been resting with a blanket, to sort the rest of the mail where she found a shiny magazine about amazing new prosthetic limbs. That was how Amy learned about the magical robotic arm that thenceforth became her golden grail.

Fast forward to October. Diane is a student at Berklee, living in a dorm in Boston. Fighting her disappointment over Julliard, she has begun to appreciate her fellow students. Zack, a freshman at Boston College, is still in the picture and they've decided they're falling in love. She's become best friends with her roommate from Minnesota, who plays a mean viola. The academic work is hard, but not too hard for fun, and the autumn days are the usual glorious Boston mix of brisk and warm, always sunny, colorful with turning trees, clumps of daisies orange and gold. Diane especially loves taking reading over to Boston Common, sitting on the grass among squirrels and children, stretching out her legs for the sun's kiss.

Diane hardly thinks about Amy any more. Mostly she feels true pity for her sister, brought so low so young. The parents talk a lot about her going back to school, but Amy has no stomach for that. What she prattles on about is her new prosthetic arm, which has been ordered, but is apparently so innovative that tests still are being conducted. Meanwhile she sits in bed most of the day, perfectly healthy but poring over veteran magazines and watching soaps on TV. She says she's depressed, but wanting to die has been abandoned as an active desire, so that's progress.

Diane has been home only once since starting school. But one lovely Saturday, hot like summer, but freshened by a good breeze from the ocean, she and Zack decide to stop by. The old house looks so shabby, Diane wonders if it's always looked that way or if she's just growing some perspective. She runs up the steps, finds her mother in the kitchen, is gratified by ooohs and aaahs of pleasure, her mother's tight embrace. Jim is out but Jamie saunters in, pretending cool, but grinning ear to ear. Immediately he engages Zack in basketball statistics.

"I'll just run up and see Amy," Diane says.

"Oh, no need for that," Carol croons, "she'll be right down."

Sure enough, at that moment in the kitchen doorway appears the Grand Amy, with two arms. She bursts into laughter when she sees Diane's mouth open in amazement.

"My new arm," she cries joyously. "How do you like it?"

"It's a miracle," breathes Diane.

"Look at this," boasts Amy, displaying her plastic hand. The fingers move. She picks up a spoon and waves it. "Just like flesh and blood."

"It's robotic," offers Jamie helpfully.

"It feels like a real hand," adds Amy.

Zack is actually touching it. "Feels kinda warm. Feels like skin, kind of."

Diane forces herself to put out her hand, take Amy's plastic one, nod in agreement. "It's so natural."

But she already feels the old familiar sting of bitter rivalry. The hand is prettily sculpted, the bright silky shirt Amy's wearing has both sleeves tidily buttoned at both wrists. Really, you have to look closely to tell. Amy is looking ridiculously happy. Plus, her fine golden hair has grown out to its old shoulder length, she's wearing lipstick and earrings. With her good hand she's stroking her revolting plastic robot imitation limb with something like sensual pleasure. Disgusting.

Alas, this is only the beginning of poor Diane's new ordeal. Half an hour later, when they're all in the living room being very jolly eating chocolate chip cookies, in walks Luke Sanders. He gets a big warm hug from two-armed Amy, and it's clear the old ardor has been rekindled between them. Luke even strokes the plastic hand with affectionate, congratulatory, possessive pride. It doesn't help that he's looking better than ever, those azure eyes of Diane's first seducer burning ever more deeply, positively mooning over spritely little Amy. Zack joins in Luke's and Jaime's enthusiasm at the miraculous mechanics, marveling over and ruminating over gross details apparently more fascinating than any sports game.

"Watch this," Luke boasts. "Come on, Amy, show them how you can pick up your cup, or here, this fork...See that, guys?"

"It's digital," shouts Jaime. "Like a computer."

"Amazing," breathes Zach, who is rarely amazed at anything.

It's a nightmare of an afternoon, but when Zach wants to leave, Diane refuses. She has a sore throat, she tells him, to forestall his kisses. She shoves him down the steps to his car, returns dolefully to the house, shoulders drooping, humiliated tears gathering. Her fabricated sore throat gets barely a mention from Carol, flushed with happiness like a girl, fussing giddily over Amy and Luke. When Jim comes home, he joins in the family revel with paternal bravado. Diane creeps up to her old room and gets into bed, nobody noticing.

She hatches the plan towards two in the morning. Amy had boasted about taking the arm on and off with relative ease, so Diane has been imagining it hanging there in the dark, Amy's stump revealed in all its gory truth. Maybe Diane sleeps a little, but mostly she tosses and turns and plots. Some pale light comes through her shades from the street lamp outside, so she can see her own healthy fists cramped with rage and purpose.

Sure enough, the arm is stored on a hook next to Amy's bed, hanging there all by itself in the gloom. Amy is peacefully and soundly sleeping, her stump covered by the pink coverlet up to her chin. But no matter, the object of Diane's desire seems to glow and expand with mesmerizing magnetism. Slowly Diane moves towards it, beckoning to her in all its arrogant beauty and falsehood. She grabs its hand, plucks it off the hook, presses it to her chest, and tiptoes out.

Back in her room, in a yellow pool of light from the street lamp, Diane crouches over her prey. It looks pretty ridiculous, curved there with nowhere to go after the elbow. Colorful wires dangle from it, red, blue, green. Fake veins, she scoffs, tweaking them in disdain. This is just a piece of plastic, right? But no, it has a life of its own, even detached from anything living. The hand curls softly as if towards an embrace. The surface glows like skin, perfect, creamy, sexy skin.

Diane yanks at the wires. First the red one, which gives only after a terrible fight. The blue one is easier, but Diane is already dripping sweat. Impatient, she grabs a chair and brings it smashing down with a sickening crunch. The arm lies in pieces.

Open mouthed, exuberant and nauseated, she listens for sounds from the others, who may have heard the crash. Silence in the old house, silence from the night street, silence in Diane's room, her ancient teddy bear a grinning witness.

What's Going On?

At first people are intrigued by the new house on the hill, especially because most of the other houses in the neighborhood are old Victorians. But after nothing ever seems to happen there, they lose interest. It's concluded from various hearsays that the person who lives there is ill, based on maybe one sighting of an ambulance. A man who delivered groceries once or twice reports he was told to leave them on the porch, and glimpsed a few folks who seemed like gardeners or maids.

The house sits low beyond heavy trees, back from the highest point of the hill, so from the sidewalk it appears a shadowy square. You can see lights on at night, especially in winter when the absence of leaves gives a better view. The grass all across the broad hill is well manicured, along with flower beds lining the pebbled drive that curves up out of sight. In any case, people in this area of Cambridge, off Brattle Street, keep to themselves and would consider it nosy to probe.

Nina Temple is a frank, forthright nineteen year old whose highest aspiration is to be a famous journalist. In the past she'd walked by the mysterious new house every day on her way to and from school. Now she's just finished her first year in college, living at home for the summer. So naturally, as she explores old haunts, she finds herself passing it again.

Nina is already a pretty good investigative journalist. In high school she was known for her daring reports in the school newsletter. She somehow found out things about teachers they were very anxious to conceal, and unearthed plans for example to curtail gym hours and strike key phrases from school policy. As an intern at the *Cambridge Chronicle* last summer, she became notorious for unmasking the mayor's tax dodges.

It's a lovely June morning. Nina strolls down Taunton Street, fresh and relaxed after recovering from weeks of exams and the stressful adjustment of homecoming. Her mother will always treat her like a child, and her father will not stop asking about her grades. Her brother is an alien, having gone from twelve to thirteen in her absence. She will need to look for a job, call old friends, get her hair cut, and hang out where she'll run into Billy Reston. But today, she's just going to enjoy herself and not think about anything.

She hardly glances up at the house. After all, nothing ever happens there, nothing ever changes. Her motto is, keep your eyes peeled for action or oddity. Then something about a black car speeding up the driveway catches her attention. It has the look and feel of secrecy, urgent anonymity. Why? Never mind, Nina knows to follow her instinct. Rather than trying to analyze her impression, she follows her nose. She boldly walks up the drive in the car's wake. The crunch of tires has stopped, so presumably the car has reached its destination. To avoid the sound of her own footsteps, Nina moves over to the lawn for the rest of her ascent.

Almost at the top, a brick-lined path leads sharply to the right. It looks shady and cool on this warm day. Besides, in front of her looms a formal entrance with several men emerging from the car, slamming the doors and arguing. And in front of that scene, a man crouching among the flowers who must be a gardener. He squints up at her with glassy pale blue eyes in a weathered face. He doesn't say anything, but he doesn't stop looking at her either. She smiles and veers off down the pretty path. Passing through a grove of bushes, she emerges into a kind of courtyard, a pleasant grassy area with several houses around it. She already has something to report! Nobody ever guessed there would be so much habitable space up here. And now she has a mission: find out if a lot more people than one sick old person live here, or at least work here. Her journalist's heart beats in excitement.

She starts across the lawn, noting the uniform imitation Colonial look of all the entrances, something a bit like a motel. Just as she catches sight of the bulk of the main house to her left among trees, she feels a presence behind her. Nina knows that at this point she can be considered to be trespassing. That has never stopped her, of course, but she gets busy concocting a soothing story for any angry owner. A few more steps, and just as she turns to see two women behind her, someone else appears in front to her left, and behind him, three others. All these people are moving towards her, slowly but purposefully, eyes fixed on her. They don't look upset, but they are not smiling either. When she stops, turns to address the dark-haired young woman closest to her, she notes four or five more men and women collecting behind her. They all seem perfectly normal, the kind of folks you might pass on any street. But something about the way they are surrounding her, as if to neutralize her, like an amoeba absorbing its prey, is unnerving.

Nina says, "I'm so sorry to be bothering you. I was looking for number seventy three Taunton Street."

The woman replies, moving up close beside her, "This is number seventy-three. What do you want?"

"Oh, I'm doing a report for school on the history of Cambridge architecture. We were told this house is an excellent example of the new fitting in with the old."

Such an excuse seems pretty good to Nina, but the woman does not relax her suspicious, cold expression. By this time maybe ten people have gathered around her, and more are appearing. She feels a flicker of fear. These people do not like her. Her cute story has not convinced them of her benign intent. Time to extricate herself, hopefully gracefully.

The woman says in an ironic tone, "You know you have no business here."

She's perhaps in her thirties, dark hair nicely coiffed, wearing a red and white patterned sundress. Her legs are tanned, her sandals comfortable but classy, kind of like Nina's own. There's nothing in her appearance to warrant apprehension.

Nina, now facing the path she'd followed, eyeing through the group the most promising route for retreat, says sweetly, "Please do forgive me. I'm so enthusiastic about my school reports. I'll just go on home now."

She starts to move, but the woman grabs her arm.

"Not yet. We want to know more about you. What's your name?"

"Nina Temple. I live over on Fayerweather Street. May I ask yours?"

"My name is Julie. This is Kevin."

Julie indicates a tall man with graying red hair wearing tennis whites. He too stands very close to Nina, and after a long pause, comments, "You are quite young."

"Nineteen," Nina obliges, hoping her smile is casual and even flirty.

He responds like a normal middle-aged man, with a patronizing but appreciative grin. Confidence restored, she again tries to step forward. But Kevin blocks her way, not entirely gallantly.

"We don't get many visitors here," he informs her. "You need to understand that."

"Sure, sure, Kevin, I certainly understand that. It must be quite a surprise, me just showing up like this. Gauche of me."

"You might be interested in meeting our Mr. Porter, the owner."

"Oh, I would, I would. But another day would be just fine."

"Today would be good."

Julie chimes in, "Today. Right now."

Each of them takes an elbow, and she is guided toward the main house. Neither roughly nor gently, merely very purposefully. As though perhaps she were disabled and needed a little help.

They pass through a gate in a stone wall. Most of the crowd has dispersed; only a few follow them. Inside the wall the grounds are less manicured, even a bit neglected, with weeds going wild among rose bushes. But the back entrance they take her through leads to a shiny hallway, then a big comfortable room sort of like a living room but furnished with desks as well as couches. They pass through this room into a much smaller one, with soft white furniture. A place with an odd feel, like a hospital or doctor's office, or a movie set.

Nina has already got far more of an adventure than she bargained for. She's frankly nervous as she sits down where they put her. There are windows but they are curtained so any view outside is blurred at best. Her chair is so cushioned she sinks into it. Someone hands her a glass of water. She sips from it, has nowhere to put it, so holds it warming in her two hands.

"May I please have your purse?" asks Kevin.

"I only have twenty dollars."

"We don't want your money." He hands the purse to Julie, who rifles through it, pulling out her cell phone. She hands the purse back to Kevin, who returns it to Nina.

"My cell," says Nina pointlessly.

"Indeed." Kevin is nonchalant. "We are interested in different kinds of communication."

"Oh, I see."

Julie laughs.

Kevin says, "You'll just wait here until Mr. Porter is free. Are you comfortable?"

"Oh, yes, thank you."

Now she's alone in this peculiar little room among these creepy people. No cell phone and doubtless a guard outside the door. For a minute, she's afraid she'll start to cry; there's that telltale tightening behind her eyes. But Nina's not a weeper. She pulls herself together. What a story she has! She can write this up for *The Boston Globe*, that should get her the summer job she covets. She jumps up, sets the glass of water on a table, and prowls the dimensions of the cube-shaped room. One of the windows yields to her push. She's able to open it, and realizes she can get out that way. Should she do it? They'll be furious, of course. It also crosses her mind that they left it open on purpose, so that she can be accused of trying to escape and get into deeper trouble. Lifting the curtain just enough, she gauges she'll land behind some bushes, which would be good.

She turns to contemplate the room, so very white and so very relaxing, to the point of mesmerizing. It almost purrs to her, return and be loved, lose yourself. The dread she feels in response is not so much its persuasiveness as her own desire to yield.

In a flash she's out the window and crouching in the bushes. She eases her way around the side of the house, towards where she thinks the front is, keeping low. But contemplating her flight down the open lawn of the hill, she stops to figure out a less conspicuous route. Suddenly she hears voices, a group of them, perhaps another manifestation of the zombie types that surrounded her earlier. Nina finds herself trembling. She really does not want to run into that crowd again. Her fingers find a door behind her. She slips in.

A long hallway, another door. A darkened room, a stuffy medicinal smell. This is a bedroom, there's someone in the bed. Nina can't tell if she can be seen. The room is large and almost opulent, with heavy tapestry drapes, plush rug, antique upholstered chairs. But all around the king size bed in the middle are the accoutrements of sickness: bedpan, vials, needles, pill bottles. Nina plasters herself up against the wall, trying to make out the shape in the bed. All at once it sits up, a very old woman, croaking, "Who's there?"

"Shhh," says Nina. "It's only me."

"Only who, only who?"

She hurries closer, begging, "Don't worry. My name is Nina. I'm a neighbor."

"What!"

"Oh please," Nina begins. Then she notices the woman's eyes are not there, but covered with film. She's blind. So Nina takes her hand. "Please let me explain. I'm just a girl from next door. I came here by mistake."

The woman peers at her with empty eyes, caresses her hand. "You feel very young indeed," she murmurs, "Nina my dear. How lovely to have a visitor from outside!"

Nina darts her eyes around, finding the window, figuring out how to escape. Meanwhile the old woman croons on, giving her name as Diane Porter, talking about her breakfast that morning which she had enjoyed, wandering around to past events, like her visit to Italy when she was young, and her two children.

"My son lives here with me," says Diane Porter. "He takes good care of me and runs the place beautifully. But," she drops to a whisper, "they don't like strangers."

"I guessed that."

"It's not that he isn't friendly, my Ricky, it's just that his mission is so important. He has to keep it pure."

"I'm sure he does."

"You're very kind to hold my hand. You don't mind, do you? I used to have a puppy, but he got old and died. They don't want to get me a new one. Say, could you get me a new puppy, Nina my dear?"

Nina finds herself, while in the throes of dread and high adrenaline, quite liking this feisty old person, seemingly with all her marbles and a kind heart. Her front teeth protrude, giving eager emphasis to her smile. Her thin white hair curls around pinkish shriveled cheeks, her bony frame is draped in a dainty vanilla-hued robe.

"I could, but I guess we'll have to clear it with Ricky, won't we?"

"Well…" Diane gets quite a mischievous look, deepening the furrows in her face. Puckish. "We wouldn't have to tell him right away." Then, excitedly, "I'm going to name him Roger. I always wanted to have a dog named Roger. Can you get a middle-sized one, like a Cocker Spaniel? Oh, that would be wonderful."

"Now, Mrs. Porter, don't get your hopes up yet. I have to figure out how to leave here first. Your son wants to interview me."

"Oh dear. If they recruit you, you may never leave."

"What does that mean, exactly?"

Diane settles herself against the pillows, her blank eyes staring into the distance.

"Well, my dear, you see, Ricky has a mission to save the world. He says it's being taken over by the Green Tide, a very large group of evil people infiltrating everywhere who reject God's plans and hate freedom. Our house is the main headquarters for Ricky's Liberty Land. Folks come from all around the country to join us. One day we will rise up and save America."

"I see."

"Mind you, I don't want to believe there are such strong forces out to get us. I've always liked to think that most people are basically good. But you have to understand, the Green Tide is determined to return our great country to a barbaric state, doing away with cars and factories and corporations and the free market. Just dreadful. Can you imagine?"

"Ricky's going to save us from them?"

"That's right. I'm so proud of him. He was a rather difficult little boy, you know. He just wouldn't take teachers' orders, as he put it. But we sent him to military school, my dear old husband and I, bless his soul, and that straightened Ricky right out. He was all for discipline and orders after that, you should have seen his darling little uniform. Now, Nina, let me tell you about the time we all went to Nova Scotia. No, that was when I was twelve, with my mommy and daddy, you see…"

Nina begins to extricate her hand, but Diane presses it closer and cries, "Oh I'm so sorry my dear. I'm off telling you stories. You want to hear more about Liberty Land."

"Yes, Mrs. Porter, I do. It's quite fascinating."

"I'm eighty-nine this September, you know. Old folks do sometimes wander. I don't want to be a burden. Ricky is so good to me. He visits me every day, you know. Do you have a granny?"

"Yes, my grandma lives in New York, upstate. We go visit her sometimes. Do you know exactly how Liberty Land is going to save the world? Will you need an army?"

"Oh, no nothing like that. Nothing too violent, Ricky promises. We'll just convert everyone by logic. Because it's so obvious, you see. The Green Tide is out to destroy our way of life and take away our freedom. As soon as people figure that out, they'll join us. Look at all the folks on our side already, a hundred of them right here in our house, all training to carry out our mission, in schools, churches, government, universities, businesses. Isn't it inspiring?"

"Oh, yes, yes, it is! Now, dear Mrs. Porter, I really should go home. My mother will be worrying about me. Can you help me figure out how to get out of here?"

Diane Porter shakes her head. "I can tell you how to get out of my room, of course, but they won't let you go until you talk with Ricky. In any case, you'll be lucky to meet him. He's a wonderful man and he'll be very famous some day. But right now, not many strangers get to know him."

Nina forcibly removes her hand from Diane's. "I'd rather not meet him today. I need to get home."

"You're a sweet girl, and a smart girl. Liberty Land could use you."

Nina stands up. "It's been lovely chatting with you."

"Ask Ricky if you can come again. I don't get many visitors. And ask him about Roger, won't you please, Nina my dear?"

Nina makes for the door murmuring assent, goes out and closes it behind her quietly. But they're waiting for her. She's seized in a steel grasp and the last thing she sees is a needle jabbing her arm.

When Nina wakes up, it's almost dark. She's back in the bedroom, lying across the bed. But Diane Porter is gone, the pillows still showing her shape. Nina feels dizzy and sick. She can scarcely sit up. All around is an incredible stillness, and she already begins to suspect what's happened.

The house and grounds are empty. Not a soul can be seen. In the gathering dusk everything looks ghostly. The desks yield no documents, the kitchen no signs of multiple inhabitants. Nina prowls weakly, more and more desperate. She has nothing to prove her stunning story. It's a journalist's worst nightmare. Nobody will believe her.

Mrs. Professor Bostwick

Ordinarily I wouldn't concern myself with a pitiful middle-aged woman paralyzed by her husband's success and charisma. But I had my eye on her son at the time, so I was drawn to study her. Let me say right off that I'm an investigative reporter and a damn good one. I confess I like to pry into people's minds and make them blurt out the last thing in the world they want to say, and then quote them. I've got quite a reputation already at the tender age of 26, not only at my paper the *Gloucester Sentinel* but also among readers. Men especially take to my rough and tumble style. Men take to me in general, because I'm that porn director's dream, a slim and pretty blond with big breasts. Men.

Anyway, Professor Bostwick had been one of my favorite teachers at Tufts University, so when his adorable son Hugh invited me to meet the parents, I knew it would be an evening to remember. But I didn't bank on how memorable. Mrs. Bostwick, Sophia that is, toiled in the kitchen the whole time. It seemed she didn't dare come out. The rest of us, the professor and Hugh and I, relaxed on the patio of the ample garden shaded and perfumed by lilacs in full bloom. The cold wine was delicious, from a remote village in Germany, the professor bragged, and fresh baked mini salmon pastries matched perfectly. The professor was flattered at how much of his course on Locke I retained. He had read enough of my articles to have a healthy respect for my scalpel-sharp brain.

"Now then, Nellie," he said with only the slightest edge of condescension, "tell us more about this study you're reporting on about fishing quotas. Hugh has told me a bit about it. Sounds fascinating."

"Well," I responded eagerly, "it's been discovered that there are far fewer fish in the wider ocean than had always been assumed. For example, Georges Bank had such a rich supply, people always thought that fish would be at least as plentiful farther out. But now that we have the capacity to reach them, turns out they're not there after all. And this comes at a time when factory ships are trawling the sea bottom and raking up nutrients as well as fish eggs. Even cod is endangered."

While I was showing off, I was watching his handsome face become intent with unfeigned interest. Though he was white-haired and well over 50, he had Hugh's gorgeous snapping black eyes and sensuous mouth. Many of my fellow students had had crushes on him, and there was little doubt he had taken advantage of that more than once.

Mrs. Bostwick appeared and hovered to one side until we became self-conscious, stopped talking, and looked at her. This was her cue to speak.

She was a short woman, rather stocky, with square hands and a square jaw. Her brown hair was arranged in tight curls, her red lipstick unrefreshed. She wore a polka dot apron over her modest gray dress. She was far from the glamorous consort one would imagine for the dashing professor.

"I'd like to serve dinner in about twenty minutes," she said, "Would that be okay?"

"Super, Soph," the professor said, handing her his whisky glass. "Just freshen that up for me, will you, when you get a chance. Dear."

I was sure he added the "dear" for my benefit. He needn't have bothered. I didn't see how he could be romantically involved with this woman; he should stop pretending. But then, maybe she ate it up? I couldn't tell what her sad, sorry expression meant. I was interested, though, that this was the mother of my newest conquest. What did that say about Hugh?

Clearly she adored him, her only child. He was jovial with her, more respectful than his father, though not much. Hugh had a way of squeezing her shoulder that made her almost giggle. I quickly figured out it was his way of making her do something she might be slow to accomplish, or maybe not want to do at all. For example, she balked at his suggestion that she serve the shrimp as an hors d'oeuvre instead of an appetizer. But as soon as he affectionately squeezed her rounded shoulder, she acquiesced. Could that be, perhaps, the only physical contact she had in life?

I am pretty gorgeous, I don't try to deny it. But at that moment as with horror I imagined my own self around fifty, I vowed never to drop my guard, and to fight aging with gusto. My momentary fear and quick scorn made me angry with poor old Sophia, so I made an effort to be extra nice to her.

I could tell Hugh was happy with the way things were going. He'd finally relaxed when his father took a real interest in what I was researching, though I could have told him the conquest had actually come when I spouted his Locke back at him. My blouse unbuttoned just far enough didn't hurt either. Sitting around the table, savoring a truly delicious pot roast with homemade biscuits, and then spectacular blueberry pie, our conversation was lively, witty, and erudite, just the combination the three of us thrived on. I made up my mind to bed Hugh that night. He'd been begging for weeks.

Mrs. Bostwick served everything and took away plates with a noiseless grace that I had to appreciate. So many wives of important men had to make some kind of statement about themselves, if only by calling attention to their culinary skills. But Sophia said not a word about her masterpieces, nor did anyone else. When I finally decided I had to compliment the pie, she only shook her head shyly, and the professor frowned at the interruption. But Hugh's eyes sparkled at me, so I knew my kindness had not gone unnoticed. Thus encouraged, I gathered blueberry spattered pie plates and followed my hostess into the kitchen.

It was an amazingly small and old-fashioned room, without even enough counter space or proper lighting. My own mother, no gourmet cook, would have gasped in horror. I wondered mightily how this woman, whose only claim to fame was serving a famous man, could function happily in such deprivation. I took a closer look at her as she labored at the sink, her little curls coming loose onto her furrowed brow, her lipstick gone entirely, her polka dot apron (an attempt at gaiety?) spattered with gravy, blueberry juice, and dish detergent. Far from wanting to linger and help her, I fled as quickly as I could. The woman frightened me. How was it possible to be so in thrall and so amorphous? Was this the way old women were supposed to fulfill themselves?

Back in the dining room, I experienced special pleasure in the awareness of both men's attention to my lovely lithe form as I resumed my seat. Normally I take those flattering moments for granted, but right then I badly needed reassurance that I myself would never disappear like the ghost in the kitchen.

About a week later I was covering a conference at Boston University on the depletion of New England fisheries. My editor at the *Sentinel* had stressed the local angle. "No showing off about global nonsense, Nellie, as you so love to do," he snorted. "I want straight story, aimed at fishermen and their wives. Your audience isn't a bunch of ivory tower academics as you so love to think." How he enjoyed belittling me just because I went to Tufts and he barely squeezed through U Mass.

So I was in a grumpy mood hanging around the newsroom waiting for the next panel to begin. The first one had given me nothing. I wanted controversy, or at least a reasonable hook. I knew my story had to interest more than fishermen's wives. I was contemplating an angle that would stimulate the Gloucester business community—that would thrill my editor and get me some wider attention. I was ambitious, and had my eye on *The Boston Globe* as my next step up.

We were on the tenth floor of a Beacon Street office building. I began to notice a group gathering at the broad window, and went to join them. Now I could hear the muffled sounds of shouts interspersed with drum beats. A huge parade of people was forming in front of the building. The participants were waving signs and looking up directly at us.

"It's the anti-GMOs," somebody said.

"GMOs aren't our fault," snapped another.

"Plenty of those biotech guys at this conference," explained a man next to me.

I nodded at him. I knew who he meant, the proponents of the latest big push in the food business: Genetically Modified Organisms, from corn and tomatoes to fish. My only thoughts about it so far included the concession that if you're losing fish populations, why not manufacture them? The idea seemed logical and of course meant billions in profits.

The bell rang to alert us to the start of the next panel. Pulling out their notebooks, cameras, and microphones, my fellow reporters were turning away to answer the call. But I'd already decided to abandon ship. The story I wanted was down there in the street.

As I emerged from the safety of the building, the roar and surge of the crowd was just scary enough to be thrilling. Protesters were spilling over the sidewalks, ignoring the cops who good-naturedly urged order. People were in an upbeat, raucous mood, many dressed as deformed fish or vegetables, all carrying signs, "Hands off our Food," "GMOs Kill," "Monsanto Go Home," "Our Kids, not Your Profits," "Frankenfish No!" Jostled here and there, I finally found a fairly secure vantage point on the steps of the building next door.

The noise was intense. Besides shouts and chants, beating drums of various sizes were joined sporadically by tambourines and party horns. Quite a few folks had brought their kids, from toddlers on shoulders to pre-teens dancing about screaming their heads off. Some very vehement protesters were shaking their fists up at the windows of our conference rooms. One stout person in particular, wearing a fish head with dreadful lesions all over it, was particularly aggressive. As I watched her take off the head to reveal an open, shouting, outraged mouth, I recognized Mrs. Professor Bostwick. I couldn't have been more stunned if she'd been running naked or aiming a rifle. Of all things imaginable, this was the least possible on earth. The woman was in an apoplectic state of rage.

The moment froze for me that lovely spring day. I was oddly aware of puffy clouds above, warm light, the roar of angry celebration all dimming, falling away, the spotlight of my amazement illuminating only Sophia's contorted face. For some wild reason, I remembered vividly the scene in my bed only days before, her son Hugh gazing down at me, eyes gone blind with ecstasy. The shock of seeing her this way seized me in a paralysis in which for a long time nothing seemed to happen. I just kept staring at her, until she saw me.

Then she burst the bubble with an awful scream. "No, no!" She was flailing towards me through the crowd. I backed up against the wall. This might not end well.

The next thing I knew, Sophia Bostwick had me by the shoulders, shaking me.

Her hands were strong. Her reddened face was sweaty so that her little curls were plastered flat. She was still shaking her head no, but she gasped, "Thank you for coming. I hope you're on our side." Trying hard to look happy to see her, I was speechless, so she went on, "I wanted to ask you when you came to dinner and talked about your fisheries reports."

Her words were reasonable, so I humbly assured her that I could certainly see her point of view. I was torn, anxious to get away fast, but also to please the mom of my adorable lover. And I was beginning to feel traces of admiration for the woman.

Someone was pulling on her sleeve, urging, "Sophia, the monitors want us to start circling in one direction, is that ok?"

Mrs. Bostwick quickly replied, "Go ahead. Get the chants synchronized, too, please." Then she turned back to me. "Why don't you join us, Nellie? We can give you a sign to carry."

"I'm on assignment," I explained. "Can't be part of the action. Sorry."

"Well then, good, give us good press." She rather sloppily kissed me adding earnestly, "Please don't tell them."

I nodded agreement, and she smiled as she turned busily away.

I must have stood mesmerized for another full minute. This was like one of those personality changes you see in scary movies. Which one was the true Mrs. Bostwick?

I had to tell Hugh. He came to pick me up the next evening for a theater date, but we never got out the door. First we had a lovely quickie on the sofa, and were freshening up when I let it slip. I was adjusting my bra, he was buttoning his shirt.

I said, "I saw your mother the other day."

His face took on that bemused, patient look he had when she was mentioned. "Yeah?"

I paused to admire his chest hairs as they disappeared. "In Boston, when I was covering the fisheries convention." Hugh leaned over and kissed me. "Lipstick," I reminded him.

"What did she have to say?"

"She was demonstrating."

"Demonstrating what?"

He was pulling on his jacket, checking his pockets, tightening his tie, clearly calculating how much time we had before the show. We planned on a late dinner afterwards.

Oh boy, he had no idea. I must admit I felt smug in my knowledge and the power I had to shock him. I couldn't resist. Besides, I was fascinated to see how he'd react. It was my damned tenacious journalistic curiosity, like a terrier that won't let go.

Assuming a kind of scientific distance, I announced, "She was dressed in a fish costume. She was protesting the biotech companies at the conference."

"What?" Hugh went so pale I was sorry at once. He sat down heavily on the sofa that was still in disarray from our passion, and stared at me coldly. "What are you talking about? Are you talking about my mother?"

Oh shit. I started to stutter.

He said again, "Are you talking about my mother? In a mob wearing a costume?"

I tucked in my blouse, adjusted it, and sat down across from him as sedately as I could, nodding. He added, "You're lying."

I was scared now, and insulted too, but I said demurely, "Hugh, why on earth would I lie about something like that?"

He was glowering at me. No charm in those normally burning dark eyes. He's not the only one with a personality change, I thought stupidly.

"Yeah, why would you?" The reply of a ten year old.

"Well, if you don't want to believe it, be my guest." Then I blurted further, "My own private opinion is that you and your father have no idea who she is. Your mother happens to be a brave, dedicated activist, while at home she's treated like a doormat."

Hugh got even paler and shouted, "Leave my mother alone. I don't know what your game is, but she's an angel and you can't hold a candle to her."

I glared back at him. "So that's how you really feel, is it? No indeed, I would never wait on you like a slave, if that's what you require."

Unbelievably, Hugh started to cry. "She's a wonderful woman," he sniffled.

"She is," I heartily agreed, surprising myself.

I realized that all my own triumphs, past and planned, had lost some of their luster in light of Sophia's brave double life. I felt like her knight in shining armor at that moment. Or was she the hero and I the rescued damsel?

One Two Three Cry

There were seven of us. A perfect number, said the therapist. We'd all get to know each other well, yet have a buffer of numbers for comfort. Providing we all were loyal and never skipped sessions. That warning was the first of many indications that Irene Norvall was a bit preachy if not downright parental.

What did I care? I was such a wreck going through that divorce, I would've grasped at any lifeline. A crisis group for the middle aged? Sure. A meditation group with a twist? Just say the word. Even though I was a successful professional man (that's the term), with two almost grown children and a bunch of good buddies, over educated and well travelled, at that point I did not feel I was anything that could possibly be called normal.

My name is Red. No, not because my hair is (it's actually dark brown) but because my dear romantic mommy named me Redmond. (My father hated the name, and said so often. He always called me Ed.) In the therapy group's first moments, I knew right away that I would break at least one of Ms. Norvall's rules.

"To preserve the integrity of the group," she informed us, "we must all promise not to meet with each other outside of session. Say you run into another member on the street. It's not okay to even invite them for coffee. I'm sure you can all understand what that would mean—confidences between you unknown to the group. So that is forbidden."

As she breathed the word forbidden, my eyes met those of Cherie Lederman. She was, I saw at once, exactly what I was looking for. A sweet young thing with loose legs. This I needed after all my cold as ice years with Amanda, and the even colder dispatches I was still getting from her lawyer. I knew I didn't look my best in those days, to say the least, but I was a pretty good-looking guy basically, broad in the shoulders, slim in the hips—or used to be before this ornery paunch—nice friendly face, and a killer of a sexy smile (so I've been told). Plus, I was making a damn good salary as a tax accountant, providing Amanda didn't take it all.

The other folks in the group were two couples, Barry and Josie and Gail and Lance, and Hal. I wasn't worried about competition from Hal, a big fat not jolly Santa type just turning thirty but looking about fifty, poor guy.

We all went around the group introducing ourselves and saying why we were there. The room was kind of small and stuffy but the chairs in our circle were comfortable.

When it was my turn, I said, "I'm going through a terrible divorce. I'm worried about my kids, and about how much money my wife is going to get. I don't mind paying their college expenses, but her trips to Barbados no. I'm losing sleep. My son Freddy's doing marijuana, he's only sixteen."

Nobody minded that this statement was disjointed and had no point. All of them were suffering in similar ways. Gail said Lance was beating her up, Barry said Josie was "out to get him," Cherie said she wanted to kill herself, and Hal confided that his mother still wanted to give him a bath. I wasn't such a kook after all. I felt better already.

Cherie didn't make it hard for me to catch up with her after the first session. She was waiting at the bus stop so I pulled up in my car.

"We shouldn't," she said when I offered her a ride.

"You don't have to take the bus."

"I like the bus." But she was smiling and heading for the passenger door.

"Ms. Norvall has a point," I said when Cherie settled herself beside me. I wanted to make it clear I was a law-abiding, sensitive person. "But a rule like that was made to be stretched."

"Yeah, made to be stretched."

Yikes, was she the type that simply repeats your words and calls it conversation? But I was compensated by her great legs, skirt to mid thigh. I dropped her off at the Union Square Starbucks where she worked, but not before getting permission to pick her up the following Wednesday so we could drive together to our therapy session. Already, I felt, I'd crafted the big brother role that would get me into her pants.

That was one horrendous week. The very next day, my daughter Linda called me all distraught from high school. I was to come right away to the principal's office: her brother had passed out. I asked if her mother knew, and yes the school had already called her, so I knew Linda was pulling another one of her ruses to get us back together. But this was far too serious to ignore, so I rushed over there. Left my secretary in a tizzy to deflect several meetings.

I had to carry Freddy home, poor kid. He was drunk. He had come to school drunk that morning.

"Where's he getting the booze," I yelled at Amanda, who was in a monster mood, trembling with that rage of hers, not even crying.

"See what you've done," she seethed at me through her teeth. "Just look at what you've done."

Linda wanted to come home with us, but none of us adults thought this was a good idea, so we left her sobbing in the nurse's arms. She would not learn much more at school that day, I figured, but it was the best place for her as opposed to our house (excuse me, I mean Amanda's house) where, while Freddy slept it off upstairs, Amanda and I duked it out with our usual poisonous verbiage. Finally I left, banging the door of course, yelling back at her, "Have it your way. He's your problem now."

I felt like a terrible jerk as soon as I got into the street. I looked up at the window of Freddy's room. We bought that house ten years ago, when they were both so little. What in God's name had happened to our family? It was a wreck. It didn't even exist anymore.

Over the weekend I tried to get my mind off things by going out drinking with my poker buddies, but they were all so damned cheerful it just made me feel worse. After about five beers I called the house and tried to talk to the kids but Amanda wouldn't let me. "Call back when you're sober," she ordered in that prickly nanny voice of hers.

By Monday I was glad to go back to work, but my boss called me in to ask for an explanation of my abrupt departure on Thursday. He ended up sympathetic but I ended up hating his guts more than ever, mostly because I want his job and the prospects for that aren't good.

On Wednesday I went early to pick up Cherie so I could watch her working. She was wearing a cute little black apron and squirting various coffee elements into paper cups as each order came her way. She had on very bright lipstick, making her look older, and long earrings like a Gypsy's. Exotic, erotic. Finally I caught her eye, and got a huge adorable dazzle of a smile. Congratulated myself.

But she wouldn't agree to a date. She said, "As long as we don't tell each other anything relevant, driving together's okay. But, Red, we really shouldn't disobey the rules. They have them for a reason."

"Irene's rules," I protested. "Her reason's just control."

But Cherie didn't like disparagement of Irene. She wanted to believe in her special powers.

"I think she's good," was how she put it.

That day we learned meditation. I was the only one in the group who'd never tried it. But Irene said this won't be like your average experience, we are going to have laughing and crying and shouting meditation. Oh boy. What kind of kooky idea is this, I wondered. But I wasn't about to turn down anything that might give me some peace of mind. And I'm no coward. I've faced my share of challenges without backing down. So there we were, each supplied with a large cushion. Not for sitting on but for hitting when we felt like it. I liked that idea.

First we had to sit cross legged on the floor, close our eyes, open our palms, and breathe regularly. It was much harder than I ever would've thought. I was really proud when I mastered it. The secret is to forgive yourself when your mind wanders, and just bring it back gently to your breathing. I actually got really relaxed doing that. But Irene wasn't finished. After we'd spent plenty of time with the breathing, she made us moan a sound like *om* with the out breath, and after that we had to learn the names and colors of the various spots in our body. My legs were aching by that time and I was starting to really lose my concentration worrying about Freddy. I was so happy to be out of there that Cherie was almost an afterthought.

That week I talked to the kids a few times on their cell phones, and then saw them on visitation day, Saturday. I picked them up promptly at noon, but they both had friends they wanted to see and stuff to do. So I drove them to their events after the three of us had a nice quiet lunch in Davis Square. We even talked a little bit about the divorce and how we all felt about it, so it was a success. I was so relieved to find that I would be able to keep a relationship with my kids after all, in spite of their mother. I felt pretty good about that.

The therapy session on Wednesday was a whopper. Cherie was looking particularly appetizing that day, wearing a silky striped jersey thing that showed off her curves. When I picked her up, I was in a good mood, and we had a lot of laughs on the way. I vowed to myself that today was the day to make my move.

First Irene had us take turns giving the group a detailed report of what was bothering us and how we had dealt with it that week. Cherie came up with a shocker telling us about a man who grabbed her in the basement of her apartment house when she was doing laundry. He would've raped her, she said, but she screamed bloody murder and another tenant came running. She was proud she'd been able to scream. Apparently, she had actually been raped some years earlier and that was one reason she was here.

"I wasn't able to scream that time," she was explaining in a strangulated voice, "I opened my mouth but no sounds came, like in nightmares. I never dared tell anybody, not even my mom. She probably would've hit me."

"Very good, Cherie," crooned Irene. "You were strong. You protected yourself. And then you were able to tell us about it. Very good."

I didn't have time to sneer at Irene's preachy manner. I was too absorbed in how I was going to share my feelings. What words could I use? I didn't want to sound like a wimp.

When it was my turn, I said, "I had a good experience this week." I looked around at all the faces, realizing they were in the same boat. So I went on, "I was really worried I wouldn't be able to be a dad any more to my kids. But we had lunch."

"Lunch," Irene repeated, nodding.

She wanted more? I was more scared than skeptical.

I said," We had a nice lunch. We all talked. I feel good about it."

"Okay," sighed Irene, as if I had fallen short somehow. "Thank you, Red."

After she got all the confessions, and all of us were kind of wrung out and exhausted, we had to get down on the floor and meditate. I wasn't too sorry. It was really peaceful listening to my breath, picturing the colors of my forehead, chest, groin. I found a place inside myself where I could go for comfort. It was pretty amazing.

But, naturally, Irene wasn't satisfied with that. She had to make us suffer some more. When she first described the crying meditation I got ready to flee the room. But I half thought it was a joke: surely she didn't believe she could get us all bawling just by giving us an order. Cheeky even for Irene Norvall. But she did!

She told us to get ready, close our eyes, and concentrate on something really, really sad. I started thinking about Freddy. Drinking all that booze by himself, getting zonked, all because Amanda and I, his parents, couldn't keep it together. Suddenly I hear this horrible wailing coming from somewhere. I can't even tell if it's male or female. My eyes fly open: by God it's poor old Hal, blubbering and pounding on his pillow. Then Cherie chimes in. She sounds awful, like a screeching two year old. I decide I simply can't stand this, I'm going to get out of here right this minute and never come back. Then I feel my own tears, squeeze them back, get so overwhelmed by the fact that I have started to cry that I sob out loud. My sob sounds worse than anybody else's, like an animal, a dog, but it's drowned out by all the agonized noises welling up around me. It sounds like a torture chamber. It is a torture chamber.

I have no idea how long that lasted. I was in and out of awareness, coming to as I was pounding my pillow, wet with my tears. How long had it been since I cried? My whole adult life. Those little old salty drops were stale from being stored up all that time, and once they got going they were not about to quit. Even when Irene finally told us it was ok to stop, most of us kept it up for a while. This I hate to confess: it felt wonderful. I've never been so drained in my memory, not after sports, not even after sex. I was simply emptied, I was a pristine and new vessel, I was reborn.

Irene passed out boxes of tissues and we sat around slobbering and blowing our noses and not daring to look each other in the eye.

In the car, Cherie was talking to herself, telling Cherie to be brave, she was safe. I can tell you, making a pass at her was the last thing on my mind. After I dropped her off, I had to sit for a long time before I dared go back to my office. For a minute I worried if I was gay. I mean, bawling like a baby and losing interest in that adorable little body! But I knew it was only Irene Norvall's clever tactics. If she had her way I'd become a wimp for sure. A ball breaker, that Ms. Norvall. For the rest of the afternoon I ordered my co-workers around like nobody's business.

It was Linda who asked me, "How's grandpa?"

It was Saturday and the three of us were sitting outside an ice cream shop. I was enjoying a mint chocolate chip with sprinkles. Freddy was nursing the same thing, but a double, and Linda scooped modestly with a tiny little spoon at a cup of strawberry yogurt. It was a fabulous fall day, colored with reddening trees and crisp but sunny. I was caught unawares by her question. I didn't realize she even remembered her grandfather.

"Well, honey…"

I waited so long for inspiration that she pushed me. "C'mon, Dad, he's your father. Don't you know how he is? Is he still sick?"

"Gee," chimed in Freddy, chomping ice cream, "how long's it been since we saw him?"

"I remember when I was eleven, two years ago," said Linda.

This was getting uncomfortable. I gave my cone a lengthy lick it didn't need, mumbled, "Why are you asking?"

The silence was enough of an answer. Why the hell shouldn't the kids ask about their grandfather?

So I said, "He's fine."

"Can we go see him? Is he going to stay in that place?"

"It's a nursing home. He's old and can't live by himself. He's not sick, just old."

"You sound like you don't care."

These barbs from my own darling little girl? I looked at her, hurt welling up in my eyes. But she gave me a comeback worthy of her mother.

"Dad, what is your problem?"

"I say we go visit him," blurts Freddy. Maybe he sensed trouble, but he was so wrapped up in conquering that chocolate mint mountain, I wasn't sure. It was probably just another ignorant asinine teenage idea.

But the upshot was, we went. The next Saturday, I picked the kids up early, giving Amanda the opportunity to sneer, "Visiting your own father? What a concept!"

The ride out to Methuen was tedious. I was tense, and the weather would have to be grey and drizzly so the colorful trees totally lost their luster. Also, I couldn't stop remembering Cherie's big drama in Wednesday's therapy session, when she told us her name was really Cheryl, and Queen Irene decided we were all going to call her that. I was forced to say Cheryl to her face, and shocked to see the gratitude and relief in her tear-stained little face. For some reason, this development meant curtains for my lust, and from then on I could only feel like the big brother I had pretended to be.

I'd only been here to this grim old institution once before. Linda got it right—two years ago. I picked Dad up to bring him into Cambridge for lunch with us. I remember that he needed a straw to drink, and his hands shook. He looked pitiful to me, but I found no compassion and hadn't seen him since. The place still smelled of cleaning fluid.

He was waiting in a sterile looking foyer, in a wheelchair. He took our tentative embraces as a matter of course, although I had never kissed him when I was growing up.

"How ya doing, Ed?" His tone was flat.

I told him I was fine, but I was furious. After all these years, with one foot in the grave, he still has to call me Ed?

"My name is Red," I suddenly said rudely. "Redmond."

But he paid no attention. He was stroking Linda's glossy blond hair. "What a pretty child. My little granddaughter. Growing up so pretty, what d'ya know?"

Linda to my disgust was loving it. Freddy shook hands with him and studied him as if hypnotized. The kids were having a ball, and I wanted to puke.

I sat there, staring out the picture window at the grey autumn landscape misted with drizzle. What a vale of tears this life is, I thought, overcome with self pity. Look at the shambles of my life. I dwelled on the river of tears old and new that I'd shed in the therapy session. Those bits of salty water, produced by my own body, seemed the real expression of all my experience, not the bombast and boasting of my public persona, the bossy coworker, the rule-making father, the ranting husband. What's the point, I wondered miserably. Someday soon I'll just be a sad sack of bones like this old man here.

Looking at the three of them smiling together, I suddenly realized I was jealous. They looked like a happy family. Wait a minute. This is my family. Why do I feel like such a jerk? I couldn't get over it. All the way back in the car and the rest of the week I planned my announcement.

On Wednesday I said to the group, "I've got something to share."

They all perked up, especially Irene Norvall. Oh boy, she's really going to crow when she finds out what I finally have to say. She's wormed it out of me at last.

"I feel like a failure," I said. I meant it to sound authoritative but it was more like a moan. "I've never done anything in my life I was proud of. My parents didn't even love me. I don't want to look in the mirror any more. I hate who I am."

There was a breathless silence in the wake of my words. Then Ms. Irene Norvall crooned, "Very good, Red. We're all proud of you."

Cheryl said, "Hey, Red, that's so brave. Welcome to the world."

I'm Dolores

The sky was that January color, more white than blue even though the sun was shining, vapid, metallic, one-dimensional. As boring and blah as I felt that morning waiting for the bus to New York, taking refuge from the biting wind in our dinky little Binghamton terminal. The bus was already late, having run into snow in Ohio. A dozen people stood listlessly staring at the schedule board, which had flashed "Delayed" half an hour ago and not moved since.

A woman next to me mumbled something to a tiny shivering dog she held in one arm, its nose sticking out from the folds of her voluminous ratty fur coat. Her gray hair was long, abundant, and curly. She was wearing tons of makeup with bright red lipstick. She looked odd, but at the same time vaguely familiar. She peered at me from behind gray curls and bobbed her head.

"I'm Dolores," she said shyly, "Remember? Dolores Barto."

"Dolores Barto! Of course I remember. Grad school, 1992, Columbia."

"Those were the days."

But I was stunned speechless. The Dolores I knew in the 90s had luxuriant black hair. She was my age, not yet thirty, with a bounce in her step and a twinkle in her eye. This woman looked ages older than me, like sixty or something, although how could that possibly be, it was only some twenty years ago. The Dolores I knew dressed plainly and never wore makeup at all. For a moment I wondered if I had changed that much as well. But my hair was still naturally brown, my body toned with aerobics, my face adorned only with modest pink lipstick. Besides, she'd recognized me right away, hadn't she?

Dolores went on talking for a while, then her subsequent silence jogged me into commenting, "Remember Professor Gambetti, Italian Renaissance?"

"Sure." Dolores was eager to respond. "Great guy."

"But a bit of a lush," I reminded her.

"Still. Entertaining. Remember George Perkins? What a hunk."

"I had such a crush on him. Did he ever make it to Harvard?"

Dolores gave a hoarse little sound, rather like the sarcastic cackle she made fun with in the old days. I was wafted back to my youth, my unrequited lust for George Perkins, what life was like when it was mostly in front of you. I was warming to Dolores just as the schedule board announced that our bus would be another half hour late.

She said timidly, "Shall we go get coffee?"

We settled at a small greasy table in the terminal cafeteria, with a view of the platform. Beyond we could see that it had started snowing. I should have known. That morning my husband had quipped, "You're going to be stranded, I can tell you right now. There's weather on the way." I'd replied that nothing in this world would keep me one more day from visiting my sister in New York. She had a new baby only two weeks old, named Linda, after me.

We both ordered decaf and Dolores made me hold the miniscule dog while she unbuttoned her fur coat, though she didn't take it off. The poor little animal shook as if in the last throes of death by terror, but Dolores assured me that was natural.

"Percy is purebred Chihuahua. He's not scared, just nobility."

I laughed but it was not a joke. Dolores did not herself laugh at anything beyond her cough-like cackle, or smile much either besides a suggestive stretch of her thin crimson lips. She regaled me with her life story: a job at New York University, a failed marriage, an abortion, an appendectomy, a hobby collecting dried flowers, and a new love interest named Rob. It was clearly drama to her, but to me simply anybody's life. As for my story, she seemed interested only in my appointment at Binghamton teaching Turkish history. Ten minutes before the bus was to arrive, Dolores shoved Percy at me again and stood up abruptly.

"Got to pee." And she was off the to the ladies room in a swirl of fur and gray curls.

I clutched the dog with a mixture of unease and pity. Its little black nose seemed the largest part of its pointy face, and its protruding black eyes suggested tears. The only dog I had ever known was a huge Husky mix who was afraid of nothing.

I felt compelled to comfort Percy. "It's okay," I promised.

But it wasn't. Dolores didn't return from the bathroom, even after the last call of "All aboard." I waited by the bus door while the driver glared and fidgeted.

"We're going to start on time," he growled at me.

"My friend is just in the ladies room, we have to wait for her."

"Go and get her, then. Two minutes tops."

Percy and I rushed to the bathroom, peeked in all the stalls. In the last one, hanging on a hook, was Dolores's fur coat, and also her curly gray hair, a wig. I stumbled out in shock, spluttering to the bus driver, "She's gone."

He looked at me like the idiot I felt, and said loudly, "Lady, you're nuts," got on the bus and drove away. As it pulled out of the station and I stood staring at it with my mouth open, a woman looked back at me from her seat at the window. She had very short black hair and no lipstick. She showed no recognition, but I did. It was Dolores Barto.

Imagining

I used to smoke a pipe. As a woman, I loved the dramatic effect. It was a big mistake, of course. It helped me give up cigarettes, but became another dirty little habit maliciously leading to asthma. So when this smallish, eager man tapped me on the breast with the stem of his pipe, I was unsurprised at the mix of repulsion and eroticism it evoked. We were standing in the sumptuous library of a mansion outside Gloucester, looking at tapestries.

I had just turned to him and said, "What's it like to live here all winter with nothing but ocean, and then experience this rush of summer tourists?"

As soon as I fully looked at him, noted his bemused expression, I realized he was the wrong person. I had thought the curator-owner was just behind me. I began to apologize but he was already replying, with that lunge of his jaw forward I came to know as his engagement with a conundrum.

"I quite agree," he said, stepping closer and jabbing that pipe stem at me. He reeked of pipe smoke and professorship. "I was thinking the same thing myself. This gorgeous spread of kings and horses everyone is so admiring, could that be enough every damn bleak January day?"

"Sorry, I thought you were…Never mind. Glad you agree."

We were almost the same height, and he was about my age, mid-forties. He had curly, graying, balding hair that was awry on one side as if he hadn't combed it since he woke up. He wore glasses and a green T-shirt printed with "Clue Me In." He had wonderful big dark eyes that gleamed with more than scholarly intent.

I'm not bad looking, I'm used to male attention, though it has begun to fade in recent years. I don't mind. I look forward to the day I can walk into a bar without being stared at. But I do admit I keep my hair blonde and my body athletic, if only so I can enjoy looking at myself.

He continued, "I imagine he comes in here every winter morning even before breakfast to ascertain his ongoing ownership of timeless beauty, historical drama. Keeps him sane when he has to dig out his car, if he can, I'll bet it snows insanely out here on Cape Ann. Would it tide me over 'til spring? Would it tide you over?"

"I would like imagining I was a grand lady in the fourteenth century admiring my dowry."

I withdrew my gaze from his luminous eyes, resting it instead on the view outside the broad window, rocks and gleaming water, boats, sweep of summer sky. It was very hot out there, I knew, but rather weirdly cool in here, as if the time warp came complete with weather switch.

"That wouldn't last through your buttered toast."

His slightly mocking tone intrigued me. He was more interested in winning than in charming. I liked that. I smiled, he smiled. I put out my finger to touch the tapestry, disappointed to feel protective Plexiglas instead of centuries-old wool.

"Look here," I said softly. "Take a look at this lovely little pear tree. You can just smell the fruit, can't you?"

"It's exquisite," he agreed, without pretense. "It just might get me through January."

"I'd like to go back to 1346, for one day. Or maybe a few days."

"I often long to do that. My specialty is the early seventeenth century but the Middle Ages are so exotic."

"The smells would have been pungent," I chuckled. Now I'd turned to face him fully. This was an intriguing man. I had one at home, but he was wearing a little thin. Besides, his clear fascination with me when mixed with his creative pedantry drove home a need.

"You would've been wearing a low-necked dress with enormous sleeves, little buttons all up the front."

I laughed in reply, "And you would've been wearing tights." I kept on laughing, he seemed so mesmerized by the inside of my mouth.

After that, we moved along side by side to view other magnificent pieces, exclaiming and sighing in unison. I found out that he and his family, a wife and two little kids, were renting a cottage in nearby Rockport. He learned that I was only up for the day from Cambridge, with a group of women friends who were at the beach. I was to pick up lunch and join them soon. He also learned of the husband and teenage daughter I was not eager to talk about. I mentioned my work as publications editor at Tufts University. But mostly we explored our mutual world of porous time, the intrigue of passing from one age to another, what it would be like to return to the past knowing what we knew in the present. The future didn't interest us. We wanted to invite Mozart to dinner, or Voltaire, or Caesar. We found ourselves at the exit, excitedly arguing how those three would get along.

The air before us was shimmering with heat. We pulled back into the cool of the building for one last exchange. We were in a sort of drawing room, plush with Victoriana, though obviously lived in. I wanted to comment on the owner's taste, but my new friend had reached out to lay his hand on my shoulder, thumb at my neck. That silenced me. I knew what he was going to say.

"Can we meet again?"

My reply was falsely chipper. "What, for more arguments about time machines?"

He moved his thumb a little. "Of course."

"Harvard Square?"

"My office is in the Yard. Emerson Hall. Coffee?"

"Next week okay?"

"We'll be back the twenty-third. Drop by any time. I'm counting on it."

"Sure," I said casually.

"Erica," he said, savoring my name. "Erica."

"Goodbye, Stan. Don't dash away to 1346 without me."

With that, I was practically running to my car, excited and embarrassed at what might result from this. It could so easily come to nothing, so it was still simply fun.

Stan and I had coffee a couple of weeks later, toward the end of July. We chose a place that also served drinks, so it was easy to graduate to a glass of wine. He was wearing a vanilla colored jacket that gave him a jaunty, sailorly air, and what was left of his springy hair was combed almost calm. I was very self-consciously showing off a lime green sheath that fit perfectly. We both confessed to be leaving soon for weeks-long vacations, he to Martha's Vineyard, me to Paris. So these few hours together felt like stolen time, the kind of stolen time we loved to imagine experiencing in other centuries.

"Let's pretend we're in Louis XIV's court," I said. "Versailles. You're a conspirator. A musketeer, maybe?"

"And you're the king's mistress."

"No, how about I'm the queen."

"Erica, my sweet, you don't want to be Queen Maria Theresa. How about a young lady's maid?"

"Ok, so I can be in on the conspiracy with you. An intrigue."

"An intrigue," he repeated sensually. "A lady's maid and a young musketeer. What shall we plot? Shall we have a love affair?"

"We shall plot to steal the queen's pearls."

"Oh, that's too materialistic. Let's murder the prime minister or the archbishop."

"I can't do murder. Too serious."

"Just like a girl. Ok, we'll kidnap them. Okay? Satisfied?"

I agreed and we shook on it, laughing like kids.

Stan walked me to my car, parked up on Brattle Street. It was a gorgeous summer evening, cooling off like a baby. I got in, and he got in beside me. I opened my mouth to protest but he was already kissing it. Our kisses were sloppy and frantic, mixed with not a little fear someone would see us. I could only get him out of the car by promising to meet him the following day. But I was determined to break the promise, and I did.

The next thing I knew, I got an invitation to a cocktail party at Stan's house, addressed to both my husband and me. What could be more on the up and up? But it excited me beyond measure. I knew I was extremely attracted to this man and should not go near him. I billed him to my husband as a stodgy old pedant I'd known in grad school. He bought it, and we went.

Here I am, walking in the door of this impressive Colonial-style house on Lowell Street, on the arm of my handsome if somewhat pudgy husband, straight into the home of my co-conspirator and his wife. Danielle is resplendent in colorful silks, but there's a great deal of her. She's not exactly fat, just plentiful. I muse, if Stan's that into buxom, what's he want with me?

Stan is cool towards me, just exactly right, very cordial with my husband, but I'm annoyed. I miss his heat, his alarming pressure, his probing, intimate gaze. I don't smile in return. The children are there. Apparently they have refused to go to bed, and mommy indulges and scolds them alternately. Stan frowns and orders them upstairs, but they only giggle. They make a terrible mess of canapés and milk on the living room rug.

There's a nice mix of folks old and young, but there are too many of them, and the food runs out. At one point, as respite from the crush and noise, I slip out to a cool shaded back porch, and there Stan finds me. His hands are on my arms, he says, "Erica."

"My musketeer."

I am too playful, he is too serious. We only have a few minutes. The upshot is, I okay his coming to my office for lunch the next day. What can be the harm in that, I tell myself. But lying in bed that night listening to my husband snoring in the next room, I know what I'm going to do.

Stan and I start an affair that graduates from fiery to routine. What holds me, after the first thrill of naughtiness and his insatiable skinny, hairy body, are the elaborate scenarios of our lives in faraway times. We build castles. I love being Anne Radcliffe, re-inventing Gothic dramas with endangered heroines. He becomes Chaucer, balancing brilliant poetry with clever power moves as a courtier. We play Lancelot and Guinevere, hiding under the covers from her husband King Arthur. I am wildly grateful to Stan for freeing me to be a child again.

We meet sporadically, whenever we can arrange suitable cover—a dentist appointment, a car fix, an important client—our invented obligations are part of our imaginary wanderings. Our favorite rendezvous is a B&B run by an old schoolmate of mine. We have keys to her suite in the renovated barn decorated country style, with actual chintz curtains and hand hooked rugs. It has a small, brass framed, ridiculously soft bed, like a cloud.

Carefree summer moves into more sedate fall, with the intensely augmented duties every university finds upon the return of students. One afternoon we're getting dressed, clucking amazement that it's already getting dark outside although only five o'clock. Stan puts on his black belted raincoat, flips up the collar.

"I've got a conference in France coming up. It's in Annecy, but I thought…"

I pause in pulling on my boots. "Paris? Are you serious?"

"You love Paris."

"Stan." I finish with the boots, get up to hug him. "I would so love to love you in Paris."

"I thought so."

We get to kissing so hard, it's an effort to stop. He has my freshly applied lipstick all over his face and we have to clean it off with soap, laughing. We're still laughing when we hurry out into the chilly dusk, a delicate rain descending. How am I going to find an excuse to go to Paris in November? This will take some convoluted machinations.

When I get home around six, with a few groceries in tow, my daughter Angela is sitting in front of the TV with her boyfriend. Now this is not forbidden, but something about it gives me pause. The girl is fourteen, pretty voluptuous already, not very adept in school, and mouthy to her parents. But she obeys the curfews, and most of the rules. This boy suddenly looks too mature to me. He's got a stubble, he must already shave, meaning hormones. My husband isn't home yet, so what have these two kids been doing all this rainy afternoon?

I flash back to my fourteen-year-old self, back home in Ohio. I had a job after school, but Wednesdays off. It was on a Wednesday that I saw my first erect penis. It was downhill from there.

"Angela," I say nonchalantly when the boyfriend has left. "Let's have a little talk."

She looks so startled I realize that I have never said this before. Immediately I feel guilty. I want to be a good mother. Oh boy. Take a big breath.

But she's all innocence and cheeky indignation, no matter what I say. She has her well-worn teenage retorts instantly ready, from "It's none of your business" to "You think you know everything" to "I didn't ask to be born." We wind up in her room, because I have followed her there. It's dark outside the pink-curtained windows. Teddy bears and shaggy dogs piled up on her unmade bed, and a huge poster of a rock star with his pants pulled down to just above his crotch. What a mishmash of pleasures! I can't get a clue of what she's thinking or feeling or who she is. I study her face while she's yelling at me, but see only the blotched and bloated red face of a stranger.

In Paris the first thing Stan and I do is visit the Cluny Museum. I'm in a little hotel on the rue Saint Severin, just around the corner, so Stan picks me up. A few months earlier, we would've rushed upstairs to make love first, but now we're more excited about the unicorn tapestry. I'm waiting in the hotel lobby that's decked out like a drawing room, graced with red velvet chairs and a hotel cat. Stan saunters in, gives me the French greeting of kisses on both cheeks, but I doubt the concierge is fooled for one minute.

At the museum we sit in the shadowy low light that illuminates only the scenes before us, larger than life: the delicate yet sexy ladies, prancing dogs and horses, gorgeously attired princes, unicorns with the grace of ethereal beings and the sensuousness of bedrooms. Gardens, flowers, fruit trees, gentle landscapes, magnificent castles. We get up and prowl past each scene in the drama, holding hands without worry. We can't tear ourselves away. Both of us have been here before, but never experienced such oneness with the imagination, passion, and humor of the people who created this masterpiece. Stan and I are there, in the sixteenth century, and we stay there when we go to bed, the rest of the day and night. Stan insists on being the unicorn.

It's only the next day, as I'm wandering the sixth *arrondissement* still catching up with jet lag, that I begin to realize. I have strolled to the middle of Pont St. Michel, leaning on the thick concrete balustrade, contemplating the velvety gray swath of the Seine. There's a chilly wind at my back but the sun is out, gilding wavelets, enhancing the sumptuous gilt of further bridges. For a small moment I treasure a memory from last night, Stan's beaming face, then the edge of dissatisfaction cuts in. I realize like a blow that I have never had what I wanted. I did not marry the man I most desired, nor did I have a child I adore, my profession is simply the best I could do with a B.A. in English, I have to live in Cambridge when I long for Paris or London. I didn't even get the parents that suited me. My mother was always depressed, my father while he lived never got over his traumas in Vietnam.

I allow the thought: Stan is not what I really want either. I dream of a tall dark stranger, a poet or painter perhaps, who will worship me. Sex with Stan has come to be a lot like it used to be with my husband, when we were still having it. I'm tired of Stan, I'm tired of everything. And I am having this illumination while blessed with a view of the most beautiful, intriguing city in the world. I'm tired of Paris.

Stan and I go back to Gloucester in January. We've chosen a splendid winter day, bright white sunshine, temperature near melting, still-clean snow padding front yards. But we have not grown cheerful speeding away from our responsibilities. On the contrary, as we follow the familiar narrow roads out to Eastern Point, we grow more taciturn. I am almost bored. Was this outing worth the elaborate skein of lies

I concocted for my family? The invention of a cousin with cancer in a Rockport hospital was almost more fun than the trip itself. I find myself hoping Stan hasn't planned a motel room on the way. He takes a gloved hand off the wheel and guides my hand to his thigh. But I let it rest there, don't take the hint.

We pull into the broad curve of driveway, no longer lined with cars, now empty. The mansion looks totally altered without leaves on the grand old trees, abandoned. The ocean seethes dark and menacing. We'd called ahead for special permission to view the tapestries. Off-season tourists are not encouraged, but the man on the phone had been more than eager to welcome us. He seems older and sadder, though it was only seven months ago we were there. Stan and I ask good questions, dutifully sigh in admiration, but the scenes that so enchanted us, the scenes that drove us into each other's arms, hang limp and uninspiring in heartless snow-bleached light.

"I was right," Stan mutters as we return to the car. "They can't get us through January."

Stan and I vowed to remain friends. But when spring came I realized we'd only had coffee a few times since our last rendezvous, which was about a week after our Gloucester trip, bordering on February. We made love in the renovated barn. Stan was Beowulf and I the monster Grendel's mother, which we dubbed a thrilling concept, but the whole thing fell pretty flat. Half dressed, we sat looking at each other and called it quits.

"I've never really had what I wanted," I offered, grandly sharing my insight.

Stan lit his pipe, though he knew it might make me cough, and commented with irritating professorial condescension, "Perhaps, then, you should want what you have."

That bitter barb hit home like an arrow. I never forgot it.

I started pulling on my blouse. "We'd better get going."

He nodded, puffing smoke. "Besides, Danielle is making pot roast tonight and I promised to be on time."

If Fish Could Cry

It wasn't a threesome in the usual sense. They worked in the same office building in Boston, and met over time in the closest cafeteria. What bound them was they all had seven-year-old daughters.

Polly, Fred, and Lloyd ate lunch together just about every day. The stress of their jobs fell away as they boasted and complained about their girls, finding endless parallels and situations in common. For example, Polly was at her wit's end because little Sophie refused to brush her teeth. Lloyd jumped in at once.

"My Angela was the same! I thought her teeth would rot. I even brushed them myself, holding her head still, God help me. And then her mother came up with a plan. No dessert. "

"Brilliant," beamed Polly. "I'll try it."

The next day Polly reported bitterly, "It worked all of one time, until my husband found out about it."

"Let me guess," Fred put in. "He nixed it. Too mean."

"You got it," Polly moaned. "His little darling has to have her ice cream no matter what."

A couple of weeks before Christmas, Fred proposed a group shopping trip after work. The three of them gathered in front of their building and sauntered over to Macy's. Snow dribbled gently catching at eyelashes; store windows sparkled myriad versions of green and red; bells and carols mingled. Dolls, games, books, trinkets, a science kit and a weaving set. Each parent came away with a gift and good ideas for more.

"Can we do clothes next week?" urged Fred. He was divorced and self-conscious about his limited know-how of little girls. He wanted to go out for dinner but Polly and Lloyd had to get home to their spouses.

"Haven't you got Caroline this weekend?" Polly asked him.

"Yep, tomorrow and Sunday. I'm taking her to the circus."

"Super. Okay, bye guys. See you Monday."

Polly hurried off towards the subway, a slim but sturdy woman in a trendy leather coat. Both men looked after her.

"Terrific woman," commented Fred.

"Nice ass too," added Lloyd.

"Now that you mention it," Fred agreed.

Over the winter months the three grew closer. Sometimes after work they met in Paddy's Bar, huddling in their favorite booth far from the door, where the din of the crowd was muted. In March they started talking about everyone getting together sometime, all the little girls and spouses included. Polly was the most enthusiastic. She even started researching houses for rent in the summer on Cape Cod.

"We'll go for a week. I figure we'll only need four bedrooms—the kids can all share one, right? How about Eastham or Wellfleet?"

Lloyd fretted over the price. "Has to cost a couple of thou."

He ran his own import business, Langetelli & Co, plus he had two teenagers from a previous marriage. While Polly and Fred were in their thirties, Lloyd was "pushing fifty," and hoping college expenses wouldn't interfere with his plans for retirement.

"I saw a nice house for $2000 a week," Polly replied. "But the one I love that has a gorgeous view is asking $3000."

"We can do that," Fred argued, "split three ways."

Lloyd was persuaded, and so Polly ordered another strawberry daiquiri in honor of their plan. The days were getting longer and spring was in the air in spite of lingering ice and cutting winds. It was still light around six or so when they hugged goodbye at the door.

"You guys are my life savers," Polly said.

They all agreed theirs was a special and uncommon friendship.

"I call it my support group," chuckled Lloyd, "when Gina gets jealous."

One stormy April evening when it had been raining buckets, Polly showed up at Paddy's late. She peeled off her dripping raincoat, pushed sodden hair out of her eyes.

"Boss give you trouble?" quipped Lloyd.

Polly administered a small non-profit whose board chair was a notorious micromanager. But both men swallowed their teasing laughter when they saw her face.

"Walt wants a divorce," she announced.

Why, they demanded, cursing the man contemptuously.

Polly tumbled over her words. "He wants custody too. The first thing I know, I hear from his lawyer. I'm an unfit mother." While her friends blustered protests, she added, "I never told you about the DUI."

Silence. Polly gulped her daiquiri and held it up like a courtroom clue. "I drink a lot of these. Haven't you noticed?"

Fred and Lloyd became solemn.

"He's serious," said Lloyd. "He's got a case."

"The man's a shithead," Fred snorts. "We knew that already. Lots of people drink, Polly."

"I got arrested a few weeks ago," Polly continued. "Driving home after dinner with the girls. Oh, yeah, I was plastered. Thank goodness I only scraped a parked car. They put handcuffs on me. They suspended my license. They're going to take away my little girl. My baby."

"Come on, be a fighter," urged Fred. "I'm a lawyer. You can beat this."

"You're a real estate lawyer," Lloyd reminded him.

Polly was crying quietly. They let her cry. Fred reached across the table to pat her hand. Lloyd supplied a rumpled handkerchief. Everything will be okay, they told her.

The big old house rambled along a dirt road in Wellfleet called Samoset Avenue. It had a lovely view across the harbor, and stone steps down to the water.

The children ran to splash in it upon arrival. Lloyd's wife Gina volunteered as life guard. She was a portly woman with a huge bosom and thinning red hair who clearly had once been a beauty. Gina was a jolly and gentle soul who had rolled with a lot of punches in ten years of being married to Lloyd. The rest of them sat on the deck and watched from above, each with a proud eye on their own little darling.

Polly's Sophie was a mythically beautiful child, with the golden curls and ruby pout Rubens loved to capture. Lloyd's Angela was a bossy, plump brunette, Fred's Caroline lanky as a colt, and as skittish. They jockeyed among themselves for importance, but sea and sand worked harmonious wonders to soothe all edges.

It was late Saturday afternoon, and the three cars had arrived pretty much at the same time for the permitted one o'clock check in. Polly and Gina went grocery shopping while Lloyd and Fred made up the beds and helped the kids unpack. Then the celebratory drinks were poured, the glorious view exclaimed over, a plate of cheese and crackers made the rounds. Close to six o'clock, when Polly had gone into the kitchen to check on the baking bluefish, there was a commotion down at the driveway. A saucy red Ferrari pulled up, and out jumped two handsome, tousled young men who made no effort to soften the surprise of their arrival.

'We're here to see Dad," they yelled exuberantly.

Lloyd was forced to shamefacedly admit he had "sort of" invited his sons to join them, "just for a few nights, if it's all right."

"Where will they sleep?" asked Fred, not hiding his annoyance.

But that was no problem. The boys had brought a tent, which they erected in no time. Vince was eighteen, Eddie sixteen. They completely changed the tone of the gathering. Polly, at first dismayed to have her peaceful prospects disrupted, ended by enjoying the fresh breeze of youth across her stale and scary life.

On Tuesday a phone call came for Polly. It was her lawyer. Everyone stopped in their tracks; they'd all been waiting with her for this call. When they heard her choking cry, they knew. Walt had won custody.

Nobody talked about it because Polly didn't want Sophie to know. In fact, after her initial shock, she pretended nothing was wrong. "I just want to enjoy this vacation," she said when pressed. But she made free with her daiquiris and presented rather a pitiful even obnoxious presence at the evening gathering. She'd been swimming and wore a terry throw over her bikini. Vince was making eyes at her, Eddie simpering in the background. Polly smiled and laughed a lot. Fred tried to get her to drink ginger ale, but she waved him away. Lloyd was grilling swordfish, Gina mixing a giant salad. Fred went to play life guard with the kids down on the shore. Polly announced she'd go take a shower, and "get properly dressed for this esteemed gathering."

Off she went, to the outdoor shower on the side of the house, where you could look straight up at the sparkling sky. Fat round clouds scudded in the gentle evening breeze. Polly made free with the privacy to have a good cry, her tears mingling with soap. After a while, sobering up a bit, she quieted, rinsing off and pondering how to tell Sophie. She would stress her visitation rights twice a week. She would emphasize all the times they'd still have together, and make plans. Suddenly there was Vince beside her, naked.

He stopped her scream with a violent kiss. "You're so beautiful," he muttered.

His passion and his praise electrified her. For a few seconds she was as eager as he to make the connection, start the magic ride in the warm gushing water. She threw her arms and legs around him. But almost at once he made a high noise in her ear and dropped her, hastily rinsed off his groin, and was gone. She staggered clumsily, and stood like an idiot as water kept on pouring over her, trying not to believe what had happened, but already disgusted.

The next morning, Vince and Eddie took off, with loud hearty goodbyes. Polly stayed on the porch, but Vince blew her a kiss from the driver's seat. She thought, the boy has no idea what he has done, and her anger melted in shame.

Later on Gina and Polly drove into town to buy fish and oysters at Hatch's.

As they parked the car, Gina confessed, "I feel bad about it, but I'm glad they're gone."

"Don't feel bad, those boys are a trial. Thank goodness you two didn't get custody of them."

"No, but they descend on us every vacation. That's no fun. Angela loves them, she says they're so cool, she picks up all sorts of bad habits and language from them. They treat her like a mascot. And they won't listen to Lloyd, and certainly not to me."

"Well, I guess they'll grow up one of these days," Polly replied lamely.

"I hope I live to see it," Gina sighed.

Waiting while Gina picked out vegetables at a nearby stand, Polly watched a pickup truck pull up to Hatch's, backing in. It was full of gutted fish, their bodies open red caves. One that lay immediately beneath her seemed to return her stare. Its silver skin shone as if still alive. The little mouth sprouted needle teeth, its fins were impossibly delicate fans.

"Blues," replied the driver, when she asked. "Bluefish. Good catch today."

He and another man began unloading the bodies, which slithered on their slippery scales the way they must have in their infinite watery home. Polly was flooded with sorrow. Something that beautiful was killed just to feed her. Why was its life any less important than hers?

Determinedly, after lunch she took Sophie on a walk looking for shells along the shore, just the two of them. Today was very hot so they wore hats and shirts against the sun. The water glimmered pale blue and mirror calm, motes of sunlight dashing off it like butterflies. Polly's grief was lead heavy. She feared she was about to break her little girl's heart.

"So, Sophie, do you want to talk about Mommy and Daddy deciding to live in different places?"

The child dug her toes into the sand, picked up a stone and threw it.

"No."

"Well, honey. There must be some things you'd like to know. Mommy's going to stay in the house we have now, and Daddy will have a new house. We will see each other all the time."

"Just not together. I know, Daddy told me. I'm going to have three new dollies in my room at his house on Maple Street. I chose them already. One has blond curly hair just like mine, and some outfits. I chose the orange suit and he says I can choose more outfits soon. I hope it's really soon. I like the pink frilly one, the party one, so very much."

"What else did Daddy tell you?"

"I will show you my new dollies, Mommy, I promise. I'm sure you'll like them."

Sophie picked up another stone and threw it. Polly waited. She put her arm around her daughter and pulled her close, but the child was stiff and unresponsive.

"Sophie, you will live with Daddy but you will see me all the time. We're going to have supper together on Wednesdays and the whole weekend every other week. We can go swimming at the Y on Saturdays just the way we do now. And lots of other things."

"Mommy, I'm sorry you can't be a better mommy. Daddy says you try but you just can't do it. That's why the judge wants me to live with Daddy. He takes care of me."

Polly sat frozen looking out at the heartbreakingly beautiful ocean. Her arm fell away from her child's shoulder. Her loss felt cavernous. But her daughter seemed already adjusted. Walt would no doubt bring other women into the picture; it wouldn't take him long to find a stepmother. And the going myth was already established: poor Polly just couldn't hack it and Sophie had to be rescued. It was somehow a more cruel version than just vilifying her. This way it was all her fault. Little Sophie would grow up believing that.

Should she tell the child this divorce was not her idea? Tell her she wanted to keep her more than anything in the world? She'd read that separated parents should try to present a united front. Hogwash. Bullshit. Polly had been cut in half and was bleeding to death and it was all legal.

So she said, "Sophie, I love you and I want you to stay with me."

"Oh, Mommy," Sophie sighed in an incredibly adult tone, "I know you did your best. Just don't make it harder. Okay?"

That evening, the group had a permit to build a bonfire on the beach. The August sun was setting earlier every day, so by eight the flames were bright against the dimming sky. The children were beside themselves with excitement, preparing marshmallows on sticks. Lloyd showed off his expertise in burying corn in the sand to roast it. Fred was overseeing the bluefish bake. Polly knew her depression weighed on all the other adults, but they were gentle with her, and she was grateful. Fred in particular made a point of including her in everything without making any demands. She was looking at him with new eyes. He had always seemed too skinny and serious, his round glasses giving him a mousy look. When she'd thought about it, she always found Lloyd the more attractive man, with his dark Italian looks. But Fred's kindness was an unexpected balm. Gina was, of course, the most openly solicitous, often embracing Polly, making free to kiss her and cuddle her like the wounded soul she was. But the warm vibes from Fred were the sweetest.

"Come over here, Polly," he said. "Tell me what you think about this old fish here. Is he done? Is he too done?"

She went over to the fireside, smiling her best. "I'm sure he's fine."

Fred put an arm around her shoulder. "Thanks."

She tried not to say it, but it came out. "He died for us. To feed us."

Fred turned to look at her face. "Polly, don't."

"I'm sorry. But I wonder, do fish cry?"

He was slow to answer but perfectly serious. "I don't know."

They looked at the fish together. It was at this point just a slab of browned flesh, grooves where bones and organs once were. There were no eyes or skin or fins to conjure life. But it was for a moment the saddest sight on earth.

Later on, when the girls had toasted their marshmallows, Fred's daughter Caroline cut her finger on something. He held and rocked her, then asked Polly to hold her while he bandaged it up. Caroline's screams were more fear than pain. In Polly's embrace she watched with fascination as the white bandage grew around her finger and some ruby red blood seeped through.

Polly felt the bony little body curving into hers, smelled its soap, sweat, and sugary marshmallow, rested her cheek on the silky hair as the child's sobs subsided, crooned nonsense about Doctor Daddy and his magic touch.

Fred and Polly sat with Caroline between them, in the rosy light of embers, listening to the sigh of the sea.

Sally Lawton

Sedgewick Swan is so young he has only one wrinkle, around the curve of a nostril. He's not even near thirty. He has a long face, but good-looking, and sandy-hued hair he teases into a modest Mohawk. We meet on a plane from London to Boston in late July. Before I gulp down enough wine and manage to stomach a really bland "vegetarian option" (while Sedgewick demolishes a juicy steak), I get to hear his life story. I guess he figures I'm at least fifty, so a safe vessel for his emotions.

Or maybe it's his recent visit to his father in Oxford, which has obviously upset him, that loosens his tongue.

"Dad's an Oxford don," he explains. "He's a big shot on Byzantine history. But I don't really know the guy. My parents divorced when I was five. My mom and I moved to Jersey—she's American—Hoboken."

I'm trying to swallow pasty macaroni. Why do airlines punish vegetarians? I start to respond with confidences of my own.

"My name's Jenny. I've just been visiting an old school friend…"

But Sedgewick ("call me Sedge") continues in mounting anxiety, "It's pretty weird not knowing your father and you have to call him Dad and he calls you my boy and it's so fake and you both know it."

Oh, I get it. I'm supposed to shut up and listen. I calculate how I can go to sleep without his noticing. The flight attendant takes our trays and I settle in to get as comfortable as I can in the sardine space.

Yawning, I add, "We went to five plays in two weeks. We were in the Drama Club together at Bromfield…"

Sedge almost yelps, "Bromfield!"

"My high school."

"Did you know Sally Lawton?"

"Don't think so. What year was she?"

"She's quite a bit older than me." Does he look sheepish? "She must be in her early 40s now."

"After my time. A friend of yours?"

"I'll say. A wonderful, dear friend. What a fine woman. Super fine."

Sedge's face has relaxed into affectionate nostalgia. He really is a sweet-looking boy when he's not all nerves.

"Wait a minute," I say, "she must be Trudy Lawton's little sister."

"Sally's sister Trudy. You got it. You know her?"

"She was in the class just below me. Played field hockey. Terrific goalie. Trudy's a TV anchor now, you know. In Chicago, I think?"

"Sally didn't care for Trudy," Sedge confides.

"Okay." End of conversation?

"Sally lives in New York now. At least last time I knew. She friended me on Facebook but then she dropped me. I guess I was bugging her."

The pilot announces our height and speed. The video showing the plane's route switched over Ireland and turned into a movie, which looks to be about war. Good, I want to sleep anyway.

"That's too bad." I yawn again, with real passion, settle the mini pillow against my cheek, close my eyes.

"Sally Lawton," croons Sedge. "So fine, such a fine lady. What a woman!"

I picture Trudy, big boned and solid, and doubt the sisters resemble each other.

Sedge goes on, "She was a friend of my mother's, the summer I turned sixteen. We had nearby cottages on the Cape. So good to me, at that awful age. I fell all over in love with her. So fine, what a fine woman. Beautiful, too. Lots of this wavy hair the color of, I don't know, amber, you could say, or sunset. You know?"

I'm doing pretty well at dozing off, manage to mutter, "Sure."

He goes on talking, but the next thing I know, my neck screams in pain, I wake up massaging it.

"You were snoring," Sedge informs me.

"Thanks a lot."

"I've been thinking."

I'm contorting my body trying to ease all the aches, but can only go from one cramped position to another.

Miserably I query, "How much does First Class cost?"

"Jenny, I've been wondering if maybe you run into Trudy Lawton sometimes. Could you ask her about Sally and let me know?"

Sedge offers me a card that says 'Sales and Referrals.' "That's my email on there."

"Your job?"

"My last job. I had to quit to go visit Dad. That's okay. I'm starting grad school this fall. I want to be an astronomer."

I look at him hard. He's not joking. In fact, his earnestness is touching. Also I'm gratified to see he no longer looks fresh as a daisy, but has a hollow-eyed look like the rest of us. So when he asks me humbly for my card in return, I give it to him, second thoughts too late.

Sure enough, a couple of months later, here's an email from Sedge Swan. Why am I not surprised? And I know what it's about before I open it. Sally Lawton. Sedge and his friends are having a party and he begs me to invite her. I want to ignore this whole thing. I have a life of my own that's far too intense at the moment for any more drama. My son's girlfriend just had an abortion. He wasn't even going to tell me, just let it slip. Of course, they've got every reason in the world not to have a kid at this point, but it would have been my grandchild, and I'm having a lot of trouble with that. Plus, my boss at the nonprofit where I do fundraising is a micromanager driving me bonkers these days. But, as fate would have it, I recently saw Trudy Lawton on a TV panel about a Chicago company I've identified as a good prospect for a sizeable donation. What a perfect opportunity for inside information. So I call Trudy.

"Jenny! Sure I remember you. Well, Jenny. How long's it been since dear old crazy Bumfeely?"

Trudy is forthright and helpful about my donor prospect. We have a jolly chat. So that's how I learn Sally's been living in Boston for two years now. And that's how I find myself at eight o'clock on a chill October evening walking down Tremont Street.

The party's in a loft on the fifth floor. The noise is as breathtaking as the climb. Young people are running up and down the stairs past me. I remind myself that it's been at least twenty years since I went to a student party. What am I doing here?

But as soon as I catch sight of Sedge, I know the answer. His youth moves me. He's a blank slate just starting his adult life. He's a damaged child struggling with old demons. And I admit, I want to see the fireworks between him and Sally. He's assured me she will come; in his many brief but effusive emails I've been regaled with the progress of his persuasion.

Sedge is grinning and glowing as he greets me, introduces me, hands me a paper cup full of pinkish liquid. There's a scantily clad brunette hanging around his neck, but he hardly seems to notice.

"Have some punch. It'll fix you right up."

"I'll stick with wine, thanks."

"We got any wine?" he asks the air.

Nobody answers, nobody's paying attention to me, and Sedge is being jostled away by the crowd. So I take a sip. Whoa. Tastes like Kool-Aid but zaps like vodka. The music is some form of rap, all drums and monotone. I move as far away from the speakers as I can. The faces around me are laughing, intelligent, lively, tipsy. I search for someone available for conversation. Couples are forming but the men barely look me over. I'm not averse to flirting, but I don't get the chance. I haven't had sex for over a year, at least not properly speaking. My last boyfriend was over sixty and couldn't take Viagra because of his heart medications. He was very enthusiastic, but could never get beyond inventive substitutes.

I'm on my second cup of punch when Sally arrives. For a few moments, everyone turns to look at her. Do I even imagine a hush? She really is extraordinarily beautiful. No magazine model good looks here, instead a face all its own, quirks like full lips that pull a bit too far over her teeth, and a slim nose that flares. Every feature is in harmony, spaced as an idealist would, large eyes thickly lashed, hair that can actually be described as golden, cascading over supple shoulders. Every movement of her body has balletic grace, she gestures often with delicate hands. She's wearing something diaphanous, white and transparent, revealing a neat and modest slip underneath, lace along the edges. On her amazing wild mouth is very pink and shiny lipstick. Accompanying her is a rather squat man with a graying goatee.

Sedge is there in a flash. He's quite a bit taller, so from a distance the difference in their ages seems minimal. She's already pushing his hands away. Doesn't the kid get it? God, he knows nothing about women yet, poor guy. I start subtly moving closer so I can catch their conversation.

"Of course I recognized you," she's saying. Her voice is low, melodious. "It's only been eight years. You're a man now, though."

"Yes I am." Puffing out his chest. "You, you're even more beautiful than ever, Sally."

"This is my friend Joel," Sally interjects.

Sedge and Joel shake hands, very coolly.

I decide to show up, but have to elbow Sedge to get him to notice. He introduces me with far too much enthusiasm to be believed. Sally is very gracious. We talk about Trudy for a minute. I'm mesmerized by the expressiveness of her beautiful face and flexible mouth, but she's obviously used to that. She's not daunted either by the circle of young men that has surrounded her. Joel keeps close by her side, protectively, and she rewards this with little pats to his shoulder now and then.

Sedge is beside himself. He practically has to slap his own hands to keep them away from her. He has not offered her anything to eat or drink. This moment is clearly all there is, nothing more wonderful can happen in this world.

"Do you remember," he says to her, "the time you found me crying in the gazebo? I couldn't tell you what was the matter?"

Sally responds with a warm smile. "Poor boy. You didn't know what was the matter. You were just sad with growing up. And you talked about your parents, how you still wished they were together."

"You were so good to me, Sally."

Sally reaches out, takes his hand maternally. "Let's go get something to drink, shall we?"

Joel and I and the circle of other stunned admirers watch in their magical wake as they stroll away hand in hand.

Joel says to me, "Quite a party."

It's an invitation to all sorts of responses. I decide on direct. "Not my style. But I'm here to witness the reunion."

"Reunion. You mean Sally and this kid?"

"He's been in love with her since he was fifteen. I suspect she knows it."

"You could be right. Of course she said nothing of the kind to me. But then I'm only her mascot. Useful for outings when there's nobody else available."

Joel's bitterness makes me turn to look at him more closely. He's hardly taller than me, and pretty ugly actually. Poor Joel.

I say gently, "Try the punch."

He wanders away, trailing in Sally's wake.

The bathroom is off a small room containing a mattress-cum-bed strewn with jackets, hats, sweatshirts and a growing pile of outer garments. I'm lingering in this space after using the bathroom, reluctant to re-enter the pounding yelling loft where dancing has begun. I can see from here that Sedge and Sally are dancing, not touching, just gyrating, waving hands about. It looks like a lot of fun but I'm ready to go home.

I sit down on top of somebody's faintly smelly clothing. It feels good to get off my feet. The light in here is dim, just one small bedside lamp. A man comes in, beeline for the bathroom, but stops short on seeing me, staggers over, muttering, "Hey, honey," falls on top of me. Finds my breasts, cries, "Whoa!" very pleased. Am I screaming for help? No. Am I struggling? A little, but that only inflames him. He reeks of alcohol, his red baby face is sweaty, his weight at the wrong angle for comfort. But his hands are on auto pilot, and they know what they're doing. Just as he zeroes in on my thighs, he suddenly leaps back, eyes bulging, flies in a crouch to the bathroom. I can hear him retching.

"Disgusting child," I say out loud.

But I only half mean it. Only my brain objects. My flesh is warm with remembering sex the way it used to be when I first discovered it, the boys consumed, out of control. Before it was ever deepened or complicated by love. The thrill and amazement, the animal thoroughness and finality, the mindless purposefulness, the cosmic trance.

I sit up, straightening my dress. Somebody has discovered the body in the bathroom, no doubt out cold. Others arrive to carry him in. Before they can deposit him on the bed beside me, I scramble up and escape from the room.

Three women dancing in a circle gesture to me to join them, but I spot Joel standing alone, and go over to him.

"At least this music is better," I say.

"Yellow Brick Road," he agrees. "I used to love Elton John."

"Me too."

I feel a companionable ease with Joel. We get some soda water and find two chairs. He tells me about his job and I tell him about mine, including the micromanager boss, who generates Joel's wise sympathy. We agree on loving swimming and volleyball, and old Bette Davis movies. But before long, Joel is talking about Sally.

"She tortures me," he confides. "She enjoys it."

We're in a sort of kitchen nook in one corner of the loft, with a small table between us, a bowl of pretzels. Joel takes a pretzel, gestures with it, gnaws at it vengefully. I nod understanding while he repeats, "She enjoys it."

I want to ask the obvious question, why do you put up with it, but I know the answer.

"I've been there," I say. "Knew a spectacular guy who loved to break hearts."

"Oh but Sally's a good person, really. I just adore her. No, her problem is she never got over her divorce. It happened that summer she got to know the kid, Sedgewick, you know. She told me he and his mother comforted her when she was feeling vulnerable and defeated."

"She was getting divorced that summer? That helps explain it. Her ego needed boosting."

"That's it. I think she'd even admit it. Poor Sedgewick just happened to be in the right place at the right time to get infatuated with Sally Lawton. It's a permanent affliction, I'm afraid."

I nibble a pretzel, look out over the room swirling with bodies, pulsating with Elton John. I can't catch sight of Sedge and Sally. I'm horrified to find I'm aware it's my usual bedtime. But I turn back to Joel, intrigued.

"Tell me," I say, "do you know why she hasn't remarried? A woman as beautiful as that…"

"Oh of course, she's had offers galore. She says she doesn't ever want to marry again. The experience was too painful. I don't really know what happened, the guy was a rat I take it. But, you know, I think she'll give in eventually. As you say, beauty like that."

"I have a husband, unfortunately," I confide, "but he's been missing in action for years. I don't even know where he is. So, worst of both worlds."

"Jenny, my dear." Joel pats my hand. "You can still have fun. Would you like to go out with me some time?"

"Even though you're in love with Sally?"

"A permanent disability, I'm afraid."

"We'll see." I smile. "I do like you, Joel."

Later, after Sally has shown up to reclaim Joel, and I've rotated once more around the loft looking for conversation, getting ready to call it a night, there's a commotion by the door. Sedge is blocking Sally's exit.

It's a pitiful scene. The poor boy is gesticulating and shouting, sobs catching his voice.

"Darling Sally darling you can't leave you can't leave." Or something like that.

Joel stays in front of Sally, hands raised at Sedge in warning and calming, the expression on his face sorrow rather than alarm. Sally is backing away, has reached the threshold. Now she turns quickly and disappears. But Joel won't budge, Sedge is nose to nose with him.

"Oh for God's sake," I cry, "are they going to fight? It's too ridiculous."

I push my way through the flabbergasted crowd, grab Sedge by the arm.

"Cut it out," I tell him. "Just cut it out."

Joel and I exchange a look, in which mutual understanding and sympathy predominate. Sedge pulls roughly away from me, but then turns to clasp me in his arms.

"Make her stay, Jenny, make her stay. She can't leave me now. Don't you see, we've just found each other again after all these years."

He's heavy against me as if he thinks he's small and I'm strong enough to hold him. Fortunately, a couple of his friends swing into action, haul him away.

"Take it easy, man," they say with amazing gentleness. "It's okay. We're here for you, man."

Joel says, "Jenny, you're a hero. What a situation. Poor kid. I'd better go."

He kisses me lightly on the cheek, is gone.

I go to find Sedge where he's being held by his pals in the bedroom, already submitting and almost defeated. Guests are crowding in to collect their garments and bid hasty goodbye. The party is definitely over.

I bring Sedge a tall glass of water, which he immediately drains. Soon everyone has left, the loft is empty. Someone has turned off the music. Silence and debris.

I say, "Sedge, you better just get some sleep."

He sits forlornly on the edge of the bed.

"I'll never sleep again."

I go get a chair to sit opposite him. "Tell me what happened."

"I kissed her."

"With her permission?"

"Well…"

"So this kiss, it wasn't exactly mutual."

"I thought she liked it. I thought she wanted me to. But it was a long kiss, and she got all upset."

"She thought she'd experiment, to see what it would be like. Then she got scared."

"I don't know. Do you think I scared her?"

"Believe me. You did. You do."

"So doesn't that mean she loves me too? She just doesn't want to admit it?"

"Not at all, Sedge. You have to give up Sally Lawton."

Tears start down his cheeks. He doesn't notice. He moans, "I will die."

"You won't die. You are going to grow up."

To soften my words, I go sit beside him, pat his back. "There are many more women in your crystal ball, Sedge. Sally's from your past. Now wake up and face the future."

Sedge leans down to put his forehead on my shoulder, wetting my neck with his tears. I find I'm cradling him, crying now too, all my own regrets and loss mingling with his.

The Difference

My name is Nina. Professor Nina Gibbons.

For my sabbatical year from Boston University, I accepted an invitation to take a guest lectureship at Cornell. I was to teach a graduate seminar in my field, exploring a new perspective I was working on and hoped to turn into a book in my newly acquired leisure time. I was anxious to get out of Boston. My beloved husband had died just a year before, my daughters were living in New York City, and my old house felt stifling and routine, no longer so much refuge as confinement.

I arrived in Ithaca on a mild September day. Nestled in the hills above Cayuga Lake, Cornell University is glorious in fall, greeting me with wildly colorful trees everywhere as I settled into my apartment near "College Town," the center of off-campus life. The streets were busy with returning students and their carloads of belongings, rosy-cheeked kids who looked younger every year. I was fifty-three and feeling it.

After my yoga class one day in early October, I hurried home to grab a bite, change, and show up at the museum opening. Cornell's museum is a grand building with spectacular views overlooking the lake. Dusk was reddening the sky as we gathered in the spacious galleries for wine and canapés. I was grateful for an opportunity, rare in remote Ithaca, to wear my sexy black velvet with the low neckline. That sort of outfit puts me in a sensuous mood, so perhaps that's why I spotted Bruno right away.

A solid young man with fiery dark eyes, a profusion of black curls, and of all things a generous moustache. I pegged him at once as the Italian academic said to be racing to the top of my field at the early age of thirty, a grad student serving as instructor. He was talking animatedly with of course a young blond. There was grace in his coiled energy, his gestures expressive, his stance alert. He moved rather like a fencing athlete, muscular and delicate at the same time.

I inched closer. Marilyn Roth chose that moment to intercept me, waving her empty champagne glass in my face.

"Ah Nina my dear, so delighted to see you at our special event of the semester, this glorious exhibition of Abstract Expressionism. I've been angling for something like this for ages. We usually have very traditional old stuff here, so tedious to the contemporary mindset, don't you think?"

This was so routine to me, the kind of chitchat pretentious people like to call conversation. It always frees me to nod happily and take the opportunity to case the room. But Marilyn was an important force in the architecture department, so I tried to appear suitably charmed.

"Oh yes," I replied, catching Bruno's eye. "I completely agree. This so speaks to our own time."

Bruno spent a lingering moment assessing my bodice, then grinned lovingly down at the blond. Never mind that she was wearing thick glasses and a droopy dress that hid any charms.

I huffily turned my back on them. "Oh Marilyn," I sang, "I understand you've got a course in the works that examines the influence of Roman architecture on Constantinople."

It was a wild guess based on something vaguely remembered, and deserved her puzzled look. "Anything that broad would take years," she answered a bit frostily. "My focus is strictly on the reign of Constantine, especially the influence of his queen."

I blurted, "My students seem really excited about the angle I'm taking on urban transportation. We're comparing ancient and modern Rome at the moment."

"How exciting," Marilyn exclaimed, so genuinely delighted with my news that I started to like her. "Just the kind of thing the kids do grab onto. I was discussing this with Bruno only yesterday, wasn't I, Bruno?" And before I knew it, she had toddled over and grabbed his sleeve. She pulled him unceremoniously in my direction, as he nodded distractedly at the girl he was abandoning, and turned to me with a weak smile.

Needless to say, I was thrilled with Marilyn's abduction. It put me and Bruno immediately in the same boat—embarrassed for her, apologetic to each other. I grimaced sympathetically, he pulled himself together into his suave stance. We bonded there and then. Conversation was witty and erudite, of course, but I don't remember a word of it. All I know is that three hours later I was in his apartment sipping a delicious cognac.

He lived on the other side of campus, in Cayuga Heights, rather too swanky a neighborhood for a mere instructor. But this was a plain apartment building housing mainly students. Plus he had a roommate, who showed up shortly and dampened any hint of romance. In any case, Bruno was holding fast to his role as professional colleague, and of course so was I. I'm no slouch when it comes to my dignity. Besides, I must admit, as a fairly new widow, I was a bit confused and starry-eyed about male-female relationships. I'd been married for almost thirty years, more or less happily until my beloved Dan got so ill.

Bruno insisted on driving me home, in an ancient Honda that had seen better days. We pulled up to my door, and as I gathered my skirts to step out, he put his hand on my arm.

"Nina," he said, "let's do this again. I don't know many people here as yet, and our fields overlap so much, it's bound to be fruitful for both of us. Don't you think?"

I nodded. "Fruitful, oh yes. Give me a call."

"Will do," he cried cheerfully.

I did not hear from him, nor even see him around, for over a week. Then one day—it was one of those spectacular autumn afternoons in upstate New York that boggle the mind with beauty—I spotted him across the street in College Town. My arms were full of groceries, but at least my hair looked good and I was wearing my adorable chocolate brown suede jacket. I pretended not to see him. He appeared at my side.

"It's Professor Gibbons," he exclaimed playfully.

I peered over my groceries. "Mr. Borelli," I countered.

"Let me carry those."

"No, I'm fine. I live right over there."

But he took one of the bags and followed me home. I did not object.

I do remember unpacking the groceries, opening the wine, and sitting down on the couch. He sat beside me, not in the chair opposite that I had indicated. We worked on the wine and elaborately evolved a discussion about the military use of the grand boulevards of Paris that grew ever more intense. Before I knew it, he was close enough to touch me, and did. His hand rested on my shoulder, then my knee.

He actually said, "May I kiss you?"

After that, my judgment and reason vanished. I remember briefly reflecting that it had been years since anyone kissed me. And as for lovemaking, poor Dan had abandoned that attempt long before. I was mindlessly hungry. I was so melted and weak from desire, Bruno had to half carry me into the bedroom.

Afterwards, while we lay still entwined, he said, hoarsely, "Wow." And a little later, "You're good."

Me? I wanted to tell him he was a god, but I refrained. I figured he was well aware what a superb lover he was.

There followed exactly ten days of bliss. We saw each other every day, often had dinner together, had long feverish discussions about our research, and numerous times ended up in bed. Then one day, after a working lunch at the faculty club, I took some respite on a bench, watching the clutches of students waltzing by. It was a bit chilly, the magic of autumn succumbing to brown leaves and gusty wind. But the sun felt warm, and so, squinting into it, I saw them.

Arm and arm, walking just below the hill where I sat, along came Bruno and one of the most beautiful women I have ever seen. It was not only her sweeping honey colored hair and perfect, classical features, but her sensuous movement and the alluring angle of her head as she sparkled up at him. Both of them were glowing. They would not have noticed me if I'd been right there. Her beauty tormented me. But much worse was the chemistry I could feel radiating from the two of them. I guess I knew right then that my little idyll was over.

Bruno introduced me to Adrianna the very next day.

"She's studying Italian city planning," he said proudly.

We were gathered in the faculty lounge for coffee between classes, as usual. I did my best to appear cheerful and friendly, asked the gorgeous one some pertinent professional questions, and squirmed at the sound of her mellifluous voice. Sure enough, Bruno did not seek me out at lunchtime. But to my surprise, he showed up after my last seminar, at five o'clock.

"Dinner?" he said in his usual casual, intimate way. "Your place?"

Was I going to say no? We picked up some takeout in College Town and made ourselves at home in my apartment. Bruno opened the wine while I got out the glasses. We delved at once into our current discussion, architecture in the context of social structure, where we'd left off two days before. It was all so familiar and sweet, I began to relax.

After dinner, we made our usual switch to the couch. The next moves would be hugs, kisses, caresses, then a stagger to the bedroom. His hand was on my knee, my thigh. But then I took a bold chance, which I may always regret.

"What about Adrianna?"

"Ah." His hand fell away. "She is beautiful. Do you see that?"

"Of course I see that."

"I will confess, I desire her. I think also that I will love her."

At this, I stood up, went to the other side of the room. But he wouldn't stop.

"Yes, Nina," he pursued mercilessly, "I do love her. I do."

I managed to croak, "Where does that leave us?"

"Should it matter?" He got up and came to stand beside me.

I could feel his muscle, his heat. I was dizzy with rage and lust.

"How could you say that?"

"But you and I are pals, Nina my dear. It's different. We have fun, we talk, we enjoy each other. Why not? What's the matter?"

"I thought…" But fortunately I didn't share my delusions with him. Instead I said, "I don't think there's room for three of us in this picture."

He looked so genuinely grieved that I almost threw myself into his arms, but I stepped back, hurried away to get his coat, handed it to him.

I said, "I'm off for Thanksgiving break on Tuesday. Let's leave it at that."

Sulkily, he shrugged into his coat.

I added, as lightly as I could muster, "It *was* fun."

I packed furiously. I'd already prepped the car for the trek back to Boston where my daughters would join me. I managed to get through my last class the next day, said my goodbyes to my students and colleagues. It felt great to be busy and to have plans I looked forward to. I avoided running into Bruno and his goddess as best I could. When I did, I waved cheerily and sped past. This was going well, I thought.

But fate decreed otherwise. Ithaca is known for its stark winter weather, and on Monday evening it started to snow like crazy. It was already a foot deep as I stomped home, wisely picking up some emergency food on the way. I pulled off my wet boots, slumped into a chair that I usually loved but at this moment hated. Out the window the snow was slanting sideways in a ferocious wind. The TV told me it wouldn't stop. I was snowed in. Oh no.

I phoned my eldest daughter, already in Boston. "I'm not going to make it," I moaned.

"No worries, you have a whole week. You'll be able to travel by Wednesday. We'll just save the turkey 'til you get here. By the way, Ron and I are getting married."

Normally—that is, in my pre-Bruno days—I would have been thrilled. She'd been going with Ron for three years and I'd always thought I'd love seeing her settled down. But this news, now, at this horrible moment, shook my soul. Tears came to my eyes as I congratulated my little girl. Never mind that she was twenty-six—I was picturing her at ten on the park swing. I did not see how my world could get any darker.

I choked down the unpalatable takeout I'd grabbed on the way, and tried to read a novel I had previously enjoyed. Outside, the streetlights went on and I watched the wild snowflakes swirling like dervishes against the light. I thought of calling Marilyn or some other woman friend to commiserate, but I really did not want to share my ridiculous situation with anybody. It was around eight o'clock when I heard a knock at my door.

I put my eye to the tiny round peephole and saw a snow-laden Bruno. No, I did not contemplate ignoring him. I threw the door open.

He stood there, boyishly and shyly dipping his head in apology.

"May I come in? I'm quite wet."

I pulled him in by the sleeve as he shed icy shards all over my rug, helped him off with his coat and went to hang it in the bathroom to drip. I was acutely aware that I looked awful. My hair was uncombed, I was clad in baggy sweatpants and a smelly old turtleneck. My poor-me clothes, hitherto appropriate for the occasion. Somehow my lack of allure made me tougher.

I faced him squarely. "Explain yourself."

"Well, I knew you couldn't travel in this weather. Hey, do you mind if I sit down?"

"Go ahead."

He pointedly did not choose the couch. We sat in chairs across from each other.

He said, "I wanted to make things right between us."

"That's thoughtful of you." But I was unhappy with irony. "Thank you for caring enough. I appreciate it. But really, Bruno, I am fine. Don't worry about it."

"I do worry about it, my dear Nina. You are a wonderful woman. I'm grateful to know you. I'm grateful we were lovers. I understand that we can't…do that anymore."

He was so serious and so sad, I almost wanted to comfort him. But I looked at myself from a new angle. I was old enough to be his mother. I was about to become a mother-in-law. Sex had been glorious, but it had been as ephemeral as a butterfly. I actually smiled at him.

"Cheer up," I said. "Let me give you one glass of wine before you venture back out into the gale."

So we sat on the couch with our wine, gazing out together at the white fury. Nature had claimed us blindly for a moment in time, and now we acknowledged her power in a new way. In that half hour while Bruno and I sat side by side in sweet farewell, we were closer than we'd ever been before, bowing to time.

Snapshots

The Cloak

From across the street I watch her come into view. She's wearing a beautiful lavender coat wrapped around her like a shawl. It appears to be very soft velvet. It's so big and she's so wrapped up, it's like a blanket. One hand holds a corner of it under her chin. Dark hair, gathered at the neck and long enough to disappear beneath the lavender folds. She's walking not briskly, but with purpose.

No other people are visible in the rather stark concrete of street and buildings, but she does not notice me. She passes by, right to left, enters a doorway, disappears. Only a few minutes later, there she is again, now wearing a short black jacket with a flared hem, walking back left to right this time.

I call to her, "I liked the other coat better."

She turns graciously, slows only a little, replies, "I'm going to wear them both."

Now I notice a man who has come to the window a few stories above her. Young, blond, he's leaning out eagerly, keeping her in sight. Just as she comes to a sloping hill and starts to descend, suddenly there he is in the doorway, striding quickly after her, following her. As another woman, I'm both excited and anxious. His admiration could be harmless, but there's also the possibility of danger, force.

Down the hill she goes, the young man behind her, getting closer. As she rounds the corner at the bottom of the hill, in the moment before he gets too close, the moment she may disappear from my sight, the shoulders of another man appear, putting his arm around her. A car is half visible, he's holding the door open for her. I see the pursuing young man abruptly change course, pass by the couple averting his gaze. They don't seem to notice him. He's gone, they enter the car.

Spiral, 2092

Everything moves quickly but nothing happens. All the water they didn't get in five years falls in five days. Right after the wildfires. The fires in May and June, in July the hurricanes and tornados. The whole area north of Portland collapses with mudslides into desert by August. Drought returns.

Blair and Ned, sister and brother, pack their wagon before dawn. They have to hurry. Making camp on a hill amid the smoking ruins of a village, just in time to watch the water come below, they've been safe now for a week. Surrounded by crowds of others in varying states of desperation. The worst off have no food, the rest have none to share. Nearly as bad are the sick; nobody wants to tend them from fear of plague. On either side of their makeshift camp the land is bare, all trees and brush felled by fire. Now, on this dull grey sweltering morning as they feverishly work, they all keep looking down over the valley for the telltale signs of approaching armies, the scouts, the flags. To the north, the water has receded out of sight. Though mud is all that remains, the horse can probably make it through.

Everything moves quickly but nothing happens. They have to hurry. They've already been delayed by the floods and now rumor roars warnings about roving armies.

Everything moves quickly but nothing happens. In the wagon, piled high, a small tent, two bicycles, three bundles of clothes, bags of chestnuts and apples, a mattress, some pans and dishes, a blanket, a bale of hay, and fourteen ancient guns without ammunition worth perhaps much or probably nothing. The sun is creeping over the horizon, a trembling, pale, menacing, persistent presence that soon will drive them all faint with its heat.

Scene from a Future

"He uses condoms made out of sheep's gut, that's all we have these days."

"My grandmother says they used to have them made of rubber, and also pills women could take."

McDowell shifts her position on the bench, chops a carrot with vehemence, and growls,

"Well, they used to have a lot of things. I'm tired of hearing about it. Now why don't you skin those fish before they rot."

"Just because you pretend to be my mother doesn't give you the right to order me around," Tree snorts. "And besides, it's my turn to take a bath, so you skin the damn fish yourself."

The year is 2097. Beacon Hill is an island surrounded by the remains of old Boston, sometimes visible under the water that has subsumed it. The beautiful brick mansions, long abandoned by their original owners, have been claimed by anybody who can offer enough muscle to protect occupation. By now Beacon Island has reached a form of stability, even a kind of village atmosphere, where neighbors know each other, and a grocer, a health clinic, and a fire station provide vestiges of the previous civilization. The only, though significant, threat comes from the enclave's dictator, who covets the island simply because it's there. With housing so limited, they form artificial families, which also helps protect rebels from being identified. This pose of Beacon Island, bland serenity and patient deprivation, is deceptive. Rebel leaders are hiding in plain sight.

The two women exchange glares that quickly fade into grudging affection. Together they gaze out over the lowering sky that presages more hot rain today. Tips of ancient skyscrapers pixilate the heaving water. Boats and rafts weave their way out to ever diminishing fishing grounds.

"Anyhow," McDowell sighs, "I'm not having sex these days. I'm tired." She tucks her graying hair behind her ears, in a gesture both weary and defiant. "He takes care of his needs with that cutesy Esme. He doesn't pester me."

"Let's try to find blueberries again today," says Tree, affecting jollity.

"We can always try," murmurs McDowell. "We can always try."

The Voyage

The cruise from Boston to Montreal began on a beautiful June day. The ship, the Noble Queen, was huge—monumental even to Ben who'd been on ocean liners in his youth. Jocelyn remarked how can that thing float, but Ben told her not to be naïve. Five years into their marriage, this was to be their second honeymoon, so she only shrugged her annoyance.

Their stateroom on D deck had a window but no balcony. That had been their choice when calculating the cost. Out this round, nautical window on the first afternoon, they watched the docks of Boston retreating in the distance, the waving farewell crowd already a blur.

"Do we have to dress for dinner? Jocelyn asked.

Ben, perusing the Events of the Day brochure, replied, "It says here 'Welcoming Gala.' Sounds kind of formal."

"Oh, I do hope I can wear my new silk dress!"

"Wear whatever you want," grumbled Ben, focusing hard on the view.

She wanted him to say, "Great, I love you in that dress." But of course he did not.

He said instead, again consulting the brochure, "Oh boy, there's a casino cocktail hour tomorrow, and a Night Deck party! And it says all the pools are open already right now."

"Plenty to do," she agreed. "I'll just take a quick shower."

"I'm starving. When do we eat?"

Thus sparring and bantering, avoiding all true communication, the young couple began their celebration voyage. They eagerly looked forward to eight lovely days and nights on the glorious Noble Queen, every moment a self-indulgent treat. They expected their marriage to revive, after which they'd return newly in love and the envy of their friends.

They met at college her sophomore year. He was a pre-med senior, restless to graduate and start his hospital internship. He pursued her avidly, confiding that he had to get married before his job started, as it would be many hours a day of grueling training. He was most taken with her larger than usual breasts, which he could not keep his hands off. She was petite, especially next to his tall frame, but she'd inherited a bounteous bosom from her mother, a hostess at the family restaurant. His mother on the other hand was an architect: thereby lay one of their obstacles to bliss. Jocelyn grew up in a small Ohio town, Ben hailed from a fancy New York suburb in Westchester County, his father head of a law firm. It was assumed between them that her origins were humble, and she would need work to rise to the level of his affluent, worldly-wise family.

Jocelyn dared not wear her best dress that night to the gala, for fear it would seem too showy. She chose the safer option of a white linen skirt and sleeveless flowered blouse. She brushed her dark curls vigorously, donned hoop earrings and high heels with open toes that showed off her recent pedicure. She was gratified when Ben squeezed her breasts fondly through the soft fabric of her blouse.

After cocktails in the casino and dinner, they found their way to the Lido Deck, where the welcoming party was in full swing. They met the captain, Ed Bryant, and the ship's doctor, Dieter Heinz. Both men were imposing in their immaculate white uniforms with gold braid. Dr. Heinz introduced them to a statuesque middle-aged woman of vaguely African descent with whom he'd been chatting.

"Mrs. Richards."

"Ruby," responded Mrs. Richards, with a dazzling smile.

They also met a very nice Canadian couple, Pierre and Becky Moreau. Pierre was heavy shouldered with an aggressively jutting jaw, but a jolly laugh. Becky was all pale blond, with the attendant pale blue eyes and creamy skin. They hailed from Montreal, so they were going home.

"We loved Boston," gushed Becky, "and we visited New York too. What a town!"

There was a lively band, and after more champagne Ben and Jocelyn danced under the stars, which on the open ocean means a very black night sky peppered all over with pinpricks of glinting light. Ben held her close. She felt safe and happy in his arms. But when they got back to their stateroom, they quarreled. Why did they always seem to quarrel at bedtime? Ben was annoyed that she took a call from her mother.

"She's always butting in."

"But Ben honey, she worries."

Ben made a vomit sound, got into bed with his back to her. She lay awake quite a while though she was very tired. Her longing for tenderness and peace was so strong, her stomach felt hollowed out.

In the morning, Ben made love to her roughly and abruptly, and went to take a shower. She sat up to look out at the view. The bed was right under the window, and the water seemed close. The ship made a soft swishing sound passing through the waves. In every direction there was nothing but ocean. It looked endless, timeless, and cold.

Breakfast was served buffet style, with a magnificent array of delicious choices. Jocelyn had scrambled eggs, oatmeal, and orange juice. Ben chose poached eggs and waffles. They talked excitedly about plans for the day. Should they go ashore at Portland, lounge on the deck, or indulge in the spa? The Moreaus joined them at their table, announcing they'd opted to go ashore.

"I've never been to Maine, you see," Becky said.

"Neither have I," said Jocelyn. "Ben has."

"Hey, it's just another American city." Ben waved a dismissive hand. "I'm saving my energy for exotic Canada."

They all laughed heartily. As if Canada could be exotic!

"But remember," Pierre countered, "Montreal is a truly international city. I think you will find it quite intriguing."

"Pierre is French Canadian," explained Becky. "I'm English, from Vancouver, way out west." She gave her husband a coy smile and added, "But I love Montreal just as much as he does."

Ben went to the spa and Jocelyn enjoyed a book on deck. It was another beautiful summer day. The ocean glinted azure in the sunlight. After the commotion of docking and departures for the day in Portland, the ship was quiet. People jogged or sauntered past. The novel she was reading eventually dropped from her hands, and her mind wandered dreamily.

It was that evening, after the ship was again underway, that the first warning came. After a dip in the pool and donning dinner clothes, Ben and Jocelyn opted for wine and hors d'oeuvres in the Forum, milling with passengers brimming with excited stories about their day. It was Pierre who commented, "Hear about this thing in China? You know, the virus?"

Ben, all medical at once, prodded, "No, tell us."

It appeared that a severe infection called a coronavirus had suddenly broken out in a big Chinese city, killing dozens within a few days, and had now spread to Italy. Television images were grim, commentators brisk. Politicians and doctors were being interviewed. Did this pose any danger to North America? That was the question on everyone's lips. But it all seemed rather a foggy notion out here on the calm ocean feathered in luxury.

First thing in the morning, Ben turned on the TV. The virus was wreaking havoc in Italy, and showing up in France and Spain.

"It's spreading," noted Ben gravely.

Jocelyn dared not ask if it could reach Ohio. Instead she said, "Well, we've got every possible medical expertise in the States, surely we won't have to worry."

That afternoon she played ping pong with Becky while Pierre and Ben went to the casino. When it was time for dinner, Jocelyn found her husband still there, playing blackjack with great intensity. Pierre was gone, and the dealer was bringing Ben free drinks.

"Leave me alone," Ben growled.

She watched helplessly for a while longer, then leaned over to kiss his cheek.

"Ben honey," she pleaded. "Come to dinner. We can have lobster."

But he shrugged away without looking at her, slapping his hand down on the table hard to indicate another card from the dealer. She crept away and went to the buffet area to get a sandwich for her dinner.

On Wednesday, the Noble Queen passed into Canada, heading for the dock in St. John's, Newfoundland. Ben and Jocelyn were looking forward to their first foray into Canada, her first foreign country. Her passport was carefully stowed in the bottom of her purse—she kept nervously checking to make sure.

Neither one of them mentioned the casino incident. Ben after showering was as chipper as ever. They really enjoyed their visit to St. John's, which was an easy walk from the harbor to the city, with just enough foreign looking things to feel like an adventure. Jocelyn would always remember it as the last time she was that person. Ben was kind and amusing, and sometimes held her hand. She felt pretty and playful, and grateful.

When they returned to the ship late in the afternoon, tension was palpable and they quickly found out why. The virus that had already devastated China and Italy was now raging across Europe. A crowd gathered in the main lounge, riveted to the big TV screen: grotesque images of medical workers clad head to toe in blue plastic, their faces completely obscured by masks; sickening shots of bodies lolling on stretchers, some alive, some not; announcers' voices strident.

Ben got a call from a colleague warning that they would soon need all medical staff on duty.

"I assured him we were flying directly back from Montreal," Ben moaned. "He seemed to be implying I could turn the ship around, for God's sake."

The loudspeaker announced that Captain Bryant would address everyone via in-ship TV at six o'clock that evening. So Ben and Jocelyn were in their room half dressed for dinner when the captain's handsome tanned face appeared, but quickly ceased to be reassuring as, in his chillingly brisk British accent, he announced that the Noble Queen was quarantined. All sorts of calming puffery followed, but the gist was that a passenger who'd disembarked at Portland had tested positive for the new virus. Thus everyone on board was suspect. Canada would not allow the ship to dock anywhere.

Ben became pale and mumbling. Jocelyn asked him to explain this wild scenario to which she could not relate at all. But he only said over and over, "We're screwed."

Thursday, June 17. The ship, now anchored off Halifax, was visited by a medical team whose gender was hard to determine through all the unwieldy plastic protection. There were nearly two dozen of them, tramping around looking like zombies. They tested every single passenger and crew, jamming a long stick up their nostrils unceremoniously. There was little sense of relief after they were gone—apparently the tests would determine if any one of them was carrying the dread disease.

Ben and Jocelyn stood at the railing watching the medical boat depart. It was late afternoon, the sun low in the sky, glinting merrily off the waves.

"We've got to get back to the States," said Ben. "Maybe they can bring us a helicopter. They should at least do that, don't you think? I mean, it's not like any Americans are infected, right?"

Jocelyn could tell he was terribly upset. She struggled for equilibrium.

"Tonight is Formal Night," she ventured. "according to the schedule. I don't have a formal, though. Maybe we shouldn't go?"

"We'll go," Ben insisted. "What's wrong with that fancy new dress you're always talking about?"

"It's not a formal," she countered stubbornly.

"Go buy another one then. There's that shop you're always gawking at."

So she hurried down to the lower deck, hoping that at four o'clock it would still be open. A few other frantic women were sorting through the offerings. The gray-haired saleslady whisked the dress out and dangled it in front of her. A silky long gown, flaming red, with lace at a low bodice. Jocelyn would probably never have dared consider it by herself.

"This is perfect for you," sang the saleslady, "Your dark hair and eyes, just the right skin tone. Perfect."

Jocelyn felt appreciated and cared about. She stroked the dress, held it gently. Clad in this luxury, she looked in the mirror with astonishment. The dress was clinging in just the right places. Her generous breasts were half revealed, peeking out from crimson lace trim. She looked like the bar hostess in some cowboy movie. But oh, she looked gorgeous! Would Ben like it? Maybe Ben would like it very much.

Back in the stateroom, their stewardess as usual had placed a little chocolate on each pillow. There was also a basket of fresh fruit on the dresser. Ben wasn't there yet so she quickly changed into her new dress, whirling in front of the double mirror, flushed with anticipation. But when Ben arrived he hardly looked at her, headed straight for the TV to watch the news. It was all bad. Thousands of dead in Europe, and the disease showing up from Russia to South America, and North America.

What upset Ben the most was that in the States they were talking about recruiting newly graduated physicians and even medical students, getting ready for the pandemic to spread widely. He sat pale and shaken on the edge of the bed.

"We've got to get back to Boston."

Jocelyn felt frivolous for being so smug about her dress. She massaged his shoulders, murmuring encouragement. He pulled her close and pressed his face into her chest. Formal Night turned out to mean extra charges for dinner, and a tense performance from a band trying too hard to cheer everyone up. Mostly, the passengers sought solace in getting drunk. Ben drank vodka straight and staggered back to the room at 10 o'clock. Jocelyn wandered out to the deck, finding a beautiful evening that failed to lift her mood. She climbed some stairs to a high smaller deck, stepped over a pile of coiled rope, leaned against the railing. The stars were spectacular, dimmed only a bit by the blaze of lights from the Halifax shore in the distance. The water below was very black except for the dancing splash of the ship's lights. The air was sharp and sweet. She felt a presence behind her, turned to see a young sailor grinning at her. She gasped, he moved closer.

"What you doing up here, beautiful?"

Alarmed, acutely aware of her inviting dress, she shook her head, looking around for a quick escape.

"Don't worry, babe, I'm harmless. Talk to a lonely sailor, won't you?"

His accent was pure Ireland. He had red hair, and his uniform included a beret with a pom-pom on top. He looked very young. She began to relax.

She said, "I'm so sorry, I must be in the wrong place."

"Don't let the captain catch you," he chuckled, coming to stand beside her at the railing. He did not pretend he was not looking at her half exposed breasts, but not leering, just admiring.

"I'd better go then," she replied, moving to brush past him.

He touched her waist lightly. "Please, stay another minute."

Something about his touch, with the soft, sharp breath off the ocean, the twinkling vast canopy of stars, gave her a jolt like joy. For just a moment she felt she was in a dream with no obligation to her actual life. She laughed out loud, fully and naturally, like a child. He brought his face close to hers, she lifted her head. He kissed her.

Even as she let him hold her close, she murmured, "I have a husband."

He pulled back a bit. "Where is he then?"

"In bed."

He gazed down at her, eyes sparkling. "You gorgeous creature, you. Will you stay a little while with Mike, then?"

She vigorously shook her head, broke away. "Sorry."

She ran to scramble down the stairs. When she dared to glance behind her, she saw only the dark and empty deck.

Lying in bed that night listening to Ben's familiar snore, Jocelyn first felt an almost unbearable surging awareness of being acutely alive. But gradually a sickening sense of guilt wrestled her exhilaration down. Before she could succumb to sleep, she vowed prodigious effort at renewed wifely devotion.

Early in the morning they were awakened by the loudspeaker announcing a vital report by the captain. She jumped out of bed to turn on the in-house TV, brushing her teeth as she watched the grim-faced captain describe disaster. The test results showed that nine passengers and four crew were positive for the "incredibly contagious" virus. Not only that, one of the cooks was already critically ill. The Noble Queen was going nowhere, but must remain at sea in quarantine for at least two weeks. The infected would be ferried directly to hospitals on the mainland.

"That said," Captain Bryant amended, "healthy passengers are encouraged to still have fun. I've ordered the costume ball to be held tonight instead of Friday. That should cheer us all up and then some! The crew is already busy getting the props ready for purchase, moustaches, veils, magic wands, clown noses, that sort of thing. Have a good time, folks. This too shall pass."

And he ended with a handsome, beneficent smile.

So that day, when the ship was supposed to be blithely sailing towards Prince Edward Island, it sat stagnant just off Halifax. But everybody temporarily stopped complaining and scampered around concocting their costumes. Jocelyn decided to be a gypsy, Becky a cat. Pierre got a kick out of going as a pirate. Ben kept his decision a secret. Moping and moaning was treated as anti-social. This was to be an event thumbing noses at calamity.

Jocelyn already had a colorful skirt and frilly blouse, and hoop earrings. So all she bought were a bunch of cheap spangle bracelets and a huge red flower with a generous yellow center. She perched the flower over her left ear. A little extra makeup, and she was done. She twirled in front of the mirror studying the effect. Ben came out of the bathroom wearing a dress.

She sat down on the edge of the bed because her legs gave way and it was the closest place to sit. Her jaw dropped and she couldn't seem to close it.

"This is my costume," he said. And then into her stunned silence added irritably, "I am going to the party as a woman, okay?"

"Okay."

The dress was big enough, brightly decorated in a garish gold pattern. He was wearing something like earrings and his mouth was painted bright red. He had also thrown on a lot of rouge. He looked terrible, and ridiculous.

"How do I look?" he grinned with an attempt at a simper.

"Oh, Ben…"

"Well?"

She managed to close her mouth, then open it again to croak, "Fine."

They joined the festive, oddly clad crowd making their way to the ballroom, which was lavishly decorated with red and blue balloons and streamers. There was a buffet feast on tables all along one wall with plenty of champagne punch, tinted pink. Jocelyn felt nervous and disoriented, as if this could all be a fevered hallucination. She gulped at the glass of champagne Ben handed her. He was smiling broadly with his ruby lips, swaggering in a most unladylike manner, wiggling something resembling breasts, which she realized were oranges from the fruit basket.

Captain Bryant came as a cowboy, in flannel shirt with water pistol hanging on his belt, real cowboy boots. Pierre's pirate had a black patch over one eye, a plastic knife stuck in his belt. He had a bandana wrapped around his head. Becky wore gloves made into claws; a band of tiger ears adorned her head. Mrs. Richards, Ruby, was resplendent as a Hawaiian dancer, in what approximated a grass skirt pushed below her belly button, a skimpy bra, and several colorful leis around her neck.

Among the hundreds of other disguises were more pirates, cats, gypsies, and cowboys. Also an assortment of nurses, clowns, magicians, and vampires. Dr. Heinz was one of the best vampires, with fangs and red streaks down his chin. There were scattered Harry Potters and Darth Vaders, and an array of animals from apes to flamingos. Wee Willy Winky wore his wife's nightgown, and Pooh Bear's wife was a convincing Piglet. One man arrived a bit late wearing nothing but a large paper fig leaf. He explained proudly that he was Adam. He held up an apple to prove it.

Everybody was becoming a bit hysterical. They shouted as if talking to a deaf person, laughed uncontrollably, pawed the opposite sex, and drank as if parched. After several glasses of champagne, Jocelyn felt woozy and sat down to devour a large plate of mashed potatoes, chicken breast, and cream pie. Ben was having a wonderful time, dancing a kind of rumba by himself, wiggling his butt and waving his arms around. The band all wore pointy New Year's hats and acted drugged, so the music was wild.

Nobody was completely sure about this later, but towards midnight the captain was seen on all fours, Ruby Richards riding on his back. Rumor had it that she was flailing him mercilessly with a little whip.

Back in their stateroom, dawn showing pale around the curtain, Jocelyn and Ben pulled off their costumes and got into bed. She lay there on her back willing sleep, nervously waiting for his snore. But in a little while, she felt fingers brushing her hair back from her forehead. She held her breath. What was this? His hand ever so lightly traveled down her breast and belly, gentle as a breeze, taking a very long time. By the time his fingers reached her legs, her breath was quickening. She turned to him.

Afterwards, she drifted to sleep on a cloud of wonder. She had never experienced or even imagined such tenderness.

Choices

The first time Rex took Carrie to Paris was shortly after the beginning of their madcap affair. He was a world-famous cardiologist, she was an underpaid journalist and single mother twenty-seven years his junior. People said they had no business being lovers; they enjoyed the scandal.

They first met in the waiting room of his medical practice, when she was sent to interview him. She'd persuaded her editor to give her this assignment. Her usual beat was community events. She longed to qualify for a better job—this one at the *Somerville News* barely paid the rent. So she was already nervous. The appointment was for five o'clock, but she had to wait almost an hour, until the last patient emerged and the nurse apologized as she donned her coat to leave. Finally, the great man appeared. He looked tired, but perked up considerably at sight of her. It shook her confidence a little to recognize his attraction to her. It was so important that she come across as capable and professional. She pressed her lips together and stood up briskly, offering her hand.

They sat in two comfortable leather chairs as the watery March light outside dimmed to dusk. He was happy to explain his specialty and to comment on the latest research. Then she deftly steered the conversation in a more personal direction. Her aim was to center her article on the doctor as a man—her editor encouraged the human angle. The doctor smiled at her delicate approach.

"Don't worry, I haven't got anything to hide. What you see is what you get." His laugh was throaty, rich.

Because she'd been so tenaciously focused on her professional persona, it only dawned on her in that moment that he was very good looking—sandy hair going white just at the sideburns, jaw square and strong, brown eyes warm. His shoulders and arms looked muscular. His hands were large and expressive.

"My wife died almost two years ago now," he was confiding. "A beloved pediatrician. Way too soon, a terrible loss."

Carrie looked out the window to spare him attention to his grief. The sky was dark now, snowflakes starting to gently float past.

He continued without prompting, "No children, though we would've liked that. It wasn't in the cards. Married thirty years, wonderful years."

"So yours was a household of doctors. Was the scheduling tricky?"

"Not at all. I love to cook!" Again that caress of a laugh.

She cleared her throat, trying to clear her head, which she seemed to be losing. "Favorite recipes?"

The doctor reeled off some of his specialties, all of them sounding delicious.

"I love breaded scallops too," she replied, contrary to all journalistic guidelines.

Alas, he responded happily to the introduction of herself. "Well, that's great. We should share them sometime."

Oh crap. How could she screw up like that? But she found herself warmed by his proposal. Realizing she already had the bones of a great human interest story, she pursued that angle with his enthusiastic acquiescence. At the door, as they shook hands again, he held hers a little too long.

"Until we meet again," he said.

She chuckled at the sentiment, drawing herself up into a dignified stance, walking away trying not to know that he was watching her. Did she perhaps give her hips just a tiny extra wiggle?

All through that spring and summer, Carrie and Rex grew close, and closer. They were dynamite in bed. She revived his youthful vigor, he taught her a thing or two. All their friends got over their initial shock, and started treating them as a couple. Carrie's ten-year-old daughter Tess sulked at first, but Rex won her over with his expertise in soccer. He even showed her a move she used in scoring her first goal ever. In June when Tess went to summer camp, the enthralled couple flew to Paris.

One lovely evening at a restaurant on the rue Saint Severin, Rex said, "You know, this has not turned out the way either of us planned."

They were at one of the little tables outside, lingering over their brandy. The look in his eyes told her this was not going to be bad news. She felt beautiful lounging there in her flimsy summer dress. She nodded casually.

He continued, "Let's be honest. We both thought this would be a quick affair. We thought it would be great fun, over with by now."

She smiled in agreement. "It's too true. Are you saying we're serious?"

"Carrie, darling, you know I am."

Carrie was flying high. She'd just had an article placed in *The Boston Globe*, amid signs they'd consider hiring her on a permanent basis. The intimate interview with the famous Dr. Rex Trevalyn had been a hit. She was gratified by her own newly aroused sexual prowess, and proud to have enchanted such a successful and wonderful man.

Up to now her life had not been easy. Her major goal as an adolescent was to escape her stagnant little town in western Massachusetts. Her mother drank too much and cried a lot. Her father distanced himself from the family to such an extent that nobody noticed when he left. Carrie succeeded with a scholarship to UMassBoston, where she flourished. Her prospects were rosy, until she met Brian. She was waitressing on Cape Cod the summer before her senior year. He just showed up on the beach one day, beaming down at her as she sat watching her friends frolic in the surf. He was so adorable she knew right away he was trouble. She didn't find out until it was too late that he was only seventeen. By the time she realized she was pregnant, he'd left town. She couldn't even remember his last name.

The years that followed were miserable and scary. There was never enough money. Of course she adored her beautiful little daughter, but that only added to her fear. Now here she was, in Paris no less, basking in the devotion of a famous, rich, and handsome man.

He leaned forward, took her hand across the table. "I know it's crazy at my age falling in love with a woman so much younger. But, Carrie, darling, will you marry me?"

Carrie's head swam with conflicting emotions. Her joy was muted with hesitation. But mostly she felt safe, for the first time in her life.

Ten years later they were back in Paris, for their ninth wedding anniversary. Rex's hair was now snowy white, Carrie at forty getting a little plump. She'd crafted a good situation at *The Boston Globe*, where she was in charge of community profiles. And she was very much at ease presiding over Rex's beautiful Cambridge mansion. Tess had gone off to college the year before.

Rex and Carrie steered clear of too much reminiscing about their first Paris adventure, when early passion raged and they hardly knew each other. This time they ate far less opulent dinners and suffered more from jet lag. Carrie could sense that her husband was on edge somehow. Finally on the third day, he blurted out huskily that he had something to tell her. They were enjoying coffee at a large outdoor café on the Place Saint Michel, with a view of the river.

"Carrie my darling, I'm so sorry. I should have told you years ago."

She stared at him, handsome as ever but showing sure signs of aging—deep crinkles at eyes and mouth, a bit of stoop in the shoulders. He'd been having some memory lapses, too. So this announcement scared her. He folded his arms, hung his head, then abruptly looked up straight into her eyes.

"I have a son."

She replied, stupidly, "That's not possible. Why would you think that?"

"I have a son. He was born when I was living with that girl I told you about, except I didn't tell you she had a child, we had a child. Of course she wanted to get married. But I was struggling through med school. How could I get married? Besides, I didn't love her. God help me, I didn't even love him. But I stayed with them almost a year. Then I left."

Her jaw dropped, she felt dizzy.

He repeated bitterly, "Then I left."

Just like Dad, Carrie thought, and the tears came. She was gazing through blurred eyes at the beautiful sparkling river. Her world rudely shaken.

Rex was done apologizing, got briskly to the point. "He's here in Paris, at a conference. I want to see him. I have to see him. He only just showed up last year, at my office of all places. He's a nice boy. I hope you two will get along."

The rendezvous was set for a tiny out-of-the-way street off rue Monge. Carrie sat back in the shadows at the little table, out of the blazing June sunlight. Now here was Rex, with a dark eyed man not much younger than herself. At first he just looked oddly familiar, and she began to search her memory. But as soon as he spoke his name, she knew.

"I'm Brian," he said, with a winning smile, offering his hand. He was dressed nattily but conservatively in pale blue shirt and purple tie.

The men sat down, ordered their drinks. Carrie sipped at her Pernod in a trance. This was so unreal she didn't register it as actually happening. The boy she once knew only too well, all those years ago. Tess's father. But of course he didn't know that. Carrie was doubtless just one of many girls he had fun with in his early youth. She understood, didn't hold it against him. But she found herself chagrined that he didn't recognize her. True, back then her red hair was in a pixie cut, and she still had a girl's waiflike slimness. Now her hair, at Rex's request, fell way below her shoulders, her body had softened, her face was chubbier too. Frozen in disbelief, she was silent while the two men talked.

Memories crowded in when she needed clarity instead, some sense of proportion. That summer—the sounds and smell of the surf, fried clams and smoked oysters, bone-tired evenings when she finished her shift and joined her friends, when one beer sent her into wild laughter. She was confident of graduating with honors the following year, achieving her dream of finding a job with a magazine in New York. She was happy then to be out from under books and exams. She didn't mind the long hours waitressing—she had plenty of energy, and two days off every week that she spent lazily getting a great tan.

Carrie fought for equilibrium, working hard to keep her expression calm while wild thoughts thrashed around grasping for direction and meaning. Brian was clearly all absorbed in the nerve-wracking and magical experience of being in the presence of his father. He'd been only a year old when Rex left them. Rex was delighted to find this meeting between his wife and long-lost son going so well. So she thought, why tell them, after all? They wouldn't ever have to know the strange and awful truth. But oh no, what about Tess? How could Carrie in conscience keep her child from knowing her biological father? Her head began to throb, she pressed her temples.

"Are you all right, darling?"

Rex forced his attention away from his mesmerizing new fatherhood, rubbed her shoulder, peered closely at her face. Carrie knew she must be betraying at least some of her agonizing stress.

"Headache," she murmured.

"It's that damn weird Pernod. Have a Coke, some coffee?"

Brian said, "Plain old water will do the trick." He turned to order a Perrier in perfect French.

She smiled at him, too gratefully, too fondly.

Brian looked at her thoughtfully. "I knew a Carrie once."

July was very hot that year, and humid with too many thunderstorms. The sticky, noisy weather matched Carrie's tumultuous mood. She busied herself getting ready to close up the house for the rest of the summer, so they could take off for their Cape Cod cottage. Tess would arrive home from her California college any day now. Theirs was the most magnificent mansion on Appleton Street in Cambridge, easily the largest and most flamboyant. They had a part-time maid who also did some cooking, and intermittent help like caterers and gardeners. Carrie had an assignment from the *Globe*, though the deadline was vague. She still had too much leisure time to agonize over her dilemma: How was she to tell her husband and child about Brian?

One day Carrie was working half-heartedly on her laptop in the den when the doorbell rang. She waited to see if the maid would answer it, then went herself. Of all the worst things she could imagine, it was Brian. And Rex was not home. He stood there looking apologetic, casual in shorts and sandals. A shiny red car in the driveway had to be his.

"Sorry, Carrie. I couldn't think of any other way to do this. I know you guys are off to the Cape soon. I had to see you alone."

"No, you didn't have to see me alone," she countered tensely. "This is a very bad idea."

They faced off there at the threshold for a long minute. She was acutely aware of her saggy sundress and uncombed hair. She did not like the expression of admiration and familiarity that came over his face.

"So you remember me," she finally said, not rudely enough.

He laughed, oh God, a laugh so like his father's! Noting that sweat was starting on his forehead, she stepped back into the cool dim hallway and he followed quickly. She led the way to the living room, sat down primly on a plush chair by the bay window. He sat on the edge of the couch awkwardly.

"Would you like some lemonade?"

What were the niceties when visited by a long-lost boyfriend who's your husband's son and your daughter's father? She almost laughed. He saw her hint of amusement.

He smiled and said, "Lemonade would be just great. It's hot out."

"Oh right, let's talk about the weather." And to her horror she burst out in hysterical laughter.

They were both laughing when the maid appeared and Carrie ordered their drinks. It was clear to them both that they were in cahoots in a wildly complicated way. So there was no point in formalities any more.

"Look," Brian said finally, taking a long swig from his glass and placing it carefully on the glass-topped coffee table, "I don't think we should tell him. He doesn't need to know, right?"

"He's my husband," she replied defensively. "I love him."

"Hey, I love him too for that matter. Though that would kill my mother—she always taught me to despise him. That's why I don't want to torture him."

"He would be horrified," she agreed. "I mean, his wife and his son… But even if I wanted to hide it from him, there's another problem."

He leaned forward, worried. "What is it?"

She looked out the window at her beautiful lawn, the row of bright pink azaleas she loved so much, her stomach hollow. "My daughter, Brian."

"She needs to know? That doesn't make sense."

"She's yours."

"Mine?" He stared at her stupidly, while her meaning dawned on him. "You don't mean? Oh my God."

She nodded sorrowfully.

Then he jumped up angrily. "Why didn't you tell me?"

"I didn't know where you were," she said dully.

He paced and cursed, red in the face, beside himself. "I have other children, my twins Sadie and Sam, I'm a good father, I support them and their mother. I'm a good person. I would've helped you."

Carrie saw tears in his eyes, and felt them in her own. She got wearily to her feet, all the pain of all those years hitting her again in one blow. He came over to put his arm around her shoulder, then they were holding on to each other for dear life.

At first Rex didn't believe her.

"You're crazy. That can't be. No, just not possible."

Then he was furious.

"What the fuck do you mean? My wife screwing my son? My son is your kid's father? What a crock."

He paced around the den, the small space giving his body a caged-lion feel. Carrie had closed both doors, but the maid was just finishing up for the day in the kitchen and not likely to hear them in any case. Rex came out with more curses than she'd ever heard him use.

"I'm Tess's fucking grandfather for fuck's sake? Are you trying to kill me?"

Tess came home a few days later. She looked beautiful with a dark California tan, stylishly dressed, radiating self-confidence. Carrie was proud and disconcerted. Hard to believe this was her baby! The perception that Tess might not need her any more lurked like a menace. Embracing their old bond, the two women set to work cooking together, reviving shared recipes. Tess started calling old friends, playing tennis, going swimming. One evening when she had a date, Rex and Carrie sat alone over dessert.

Rex had seemed self-absorbed and distant since her revelation about Brian. She was content to wait it out—of course he was having trouble processing, who wouldn't? She was gentle, tiptoeing around him, trying to silently convey sympathy and affection.

"Tess made the cherry pie," she said.

He scooped up the last of his, nodded but didn't smile. "My favorite, she knows that."

"She does. You're still her Dad."

Outside the broad window at the end of the dining room, rain pelted the lawn into obscurity, thunder rolled in the distance. Around them, shadows shifted in the darkening room. Rex looked very tired, shoulders stooping.

"Carrie, I've been thinking."

"It's not my fault, you know," she started defensively, "none of it. I raised my baby alone, and well. I have no regrets. I did what I could."

"Of course, darling. I'm sorry I was angry. But I need you to know that I want to be a father to my son. You can understand that, can't you?"

She wanted to get up and go around to hug him, but she was wary now.

"What are you getting at?"

"First of all, I'm only too aware what my memory lapses can mean. I'm not fooling myself. Maybe a serious stroke. I'm going to be seventy in a couple of years. I don't want to waste any time now."

He pushed away his empty plate, sipped coffee, shaking his head. He went on, "We can be a family. I want us to be a family."

"That will be awkward," she replied a bit coldly. "But we can try."

"Tess has to be told."

"No!" She wanted to be furious, to fight, but she felt helpless.

"Carrie, cut it out for God's sake. You always think everything that happens to you is a planetary event."

His harshness crushed her further. She sank back into her chair as if from a blow.

But he persisted, "Think of me, how about that? Think of me now. Look, I've got medical problems. I've got a child of my own to care about. I'm a grandfather! I never thought I'd have grandchildren, but now I have three. Tess, and Sadie and Sam, youngsters who can use my influence, my guidance. My own flesh and blood."

He was high, he was bragging, he was practically elated.

She begged, "Stop it."

"Listen up. We've talked. My son and I worked it out between us. He agrees we can be a family. He and I are going to the game together tomorrow afternoon. We're both Sox fans, it turns out. Yeah. And afterwards, I'm going to bring him back here, and we can all sit down together."

She rallied, cried, "What about Tess? What will this do to her?"

"Oh for God's sake, Carrie! Tess is a grown woman. Stop trying to protect her. Let her go. She and Brian deserve to know each other. Listen to me. Listen now. We're going ahead with that whether you like it or not."

He glared at her triumphantly, smugly. So he was going to tell Tess anyway. Carrie's feelings about it no longer mattered. In despair, she looked around the beautifully appointed room, out the softly draped window where the July dusk was gently prevailing over the last of the rain storm, sending shoots of misty sunlight over the broad green lawn. This house, her sanctuary, her refuge, her pride and joy, a mockery.

The next evening, all four of them gathered in the living room after dinner. Rex had waited until dessert to break the news, which elicited from Tess only a wall of stony silence. Carrie sat on the couch, gestured to Tess patting the seat beside her. But Tess chose a chair opposite her. Rex and Brian took the armchairs on either side of the bay window. Lamps were lit against the murky twilight. Rex cleared his throat, but it was Brian who began.

"We're all caught in a web," Brian said, "of our own making."

He was looking around the room at everyone directly, seriously. Wearing shorts, T-shirt and sandals, tanned, his casual look belied by his urgent tone. Carrie began to reassess him. This boy was a mature man. Why had she been so desperate to deny him Tess? Because Rex was the only father she'd ever known? No, more likely because she wanted Tess all to herself, her own. The child sat opposite her now, leaning back in her chair almost laconically, eyes defiant. She seemed to be dismissing the rest of them as unworthy of her concern. This young woman did not belong to her any more. The realization both appalled and relieved her. In all those twenty years, Carrie had been coiled in fear and worry, pulling the protective cocoon of motherly love tight around her. In this fraught moment, Carrie's deep feeling of loss was overwhelmed by the release of that coil.

"Not me," Tess said in her clear, bell-like voice. "I haven't woven any webs around here. You people just made some bad choices."

You people: Carrie frowned at her rudeness. Rex looked wounded. Brian tried on a shadow of his winning smile.

Brian said, "Good for you, Tess."

"I will never call you Dad," Tess shot back grimly. "I don't even know you. I have zero interest in you at all."

"Tessie," Rex pleaded, "it's not his fault. There's no need to hurt him. He's trying his best."

Tess snorted. Even in her high and mighty offense, she looked beautiful, so fresh and ripe just entering womanhood. Like a butterfly still damp from the cocoon, glistening in new light.

Dark Matter Mansion

Grace Wilson had seen hard times already. At twelve the death of her parents and the abduction of her sister, at twenty the death of her first love in the War. Not to mention now and then the floods and famine with little to eat besides bread and the occasional root vegetable. She had no children of course—very common now that pollutants were making people sterile. So at thirty the latest virus had carried off her grandfather, her cherished Gumpa, the last person she loved.

There wasn't much of a funeral, with quarantines still in place. She stood almost alone in drizzly rain, October dusk falling fast. Gumpa lay there beneath the muddy soil, along with half a dozen other people; individual graves could not be purchased even for a large sum, there was just no space left.

An official of some sort intoned a brief farewell, his eyes above the mask bored and resentful, hunched under an umbrella held by a sallow-faced teenager. Sobs now and then escaped the few other mourners. A sickly smell of decay lingered even after the bodies disappeared. The two grave diggers shoveling the mud were skeletal old men looking like they were about to collapse, sparse gray hair plastered to bony skulls in the steady rain.

At the horizon of the vast graveyard, the sun struggled to glimmer faintly, then abruptly succumbed to a watery dusk. Grace in her threadbare jacket shivered, swiped at tears mingled with raindrops on her face.

It took her an hour to walk home. Not to the place that since childhood she'd shared with Gumpa, until he was carted off to the Virus Tank. Now she lived with her boyfriend in one small attic room in a sprawling old house on Appleton Street. They were lucky to be able to afford even that. Her street sweeping job had ended a year ago. Cal played in a band that sometimes got paid. He also showed up from time to time with money from some unknown source that he was cagey about.

He'd say, "Don't worry about it, honey. You don't want to know. Just kiss your old Cal."

She was willing enough to kiss him. Broad shouldered and sweet, Cal was the one certainty in her life now that dear Gumpa was gone. She felt not love, but great gratitude and caring.

Suddenly ahead of her on Reservoir Street, Grace spotted the body of a woman splayed across the crumbling sidewalk, dressed in a tattered nightgown. She looked very dead. Grace's heart wanted to stop and try to help but her brain signaled clearly and coldly, danger. Virus victims sometimes stumbled out of their houses in a last lunatic frenzy of pain and fear. The patrolling Tank Wagon would be along soon anyway to pick the body up. Grace stepped aside quickly.

The rain had dwindled to a damp mist and it was nearly dark as Grace climbed the last hill, and her home rose into sight. Sprawling and ramshackle, the house had once been an elegant Victorian. Decades of neglect had diminished its allure, though not its old world charm, in spite of peeling gray paint and tousled, overgrown lawn. A large sign hung crookedly on the high front fence, reading Dark Matter Mansion. This alarming and intriguing name was explained by her landlady as a tribute to her deceased son, who had been a scientist studying the mysteries of dark matter in space.

"Well, he was just the best boy," she liked to intone, "always good to his mama. And such a success, you wouldn't believe. He was famous, I tell you. And handsome, oh my!"

Mrs. Sutter was a dumpling in shape and texture, invariably clad in a roomy apron, with large froggy lips and shiny little black eyes like a crow's. She was good natured and dull, just what Grace needed, a comfort of sorts.

Grace ran up the three flights of stairs and found Cal cooking eggs on their hot plate. He dropped the spoon and came to embrace her.

"How was the funeral?"

"Gruesome." She threw off her jacket and plopped into a chair.

He whipped out a bottle of grape vodka and poured two generous glasses. She refrained from asking where he'd got it, raised her glass in a toast.

"Thanks, Cal. I feel better already."

"Then wait 'til you hear my news." He lifted his glass, took a generous gulp. "I found you a job!"

"No way."

"Well," he said, "you know that gig I played on Friday? On the river boat? I met a guy there, one of the waiters, ran into him today. He says they're looking for maids over at Colonel Marcham's."

"What kind of maid?"

Cal scraped scrambled eggs onto a plate for her, and sat down with his own, shoveling it in. He answered with his mouth full.

"Hell, honey, I don't know what *kind* of maid. Do we need money or not? You kept house for your Gumpa all those years. You can do whatever it is."

She took a swig of vodka. "Gumpa was a good cook, and he could scrub a floor like nobody's business."

"A terrific man. Course you miss him like crazy. Like your eggs?"

She took a dainty bite. "Oh, it's got mushrooms! Oh, Cal."

"Yep, your favorite. For you, honey. Now cheer up."

That night Grace lay sleepless with the waking nightmare that always plagued her when she was upset.

She and her little sister Deirdre are tending the farm stand their family runs to sell everything they can scrounge. Rusty nails, scrap metal, string, wire, moss, asphalt chunks, soap shards. Grace tells six-year-old Deirdre to take charge while she runs to the outhouse. Looks back once, to see the little girl sitting primly, taking her responsibility seriously, her beautiful dark red hair tied up in a blue ribbon.

That was the last time she saw her sister. When she returned, after just a few minutes, Deirdre was gone. Just gone. Forever. Now when Grace screamed, reliving again that dark terror and rage, Cal reached over and pulled her close, hushed her with caresses.

The morning she was due for the interview, Grace trudged downstairs to the bathroom carrying a kettle of boiling water, knowing the faucet would produce lukewarm at best. With another tenant knocking on the door, she sponged quickly. On her way back upstairs, passing the window on the landing, she noticed that the old garage in back was getting renovated.

Cal was just getting up, yawning and gulping down chicory coffee. When she mentioned the garage activity, he told her Mrs. Sutter said her nephew was moving his business in very soon.

"Who knows what it is," he chuckled. "But it's lucrative enough to excite her. And she's on and on about the charms and talents of the nephew."

Grace, in the new blouse and earrings Cal had magically produced, brushed her cap of reddish brown hair vigorously, preened.

"How do I look?"

His answer was a leer and a hug. "Spectacular."

Out in the street, she was greeted even this early with a murky wave of heat promising a suffocating day. The autumn rain, far from cooling the air, had only increased the heavy humidity. She crossed Brattle Street, where tents and lean-tos had taken over the lawns of the former grand mansions, now in complete disrepair or occupied by squatters. A Tank Wagon passed her, going very slowly to keep an eye out for new cargo.

Straight ahead now she could see the river, and the outline of the old boathouse that served as Colonel Marcham's impressive abode. The perhaps 200-year-old picturesque façade, two broad cupolas and wide doors for boats, was augmented on both sides by recent additions with windows and balconies. Once perched at the edge of the river, it was now surrounded by marsh, the abandoned dam having let in the ocean. Marcham was one of only five colonels who answered directly to the Chief of Police. They topped the elite, you might even say royalty, of this area ruled by Chief Rey. At this time the various chiefs maintained a tenuous peace among themselves, coordinating laws and policies. It had not always been so: brutal wars had once been fought over each one's territory. Eventually they settled on the boundaries of this land west of what had been the old city of Boston, before sea-level rise took its toll.

Half a dozen boaters vied for her business. She chose a tall turbaned woman for both her price and her sinewy self-confidence. Grace tried not to be awed by the grandeur looming up ahead. The massive broad-faced boathouse retained its original red brick color, brandishing elaborate filigree over windows and archways. Grace worried about sweat showing under her arms, her scruffy shoes. She lifted her chin defiantly when asked her name by the guards on the dock. They directed her without interest or ceremony to a back entrance.

Inside, she joined a line of other people waiting in front of a heavy door. The few chairs were taken. Most had pushed their masks down over their chins; nobody had much faith in masks anymore and they were no longer required. The viruses came and went, every year, without a rational pattern.

At least it was cool in here. So the rumors that the elite had air conditioning were true. Eventually she found herself face to face with a large woman in uniform, not fat, not muscular, just large. She wore the same uniform as the guards and other police: high-necked dark green jacket, black pants, black boots.

"Lieutenant Bunt," she said. "Call me lieutenant."

"Thank you," replied Grace, gazing up at her with as much dignity as she could muster, "Lieutenant."

They did not sit down while Bunt looked her over critically with quick and beady eyes.

"Street sweeping," the woman muttered."Some experience with sales. Not much to recommend there. But looks good. Healthy. Not too young. Did some school, did we?"

"Yes, Lieutenant. Finished tenth grade."

"OK, wait here. You'll see the captain next."

Lieutenant Bunt turned abruptly and went out. Grace waited some more, finally was fetched by another guard and shown into a large office with a window overlooking the marsh, a burly officer seated at a desk.

"Sit down," he ordered.

Grace sat, not too hurriedly, folded her legs demurely. Her growing annoyance was helping to quell her nervousness.

The man peered at her as if looking through a microscope.

"You'll have to grow out your hair."

She nodded, without enthusiasm. "I can do that, sir."

"Of course you can. I've never understood why these women chop off their hair. It's very unattractive." When she was silent, he cried, "Can you tell me why they do? Give me one good reason."

His vehemence, and the real interest in his tone shook her confidence. "I don't know, sir. Maybe it's easier to care for?"

"Nonsense, young woman. What's your name?"

"Grace Wilson, sir."

"Well, Miss Grace Wilson, you don't know a thing, do you?"

When Grace smiled apologetically, he added, "But you do have spunk." He produced suddenly a wide and generous smile. "And I will say, you seem intelligent enough. You're cute, too. Tell me, do you like hard work?"

"I've seen plenty of it," she replied, leaving out the "sir."

The captain laughed pleasantly and got to his feet.

"You'll do. The lieutenant will give you your instructions."

And that was it. Grace found herself getting measured for a maid's uniform while being briefed by Bunt. Then she was back in the rowboat again watching the sinewy turbaned woman ply her oars with grim vigor.

A light fog lingered as the gray sky released its blazing October sun. Looking back at the colonel's imposing buildings presiding over muddy water matted with weeds, Grace tried to be thrilled at getting a good job. But she found herself instead newly mourning Gumpa, and all her old family before everything crashed. Back then, the five of them happy together, the river still contained in its winding banks, the weather predictable, even a winter of sorts. Then the heart-rending, agonizing loss of her little sister. Then the plagues. What a difference in those twenty years!

When Grace got home, she noticed a new sign posted on the high fence, side by side with Dark Matter Mansion. But the new sign was merry and colorful, proclaiming, Hearts Angels. Jaunty red hearts danced around the words. It added a cheerful note to the otherwise somber presence of the looming house. So the nephew's business must involve something nice, Grace concluded, maybe matchmaking or pets.

As she passed the kitchen on her way upstairs, Mrs. Sutter emerged grinning.

"You got the job," she smirked, flapping her voluminous apron enthusiastically. "I can tell, you look that happy." She beamed at Grace's nod. "You'll pay that rent right on the nose now, won't you, dear. Well then, good news all around. Volfie's business opens tomorrow. He already has orders!"

Grace turned on the stairs to acknowledge their mutual successes, politely asked, "What's he selling?"

"Children," replied Mrs. Sutter.

Even the kitchen in Colonel Marcham's estate was magnificent. Enormous solar heated ovens and freezers, pots and pans for every occasion hanging from the ceiling, rows of spices, chutneys, baskets of carrots and turnips. Steep stairs leading down to a luxurious root cellar, piles of apples and potatoes, shelves of bottled jams and pickles, bins of dried and salted fish. One day three weeks after starting the job, Grace was sorting through the jams for strawberry, specially ordered by Miss Trilly, when Bolton Fleming showed up beside her. Of course there was no reason for him to be in the root cellar except to pester her, but she was not entirely sorry. He was an important adjunct to the colonel, on his way up in the police hierarchy, just over thirty and handsome in a rough and rugged way. He was fond of squeezing her waist with both hands, laughing boyishly to indicate just fun.

"Ready for the big party?" he inquired.

"Yes. It's exciting. I've never been on a yacht."

"Oh, you're such an innocent."

"That I am not!"

They laughed together. He certainly did look good, Grace conceded, in his spiffy uniform, badge and buttons shining. He disturbingly reminded her of her beloved sweetheart killed in the War who still visited her in dreams. Same flashing brown eyes and playful shrug of shoulders. She reached from the shelf two jars of jam, turned back to find he had only moved closer. She was hardly seductive in her bland uniform—black leggings, small black apron, blue blouse buttoned up to the neck—but she felt vulnerable. She wriggled around him, moved off.

"Got to go," she said.

"Good to see you," he replied simply.

"I'll see you on the yacht. But we'll both be pretty busy."

She hoped this remark conveyed her friendly intentions but suitably professional stance. She certainly didn't want to be the dalliance of an ambitious official. But more importantly, she didn't want to be unfair to Cal. He was such a great support to her, especially during this time of mourning for Gumpa. In his arms she found warmth and reassurance.

Grace quickly climbed the stairs to the hubbub of the kitchen. The upcoming party on General Rey's yacht was to be a splendid and very special affair, celebrating simultaneously the birthday of his wife, and the official end of this particular pandemic. No masks allowed!

It was only a matter of hours now, and the preparations were frantic. She hurriedly passed the jam jars on to the girls' special chef, and turned her attention to chopping mushrooms for canapés. Then Lieutenant Bunt showed up and summoned the maids chosen to serve the guests. Grace and six other women clustered around her as she barked out orders. Along with warnings to adhere to ladylike and obsequious behavior, she told them all to unbutton their blouses three buttons in the front, just enough to show a hint of bosom.

"We want them all to relax," she declaimed. "This is the cream of society cream. Honor them, please them, obey them."

Grace as usual secretly smirked at the royal presumptions so flagrant in this elite house, but at the same time she couldn't help being impressed at the affluence and ease of the lives of these privileged people. The world outside was so horribly different, it felt increasingly unreal to her. That world of terror, sickness, want, of children bought and sold, of corpses and mass graves. That world, where half a rabbit for dinner was a feast, where Cal's triumph at securing a bunch of turnips occasioned joyous prancing.

No, how could she want to be part of a world where Volfie could sell infants and toddlers to anyone who had the money? He called Hearts Angels an orphanage, but nobody pretended his business was rescuing them—more like manufacturing them. Most of his "assistants" were pregnant women. Mrs. Sutter had let slip that he was the father of most of the babies: she was proud that her entrepreneurial nephew was one of the few very fertile males left, who had the smarts to make the best of it.

Grace's title was Girls' Attendant. As such she was pretty much at the beck and call of the twelve young girls alluded to as princesses, because they were the colonel's daughters. At first their diversity of coloring and physique made her assume they were mostly the offspring of his mistresses, but recently she learned that some had been purchased. This was not mentioned overtly, as his masculine prowess was so clearly proven by that many children. There were in addition twelve sons, housed separately and slated for police training.

Chief Rey's yacht was already docked outside, an awesome sight, immaculate white with several decks. Its name, elegantly scripted on its massive prow, was Dream Queen. On board, Grace took her place at the serving counter, top blouse buttons duly unhooked. A lively band was playing popular and patriotic songs while a lithe woman all in sequins belted out the lyrics.

The giant boat heaved away from the dock and headed up the marsh towards Watertown. Grace was moving from guest to guest on the open deck balancing a tray of appetizers, trying not to gawk at the extravagant gowns, when Chief Rey and his wife were announced, making a dramatic entrance.

"Our fearless, invincible leader, Chief Gustav Rey, and his beautiful wife, Lavinia."

The chief was a corpulent man with an arrogant swagger, a heavy, clever face and snow-white hair. But Grace was at once mesmerized by the beauty of his wife. In her twenties, as regal and graceful as a swan, clad entirely in bright green silk, a sparkling tiara crowning brilliant red hair, a face of harmonious perfection, skin fairly translucent in its delicacy, Lavinia was breathtaking. The guests made no pretense about staring at this lovely vision, even though many had no doubt seen her before. The band struck up a waltz. Chief Rey led his spectacular lady onto the dance floor.

Grace and the other servers retreated to their stations. The horizon was offering a satisfying sunset of violet and rose. The ship eased into a cleaner and narrower slip of river lined with houseboats in various states of disrepair, peopled with families, lines of laundry, pots of ripening tomatoes and chard. On either shore could be glimpsed campsites of tents and lean-tos. The air was noticeably fresher here upriver. There were trees here, some quite old, with thick beefy branches, halos of autumn colors.

Bolton Fleming, all spiffed up and shining in his impeccable uniform, materialized by her side, acknowledging with a full stare the attraction of her cleavage.

"Lovely evening," he said.

"I hadn't ever seen the chief's wife. Isn't she gorgeous?"

"Just acquired a few years ago. Promoted from mistress, which does happen. Yes, she's gorgeous, our Lavinia."

"What's she like?"

"Well, I have chatted with her occasionally, but very formally. You'll find out more from the other servants. I take it she's good at giving orders. I don't think she's much of a favorite with them."

Grace was busying herself arranging glasses of champagne on a tray. But the smile she threw at him was not as dismissive as she intended.

"Look," he said. "I have to go dance with somebody now. Duty calls. But I need you to know, I find you very attractive. Tell me, Grace my dear, would you like to visit my rooms?"

She reacted to this with the indignation it deserved. "Certainly not. What for?"

Bolton moved close enough to whisper in her ear. "You know what for. Will you please, please have sex with me?"

This time she laughed. "Well, you are honest!"

"Honest. That's me." His breath was hot on her neck.

Grace knew she was flushing. She retorted, "I'm already taken, sir. I have a partner. I live with him. So thank you very much, you are dreaming."

Bolton Fleming made a little bow that pretended to acquiesce, but his satisfied grin said otherwise. Later on, she saw him dancing with several different attractive women, dressed in gowns she envied. Their world was far from hers, she scolded herself, she should stop imagining.

Grace hurried home much later than usual that night, only too aware that the dimly lit streets held unknown risks. As she reached the safety of Dark Matter Mansion's front gate, close behind her appeared a burly man carrying two young children, one of them screaming. The other one lolled with catatonic staring eyes. Beside them scurried a skinny woman in black, who kept hushing the child with curses. Grace stood stock still as they pushed past her and continued down the path around to the back of the mansion. The piercing screams were animal-like in their wild desperation. Grace felt her heart bursting.

When Mrs. Sutter opened the door to let her in, she asked, "I just saw somebody carrying two kids to Hearts Angels, is that ok?"

"Oh, yes, dear, very ok. We do take older children, maybe even age three or four. There's quite a demand for them."

Grace paused at the foot of the stairs, daring to pursue it. "But why late at night, why was it screaming?"

Mrs. Sutter surveyed her for a moment, disapprovingly. She was draped in a blousy bathrobe, but her eyes were alert, both cautious and merry.

"Oh, say, what do you know, we got twins tonight. One of the girls had twins. We struck pay dirt. Be happy for us, girl."

Grace knew she'd gone too far. "That's great news," she managed to mumble, as she turned and ran up the stairs.

At the beginning of November, Bolt was promoted to lieutenant, and Grace was proud of him. They'd become pals of sorts, he respecting her boundaries, she seeing him as the representative of a brighter world. They discovered a corner of the root cellar where two wooden boxes provided seats of sorts. They met there a few times a week. One day shortly after his promotion, Bolt announced important news. She took up her basket of salted fish, and sat down beside him expectantly.

He started by asking her how her job was going. She reported progress in placating Miss Trilly, who was her most trying mistress among all the girls. A pleasant odor of apples, both overripe and fresh, emanated from the bins behind them.

"Too bad you have to humor that spoiled little girl," he sighed. "Wouldn't you like to try for another job?"

She smiled at him warmly, knowingly. "You have something in mind."

"You guessed it," he laughed. "And I'm sure you figured out right away that it concerns our friendship. I've just found out that along with my promotion comes a new assignment. I've been honored to join the chief's personal guard."

"That's wonderful, Bolt!"

"It is, it is. But that means I have to move to the main barracks not far from his estate. I won't have many chances to visit with you here anymore."

She took in his sad face, was chagrined to find herself feeling a similar sense of loss.

"I will miss you," she confessed, but hastened to add, "maybe it's for the best."

"I don't see how it can be good in any sense," he remonstrated. "Except…" He took both her hands in his. "Now listen to this, my dear. There's an opening for a maid on the chief's staff. I hear it involves young children. You have experience there, and good references I'm sure. Why not try for it?"

Grace held her breath, let it out slowly. She did not pull her hands away. Cautiously, she ventured, "So you and I could keep on meeting like this?" His answer was the fire in his eyes. She added, "I'd like that."

And so it happened that Grace Wilson found herself in the presence of the beautiful Lavinia, wife of the most powerful man in the region. The interview took place on the second floor of the family residence in Chief Rey's sprawling estate. It had once been a country club, carved out of the woods just north of Concord. Grace had to be vetted at the big iron entrance gates, then escorted in a pony-drawn golf cart up the long drive, where the dead trees blazed with colorful flags and streamers.

Lavinia was seated regally by a lace-draped window. Even in her far less fancy dress, she was radiantly beautiful. The room was large and long, all the furniture a small size suitable for children. Grace had been told she was being considered for the position of nanny and teacher.

"You come highly recommended," Lavinia said, her voice as resonant and melodious as the rest of her.

"Thank you, Madam."

"You're Grace Wilson. Where have I heard that name? I'm curious—it rings a bell."

"I hope in a good context, Madam."

Grace was standing there awkwardly, since she'd not been asked to sit down, her hands clasped tightly together in front of her.

Lavinia said, "You are highly praised by Lieutenant Fleming."

Grace hoped she wasn't flushing. "That's very kind of him."

"You could do worse."

Lavinia allowed a small smirk to loosen her proud mouth. In that moment, Grace saw lightning. The vision before her exploded into the mischievous face of her lost little sister.

"Deirdre," she breathed.

"What did you say?"

Grace stared and stared. Then she opened her arms, repeated the cry, "Deirdre!"

Lavinia started to her feet, glowering at this impertinent servant, but eyes wide with terror.

"Go away, go away," she shouted.

Grace started to back away. But now Lavinia was upon her, grasping her arm fiercely, shaking her, pushing her reddened face into Grace's.

"How do you know that name?"

Grace put her hand over hers, crooning, "Oh my precious sister!"

The porcelain face cracked open, and Deirdre was sobbing in her arms.

Crescendo

Some say the world will end in fire,
Some say in ice.
—Robert Frost

It worked out quite well. When all those tsunamis hit the northeast coast in 2089, folks fled west to cities like Worcester and settled in abandoned office buildings. There was no gas for their cars, which were mostly waterlogged anyway, so they came in solar-powered school buses. They had to camp in the parks for a few months, and that's where Eden's mother caught the dysentery that killed her, but her grandmother took over that role, and anyway Eden was already sixteen. The rest of the family consisted of her father and little brother Tex. Their apartment had three rooms that once housed an insurance company, looking out over a park with a pond, lots of sun in the morning. All of them were groggy with trauma, but the needs of daily life soon shifted their mood to determination.

Over the next two years, most folks relinquished vivid memories of the comparative ease they'd left behind, as well as their sorrow at the loss. Eden and her father Jack found jobs, as seamstress and baker; grandmother Nana picked up odd jobs making yogurt and baking pies. Tex went to a school of sorts, learning basics from math to biology. Nana filled him in on things he wasn't learning, like there used to be machines in the sky, and spring came predictably every year in April. He humored her.

With all the instability and chaos of millions of displaced people migrating, local governments were enfeebled and faded away. There wasn't a police force to speak of either. Instead, small areas were organized haphazardly, usually by groups resembling gangs, with powerful leaders and strong-arm tactics. Eden's building was run by Mr. Burns and his staff, who called themselves The Eagles. They collected rent, and from time to time requested other favors. For example, Tex had to brush down their horses, and Eden was required to help sew their clothes. But the family wasn't complaining. The comfort and safety of this haven was worth the autocracy.

1

When he turns fourteen, in fact only a few days after his fourteenth birthday, Tex springs an ugly surprise on his family. They're all sitting around the table in the main room, dinner finished. Eden gets up to clear the table.

"Sit down, sis," says Tex. "I've got an announcement."

Tex is not a young man of many words, so "announcement" is heavy with meaning. Eden, already alarmed, sits.

"You know the Eagles." Tex starts, then blurts, "I've been chosen." As they're all mute, he adds, "Mr. B chose me."

"What the hell," Jack shouts, turning red. "Who says? What're you talking about?"

Jack's eyebrows are twitching, a really bad sign his children have learned to fear. Eden puts her hand on his shoulder, he shakes it off. Nana sits up straight, stiffens with resolve for whatever's coming. Her abundant white hair reigns proudly over her small anxious face, providing a dignity her bony body would otherwise lack.

Tex goes on, swagger dimmed by filial habit. "Look, Dad, it's no use you getting all worked up. This is my chance for a job. You're always saying I need to provide more now that I'm a man. Well, Mr. B sees a lot of potential for me. He says I'm really good at noticing things and remembering."

"My foot," snorts Jack. "He wants you for spying. You're supposed to come into the bakery with me. I've already taught you a lot."

Tex snorts back. "Oh goody, goody, I can bake potato bread."

His father jerks out of his chair. "Don't you dare insult my business, don't you dare…"

Tex cringes automatically. But getting slowly to his feet, he remembers that he's now taller than his father, shrugs. "Not insulting anybody. Just going my own way."

Nana says, "Jack now, take it easy."

Eden says, "Dad."

Jack stares up at his son, deflates. "Fine. See how you like it, pushing folks around, hurting them, taking all kinds of kinky orders, ending up with your knees broken, most likely."

"Those are just rumors, Dad," Eden intercedes. "Nobody ever proved them. Mr. B's pretty honest in most of his dealings, right, Nana?"

Nana, continuing the upright stance of her spine, concurs tartly, "He has a lot of power. People resent that. So they talk. How much will he pay, Tex?"

Jack says softly, "Son, you'll never get paid enough to make up for their making a thug out of you."

Tex is mollified by the sorrowful affection in his father's tone. "Dad, I won't do anything wrong. I promise. I'll make you proud."

"Look at what we've come to," laments Jack. "We used to be respectable people, we had a house, money, voting, good food, we were happy…"

"Jack," cautions Nana, "don't go there. Don't mourn over the old days, it only gets you gloomy."

Tex scoffs, "What about all your terrible hard times in the 2060s you're always moaning about?"

"Dad, we're fine," Eden argues, annoyed. "We're lucky."

"Dad," pleads Tex finally. "This is a great chance for me. I'll work hard and get to be a leader."

But Jack hangs his head.

The next day, Eden says to her boyfriend Nesto, "I think I should go see Mr. B and persuade him Tex is too young for that kind of work."

Nesto, a lanky, dynamic young man with blazing dark eyes, has firm opinions on everything. "Oh hell, Eden, why? It's a job. The Eagles are big shots nowadays. Your dad is old school."

"So okay. He cares about how the world is going."

They're sitting on a bench near the pond on a hot March afternoon. He puts his arm around her and her head falls to his shoulder. Just weeks ago he persuaded her to make love, and they are both still in the first stages of amazement about it.

She gently reminds him, "You yourself didn't join a gang, did you? You aimed higher. And now you've got a chance at cheese factory manager, right? Because you wouldn't settle."

"I wouldn't mind Mr. B's situation. He's rich, damn it."

"Rich isn't everything."

"My, aren't we little Miss Goody Two-shoes." He caresses her breast briefly. "Kiss me."

So she does.

But that afternoon she heads for Mr. B's office.

Mr. B is doing well. The Eagles have expanded to take over two adjacent office buildings, so he now controls the whole block, totaling some three hundred people. He's a hefty, solid forty-two with balding reddish hair, a charmer when he wants to be. He looks Eden over with warm eyes. He comes from behind his desk to motion her to a comfortable chair, sits opposite.

"What can I do for you, little lady? My how fast you've grown up! How long is it now? Two years since you came here? Do you like it ok? Is there anything we can do better?"

"Oh no, Mr. Burns. Everything's fine." Eden has worn her most sophisticated jacket, hoping it will give her a serious and capable air. She crosses her legs self-consciously. Worries, are her shoes appropriate?

He keeps on nodding, not impatient, just encouraging. "Fine, fine."

"Well, you see, it's about Tex. My brother Tex."

"Is it." His tone is perceptively cooler.

"You see, my dad…well, he thinks Tex is too young to work for you."

Mr. B laughs heartily. "Has he looked at our Tex lately? He's tall, strong, and smart. He's no kid anymore."

"Sure, I know, but…"

"Now look here, little lady. Don't you worry your little head one more minute over this. Dads are always looking after their own. I'll have him in for a talk and we'll work it out, what do you think?"

Mr. B is standing up, in the process of dismissing her.

She says, "I don't think that's a good idea. He has a temper."

"Does he."

"Won't you please reconsider?"

Mr. B gazes down at her, smiling benignly. "What are you willing to do for me?"

Eden replies sweetly, but refuses his invitation to lunch. He's pleasantly noncommittal, polite, with a kindly and conspiratorial grin. He ushers her out as if they are the best of friends. Eden is experienced enough to perceive that Mr. B has proposed exchanging or mitigating Tex's role for her favors. She debates whether to consult Nana on this dilemma, but Nana might tell Jack. Jack will want to leave town. Nesto will have a fit. Her best friend Thea says, "Find out what he wants. You can draw the line. Doesn't he already have a bunch of women at his beck and call? Maybe you can be, for example, the storyteller of A Hundred and One Nights."

"Dream on, Thea. You're such a romantic."

"Hey, you could get a lot from him for not so much if you're crafty. He's got a lot of money. Also, you sure don't want to get on his bad side."

Eden laughs, disguising the sour taste in her mouth. Does not confess that she's afraid.

A few days later a young man wearing an Eagles T shirt accosts her in the lobby on her way home. He informs her that Mr. B wants to see her right away, on an important matter. She doesn't dare disobey. Besides, this personal summons makes her feel special.

Mr. B says, "Thanks so much for coming, my dear little Eden. Sit down over here. Will you have some ice cream? No? Don't you look nice today. Where did you get that pretty blouse? Sewed it yourself, I bet!"

Mr. B is looking spiffy in a freshly ironed white shirt, his big red hands sporting rings. He's not really a bad-looking man, she thinks. He looks strong and kind at the same time. She gives him a genuine smile.

"I've had an idea," he says. "I hope you like it. Tex can wait and join my staff next year. That's if you'll be my girl."

Jack's warnings ring in her ears. She envisions him and Nana in furious fits. She confronts her own feeling of shame. But she just looks at him with wide eyes, whispering, "What do you mean?"

Mr. B comes over to her chair, takes her arm, pulls her to her feet. "This."

He kisses her fiercely and tenderly. His passion feels real. She's horrified and flattered. She pulls away, panting. She's saying, "No, no…" But she's so weak he has to hold her up.

Before she leaves him that day, an arrangement has been made, not in so many words, but without any doubt. Eden will visit Mr. B from time to time for sexual purposes, and Tex's employment will be put on hold. She's thrilled that she has spared her brother. At the same time she's burning with excitement. Playing the role of mistress to the king is kind of like a fairy tale.

When Tex announces the postponement of his job, Jack is jubilant with congratulations and encouragement.

"I'll get you into the bakery right away," he promises. "No more school for you. I think you'll make a great chef some day, too. You'll never need to cater to that thug. Way to go, son." To Eden he says smugly, "You see, no compromises with dictators. This family's above all that. Times may be hard, and other folks may have to settle, but Jack shows them all how to live with honor."

2

At first they welcome the news about General Starr. Right now, he's marching from Buffalo with a thousand of his elite troops, to calm the chaos that has ensued from years of drought followed by months of one hurricane after another. Everyone clusters around radios, entranced, murmurs of hope growing to cheers. Worcester is constantly besieged by hordes of starving migrants, and gang conflicts are increasing daily. The bosses have tried to pool their gangs into a police force of sorts, but cooperation flounders.

"The general will fix it," Mr. B assures Eden. "He's a man's man. Won't take any crap, you'll see."

One of B's wives—a charmer named Lydia—is serving them breakfast in bed on this sultry September morning. Eden picks at the mushroom omelet. She's covered herself with a gauzy robe over B's objections, still not used to Lydia's seemingly gracious attentions. Lydia has assured her that she and the other three wives welcome being spared too much of B's voracious sexual appetite. "After all," says Lydia, "it's not as if he wants to marry you. Just like the other stray girls, you'll soon be history." But Mr. B is a very good lover, and Eden has to doubt their indifference.

Eden herself has no emotional stake in the matter. She's only here to protect her brother Tex from being recruited into Mr. B's gang of Eagles. She's been the Wednesday girl for nearly six months now, so Tex remains safe in his job at the bakery.

"That General Starr, believe me," B continues to pontificate, devouring his omelet with gusto. His ruddy face, already flushed from love making, turns even redder with enthusiasm. "There's a man. Don't come up against him. He gets what he wants, I'm telling you.

These crazed crowds trying to take over, they'll wish they never left home."

Eden sips chicory coffee, vaguely pitying the migrants. She has seen their faces, people just like her own family once were, wretched, terrified. But she shares B's confidence in the general's ability to restore order, and begins to plan her day. Nana will have covered for her absence with lies to her father about staying with Thea, but how will she explain the pretty new dress B gave her last night? She'll have to hide it until she and Nana think of something plausible. Jack is getting a little wary, although he suspects her old boyfriend Nesto, never dreaming of Mr. B as the culprit.

Eden meets Thea in the marketplace by the cabbages, as arranged, not long after kissing Mr. B goodbye at around nine, when his workday starts with a team meeting. He has assured Eden that gang violence can be controlled until the general gets here. "You're a good girl," he tells her at parting, his highest praise.

Thea is selling vegetables that her family helps grow. She's wearing a huge apron that emphasizes her skinny form. Eden, proud of her own ample proportions, does not envy the effect.

Peeling wilting outer leaves from a cabbage, Thea asks, "How's old horny bones?"

Eden hands her the new dress in a package, says, "Keep this for me. I can't let Dad see it yet, before I find an excuse."

Thea takes the package with a smile. "Sure. Old B still turning you on?"

"Enough. Nesto could learn a few things from him."

"Give Nesto time, he's only twenty. I saw him yesterday. He was flirting with that Mrs. Teller. But you know he still loves you."

As a matter of fact, Jack is so distracted by his rage at General Starr that he stops quizzing Eden about her overnights.

"Listen up, kids, and you too, Mama." He's holding forth after dinner, his favorite time, when they are all still at the table. "And," he shoots at Tex, "don't roll your eyes or I'll wrap your legs around your neck."

Tex smiles conciliation edging on condescension. Jack, still in his blue bakery smock smeared with flour and grease, wiggles his grey-tufted eyebrows in further warning, and continues.

"This is important. You all need to know what this monster's doing. You've got romantic ideas about his swaggering brutality, you call it leadership. Let me tell you, leaders don't go around killing innocent people at a whim, filling up mass graves, torturing folks who speak up, inventing decrees every minute to get us more enslaved…"

"But, Dad," ventures Eden, "Mr. B says he's going to solve our problems."

"Oh, sure. B has an interest. Starr will make or break him and his little empire. You watch. The likes of B stand to gain a lot by throwing in their lot with the dictator, the lizard."

"Now be careful, son," intercedes Nana. "The bosses forbid us to call him that."

"The lizard," Jack shouts. "I'll call him whatever I want. It suits him, with those big staring eyes. Lizard! Now you listen, we average folks have to stand up against this. Our friends and our planet have been through hell what with the fires and floods and crop damage, and the raging priests and petty tyrants and cults brought by fear and chaos. This is a time for brave folks to stand tall."

Eden watches his beloved face contort. He really is so upset. She knows that the general is rumored to do bad things, sure, but that pales in the light of peace and stability. Her dear father is of another time, she feels, touting values long proved useless.

She says, "Okay, Dad, consider us warned. Don't get all worked up. Our lives won't be disrupted if we just stay under his radar. We'll be fine."

"Sure, that's what they say at first. Then the noose comes around to them eventually and they wonder why they didn't get wise sooner."

"Dad," says Tex in a surly tone, "Cut it out. We can take care of ourselves."

Jack glares at him, looks around the table at the faces of his family, his eyes welling with tears.

Nana says, "Jack, Jack. You're too good. There's no place any more for good men. Try to forget about it. You'll get in trouble."

"Mama," he begs in a thick voice, "you don't think we're already in trouble?"

"Not if we shut up," Tex retorts.

Eden goes out after cleaning up the kitchen, into the misty sluggish evening, the sky a deep uniform grey. She's hoping to intercept Nesto as he returns home from the bakery. It's been weeks since they talked, Nesto distraught and furious.

He catches sight of her as he turns the corner by the marketplace, just closing down for the day. He tries to brush past her. She murmurs, "I miss you."

He whips around, starts to yell, his face close to hers, stops, grabs her into his arms. Their kisses are full of hunger, sorrow.

"Why, why," he's breathing. "Why are you doing that? Don't you know it's killing me?"

General Starr has been quartered in Worcester for one week only, and has already managed to arrest over two thousand people. Nobody knows exactly where they're being kept. So far they've been mostly migrants, so at first nobody cares a lot either, for isn't this just the "law and order" he promised? The general makes numerous fiery speeches, breathtaking in their confidence and menace. If you aren't horrified, you rush to embrace his comforting promises. No more street violence, no more food and water shortages, no more hordes of needy migrants, no more paralyzing fear.

"I will take care of you, my people," he trumpets, "I am your leader for all time. Hold your heads up high and follow me. Follow me, my people, and all will be well."

He's a tall man with long blond hair, and a clutch of blond hair on his chin. He always wears the immaculate uniform of his reign, in the blood-red and gold of his colors, flags flying around him bearing the now familiar insignia of a hawk with outstretched wings. Most folks are entranced, awestruck, swallowing their doubts in heady acquiescence.

Mr. B and his ilk rush to join the great general in his worthy mission. For the first time, all the bosses meet amicably, and jockey to praise Starr the most glowingly. Then the general's guards start rounding up any protesters. It's not long before they come for Jack.

It starts as a normal November day. Sweltering, suffocating, overcast, with a hot wind from the west intensified by wildfires raging around Albany. Downtown, the marketplace is busy as soon as the sun's up, people hurrying to shop before the wilt of high noon. A television set has been magically restored—the general finds parts for it somewhere—and blares beautiful pictures of Starr holding forth, his red and gold hawk flags waving, crowds yelling devotion, scenes of fields rich with crops like lettuce and strawberries that nobody has actually seen for years. Who could not be thrilled with the promises of such a man?

Eden gets to the market around nine. There's Thea, rearranging turnips into an attractive display. Her gritty little hands move swiftly like an artist's, hovering, adjusting, brushing lightly. Eden stops to eye the turnips, chooses a handful for her basket.

Thea, eyes flashing, murmurs, "Ten more arrested last night."

"I know." Eden glances quickly at the customers nearby, conscious of her own trepidation. "Better not talk about it now."

"Later," Thea concedes. "Meet me at the pond for lunch?"

Eden agrees, moves on to the fish bin, deciding on some fairly fresh looking carp. Next she finds a pile of breads of different sizes, no doubt many baked by her father. After further loading in pickles, cheese, jam, chestnuts, and a dozen eggs, her money's nearly gone and her baskets are heavy. She treats herself to an apple juice, heads home.

In her lobby a cluster of red and gold uniforms. They wear helmets that shade their faces, expressionless. In their belts a few pistols, but mostly knives. These are not the unruly thugs she's used to; alarm surges. As she heads trembling for the stairs, she looks up to see her beloved father descending with chained wrists, hustled on either side by the terrifying uniforms. He sees her but pretends not to. Eden takes the warning, stays silent, only staring with dry and frozen eyes, as the soldiers hustle him past her, out the door, into a waiting van. Only after they have all disappeared does she allow a scream. Nana is standing in the kitchen, a spoon still in her hand, like a stone statue. Eden takes her by the shoulders, eases her into a chair, offers water. Nana's sweet, haggard face can't seem to form an expression. Eden talks to her gently, massaging her back, kissing her forehead. Gradually Nana melts, folds into her granddaughter, starts to shake.

Nana moans, "They took him. They took my Jack. He never did anything wrong. He was always a good boy. He was a good man, too good I always told him. Cared too much. They took my boy."

The two women cry together, but not for long. The situation calls for action, and they are used to crises. Within another hour Nana has bustled out the door determined to follow the prison van, and Eden heads over to her rendezvous with Thea to get advice. It's close to noon now, stultifying sun sucking out the air. People in the street walk slowly, shoulders hunched, sweat dripping under straw hats. Nearing the park, Eden encounters crowds of bedraggled migrants newly arrived from the east, sleeping in doorways, clutching wailing children, begging for water, huddled in despair. It's only a matter of time, everyone knows, before Starr's troops collect them into wagons for an unknown and even more dreaded fate. Probably the camp set up for them in the old subway, rumored to be as good as a death sentence.

She's not surprised to see a distraught Nesto waiting by the pond with Thea.

"Sorry, Eden," Thea starts, "he made me bring him…"

But she stops as Eden falls into his arms, falters, "Oh Nesto, what's the matter?"

He stands back, grasping both her arms. "They have your father, and I'm next. I've got to leave, my darling. Right now. A horse is waiting for me behind the factory. Come with me?"

Eden fights tears and panic. "What about Nana, what about Tex? I can't leave them. B would punish them, don't you see?"

"Then come with me now, just for a little while. Let's make love one more time." She's shaking her head as he pulls her roughly towards him. "My darling Eden."

When Thea sees their hot embrace, she backs away. "Go ahead," she urges. "Take it." And she hurries off.

Eden and Nesto, in a tool shed on an old mattress, make the frantic, mindless love they've both been longing for, over many months. The smells around them are musty, rusty, and moldy, but their flesh on flesh blooms sweetness.

Afterwards, holding her close, Nesto urges, "Come find me. I'm headed for Cod Island, off the coast, where a bunch of buddies will keep us safe. Come to Cod Island, Eden."

"I will, Nesto, I'll try."

"Bring Nana and Tex if you want. But keep your mouth shut about where you're going. Just come."

In the end, she's urging him to flee, pushing him away, even turning her back on him, overwhelmed with foreboding. When she dares to turn around to look at him again, he's gone.

Eden sits alone at the table, her hasty supper mostly untouched. Neither Nana nor Tex has yet shown up, and it's already eight o'clock.

Tex of course could be playing one of his leave-me-alone cards, but Nana's absence is worrisome. Oh, could they have taken her too? An image of the bent little body being pushed around by hefty guards, her proud white hair in disarray, shakes Eden to the core. She determines to appeal to Mr. B, even though this very afternoon she promised Nesto not to. She forces down bites of potato and turnips, tasting nothing but needing strength. Outside the window it's dark now, a few lamps flickering here and there. She hurriedly dons a silky blouse B likes. She knows without acknowledging it what she's willing to do.

Mr. B's guards ask her no questions, and she slips into his inner rooms where Lydia is combing her hair, wearing a short nightgown.

"Go on in," she says laconically. "But I don't think you'll interest him tonight."

Eden meets this reference to Lydia's powers of satiety with a sweet grin. Mr. B is already dressed, and has summoned two of his advisors. The three of them are chatting over glasses of port. One of them pours her a glass.

"Well if it isn't my little Eden," gloats Mr. B "Sit down, my dear. But I don't have long. Big stuff is happening. General Starr will be making an announcement soon. You will love it. I told you he's a real leader."

Eden sits carefully, sinuously, just shyly enough. The men all watch her with the proper predatory admiration. She licks her lips seductively, though her throat is dry. Playing sex queen while hollow with fear for her father makes her queasy.

"I've come to ask about Jack," she says simply.

"Ah yes, your dear old dad," Mr. B grins. "And?"

"This Jack," puts in one of the men with a wave of his glass in a hairy hand, "he one of these creeps trying to organize?"

"He's not well," tries Eden. "Sometimes he gets carried away."

"Carried away, that's right," chuckles Mr. B, and the men all laugh together. "I take it he's got himself in trouble?"

"Arrested this afternoon. I saw it."

"Come now, little Eden. Drink your port, it'll do you good. Listen, my dear child, this can't be helped. I'm sure the general has only removed him from danger, wants to explain things to him. For his own good. Don't worry your pretty little head about it."

Eden tries to smile at him, but knows she looks sick. "Please. Please help."

"Tell you what," says Mr. B, getting up and coming over to pat her head. "I know it's only Monday, but why don't you come on into bed, make old B happy the way you know how." He squeezes her breast. "Don't take off the blouse."

January. Eden has not yet been allowed to visit her father, or even know for sure where he is. She's seen Nana once, held in a ramshackle house with a dozen other harmless old ladies, guilty of crimes nobody can readily identify. They are not exactly mistreated, but there's no heat, and the food is runny cornmeal. Nana looks terrible, her lovely hair matted, her sweet face pasty and ravaged. She tells Eden she will die soon, and Eden believes it. Eden has to summon all her defenses to keep from sobbing. But she has promised her grandmother to rescue Jack, no matter what it takes. Only she knows she has already tried everything.

In the barely two months since Jack was taken, General Starr has established an iron grip on Worcester. There are no more migrants to be seen. Nor any beggars or sick people at all. Gang warfare is a distant memory. The streets are clean, immaculate, with teams of folks sweeping and scrubbing them diligently. Parades are frequent—mostly festive, with colorful garments, trumpets and drums, although always accompanied by rows of armed troops. The glorious red and gold Starr flags with their soaring black hawk wave everywhere, drape giant-sized from windows. The radio keeps up a continuous roar of ecstatic crowds amid breathtaking shouts from the General, whose high but resonant voice never seems to tire of its own magnificence.

One foggy evening Eden and Thea are at Eden's kitchen table waiting for a couple of pigeons to finish roasting. The little stove chugs bravely with its sparse ration of twigs and charcoal. The room is cozy with warmth and the roasting smell, gamey but crisp. A bowl of steamed and buttered carrots awaits. Thea has been talking ever since she arrived about the food that Starr requisitions from her family's market stand.

"They said they'll pay for it, but they never do. We just have to give it to them. We're feeding the whole damn army, it seems. My sister's going nuts. I'm afraid she'll say something that'll get us in trouble."

Eden sips wine, blurts, "Thea."

The heavy tone startles her friend. "What is it?"

"I might be in the worst trouble of all." She waits before she goes on, as if silence could contradict her conviction. "I'm late. My period was due two weeks ago."

Thea takes a sharp breath. "But you're always so regular." Pause, while her eyes widen. "It can't be B's. He's never had a single kid in all this time."

"Remember the day Nesto went away? If I am pregnant, this is Nesto's."

Voluble Thea speechless, clutches Eden's arm.

Eden shivers. "If Mr. B finds out…"

"Wait, wait," breathes Thea, thinking fast. "He doesn't need to know yet, not for a while. We can make a plan."

"Abortion? Girls die from that butchery these days. Besides…"

"You want to keep it? That's not wise, Eden. Mr. B will have a fit. You just can't do that. I won't let you."

Eden sits gazing at her dear friend, the only person left in the world it seems who cares about her. "Help me?"

"How? What can I possibly do?"

"I think I need to leave town."

Before Thea can finish gasping protest, a key in the door startles them, Tex's voice reassuring. And there he is in the doorway, tall and strong and smiling broadly, so full of his youth he's a breath of fresh air. Eden jumps up to hug him. He sits down, in his old accustomed place.

"Any food left?" he says grinning, knowing he's playing his old teenage role for them. "I could even eat a carrot."

Eden and Thea laugh with him. Eden teases, "You look as if you're getting plenty of food wherever you've been."

"Well, yeah, what I want to tell you. I'm not at the bakery any more, they shut it down. Dad really made a mess of things challenging the general like that. But look, guess what I'm doing now."

Eden suddenly doesn't want to know. Hopefully at least he hasn't a clue that she's been serving Mr. B for the sake of his safety.

Thea urges, "Tell us, Tex. Is it exciting?"

"Sure is. I'm a recruit."

"Meaning?" says Eden sourly, anxiously.

"You know, a recruit for the army. I've been accepted into General Starr's Magnificent Force."

Thea replies weakly, "Is that wise?"

Eden's shoulders collapse. "Tex. They kill people."

"Kill or be killed," retorts Tex. "Besides, I'm hoping it'll help Dad, though he sure doesn't deserve it, after all the trouble he made. He really tried to put a dent in the general's grand plans, they explained that to me. But look, if I'm on the inside…"

"Shut up," says Eden, but helplessly, with ominous sorrow.

"Oh, shut up yourself, Sis, you just don't want me to grow up."

Thea puts in, "Tex, listen to us. That man is dangerous."

"What a bunch of wimps," he scoffs. "Wait 'til you see what I can do for you, too. You'll eat better, that's for sure. You know, they actually gave us bacon this morning. Imagine that!"

The two young women gaze at him in bewildered dread.

On Saturday morning there's a festive parade, followed by public executions. Bullets are too precious to waste, so some thirty prisoners, hands tied behind their backs, are seated tightly along a freshly dug trench, and knocked one by one over the edge. Then the dirt is shoveled quickly back in. No blood, no corpses, just a huge mound of drought-pale earth. The band plays a triumphant tune, heavy on the trumpets. Thea recounts all this to Eden on their way from the marketplace to the park at lunchtime.

Eden asks, "My father? Your sister?"

"No. I didn't see them. I looked."

"Could you see the faces?"

"Not well. But then I was throwing up."

Eden puts her arm around Thea's thin, shaking shoulders. Young men in brisk red and gold uniforms pass them, laughing, full of energy and confidence. Some make suggestive comments, elbowing each other. It seems the killing has invigorated them. The women sit on their usual bench overlooking the fish pond, unwrap their little cheese sandwiches. Sun breaks through the mottled winter sky.

"I wish I could cry," says Thea, "but I just feel numb."

"So now are you coming with me?"

"Yeah. They took my sister. Maybe I'm next. But have you got the horse?"

"Not yet. I'm worried. I'm due to show up at Mr. B's in four days. I faked a period last Wednesday. I don't know if I can go through with it. Oh, sure I can. I just don't need to any more, now that Tex has gone and signed up with the general."

"You kind of have to. You can't get B upset now, especially now. We have the wagon, just not the horse."

"What if we can't get one soon?"

"Bikes? Or I think I know where I can get an old pedicab. We don't have a lot of stuff. We could make do."

"Could we possibly leave next week?"

"Possibly. Two weeks more likely. Are you packed?"

"Pretty much."

"I'll find out about the pedicab. I'll get it over to the east side, so we can leave by the route we planned."

The pond sparkles in sunlight. On the other side, workers are harvesting the last of the squashes and cabbages. In the middle, a boat is squirming with newly caught fish. Eden finds her hands on her belly, a protective gesture she will often repeat in fears to come.

Tex shows up again the morning of February 8. Eden is finishing sewing a batch of aprons ordered by market folks. Her right foot is tired from pumping the machine, fingers stiff from pressing down the material along the needle. Her jobs all seem so tedious now, with escape in sight. She just needs to follow up one more lead she wormed out of B, vague as it is, vague as they all have been. She's begun to realize he really doesn't intend to tell her anything of value. Out the window she tracks mottled gray clouds streaming across a blank sky. In the street below, the usual market bustle, wagons and bicycles, many soldiers—more and more every day. Her breakfast has been frugal, so she's contemplating having another slice of bread with her tea. No butter, though. The price of butter has soared because the goats don't get enough water these days. Maybe some gooseberry jam?

Tex bursts in, strutting rather than bounding this time, resplendent in his red and gold uniform, shiny black boots, and a shiny gold helmet that he removes and places lovingly on the table like an icon.

"Well, Sis," he says, still standing. "You're looking good."

"Sit down," she says. "Want some tea?"

"No tea. They give us good coffee." He paces a little. "I have news."

Eden starts to worry. He hasn't smiled once. She gets up from the sewing machine and takes her cup over to sit at the table. "Go ahead."

"Bad news. Nana's dead."

Eden's tears start at once, burning and blinding her eyes. "I knew it."

"Pneumonia. Thursday, but they just told me. Dear old Nana." Tex betrays a hint of sorrow, pulls himself up tall, then succumbs, sits down. "She was always good to us, especially after Mom died. Remember?"

Eden nods, blowing her nose. "Can we bury her?"

"Err, no. I asked."

"But why? She's no trouble to them anymore."

"Against regulations."

"What the hell is that supposed to mean?"

But her fury is lost on him. He repeats mechanically, "Against regulations."

Eden stares out at the ugly sky, heart swelling.

In the pained silence she whispers, "Any news about Dad?"

"Oh yeah. He's on his way to the big project in the Cleveland Settlements. Rehabilitation."

"God no. That's a slave labor project and you know it. Rehabilitation my foot."

"Now, Sis." Tex puts on his patronizing face. "You just don't understand. Dad needs to learn how to be a good citizen. You know how he used to act. Like a god dam rebel nutcase. It'll be good for him."

"He's fifty years old. That backbreaking work will kill him."

Tex stands up, takes a military stance. "Now, Sis…"

Eden jumps to her feet yelling, "Don't give me that, you idiot. You are so brainwashed. Get out of here. I never want to see you again. Go kiss the feet of your damn lizard Starr."

Tex gazes at her in horror. She has not only repudiated him, her precious little brother, she has also insulted his hero to the point of heresy.

"You can't…" he breathes, "I won't…I'll have to report you!"

"Get out."

Tex grabs his helmet, turns on his heel, and slams out the door.

On the following Monday, very early in the morning when folks are just beginning to head for jobs, Eden is trotting across town with a heavy backpack. At one point she passes soldiers hustling a group into a wagon, women and children, all crying. She doesn't look at them, keeps her head down, averted. She can't afford any feelings of pity right now. Or fear. All her energy and concentration is geared toward escape. She tries to walk casually, but her steps keep quickening.

The day has dawned grey and windy. Eden catches sight of the old overgrown factory where Thea should be waiting. She starts to run, and in that instant several figures around her are running, too. She'll be captured, they'll find the telltale supplies in her backpack, she'll be hauled in front of officials…but almost in the same instant, she sees a furry heap by the side of the road, decides on a wild ruse, heads for the animal.

She kneels, scoops up the injured dog, caressing it, turns to walk in the opposite direction, towards home, murmuring into the fur, "You angel, you angel." And loudly, "Now you naughty dog, where have you been? I've been looking all over."

Vaguely detected figures fade back, stay behind her for a time, hopefully confused. Eden keeps on plodding homeward, aghast at her near miss, and at the time she's wasting while Thea waits, no doubt anxiously. Precious time they need. The dog's a dead weight, something wrong with its leg, but passive, grateful for attention. Finally she decides she can stop, sits on a bench, all the while kissing the very smelly, dirty fur as if it were a long-lost treasure. Her pursuers are nowhere in sight. Hopefully, they have given up the chase as a false alarm. How long should she delay resuming her way toward Thea? She chooses a different route that will take her in a roundabout way back toward the factory. It turns out to take another whole half hour. The dog is snuggling into her, and she can't bear to abandon him, at least not yet, he's been such a savior to her.

By the time she spots Thea and hurries to her, a watery sun has emerged in the sky. Thea, distraught at how late it is, only cries, "Come on, let's go." Eden jumps into the pedicab and Thea quickly guides the bicycle onto the side road they plan to follow. The dog falls asleep on a bag of belongings, oblivious to his heroism but not his good luck.

3

The two young women have made a home for themselves and the baby near a small encampment on Pinnacle Mountain. Having endured near-misses with Mr. B's pursuers, then floods and mudslides, they feel lucky to have made it up here where they can oversee the nightmare scenario they so narrowly escaped. Rivers of mud took a chunk of the mountain along with anything else, trees and houses included. Baby Mira was born in the middle of a rainstorm just as the flooding began. They had to climb all night, a sea of mud at their heels, only shortly after her birth. Now just a year old, she's a cheerful, rosy child who never guesses that she's on the run in a world gone mad. Eden and Thea keep her healthy supplementing Eden's milk with soy cereal and vegetables they have planted themselves. But their bounty would not have stretched far without Thea's fortitude in recruiting young soldiers to bed. They give her supplies when they can't manage money. So the little family even has some goodies now and then, like wine and pastries.

The structure they call home is an old yurt—one cone-shaped room with just a hole at the top for stovepipe and skylight. It was dilapidated when they discovered it, half hidden by brush. But with the help of some of Thea's clients, they've made it quite cozy by now. Eden is delighted with her child, but frets more and more at their inability to travel further. Her heart is still set on somehow reaching Cod Island and Nesto.

One September morning Eden and Thea are sitting at the little table in front of their home, baby Mira ensconced in a makeshift highchair, absorbed in spreading applesauce on her hair, cooing with satisfaction. Not far away, the tents of their neighbors are busy with cooking and kids as usual. The early sun is mercifully mild, with only a hint of the heat to come later in the day. Months now without rain presage another drought, but rain cisterns are still full enough to forestall panic. The camp also has a generous supply of apple trees, goats, and chickens; every tent has some kind of little home garden. Access to this refuge is still only by horseback, as the washed out road remains otherwise impassable. That means a minimum of interference by authorities; the guards, ubiquitous elsewhere, only bother to patrol up here on Pinnacle Mountain now and then.

Thea holds out her buttered toast in a gesture, sighing, "I'd better get over to the Granby's tent or their cheese will be gone soon, it's so popular." She's wearing outsized overalls that make her slim form appear even slimmer. Her dark curls are contained by a red bandana. "What shall I take them? We have plenty of tomatoes."

Eden pauses to speculate. "One or two should be enough for a hunk of cheese. Take green ones, don't you think?"

"Oh, yeah, they'll last longer too." Thea drains her mug and stands up stretching. "I'll be right back."

"Or maybe you'll wander over to the cookie tent," Eden calls after her, laughing.

So it happens that she's sitting alone with Mira when the mysterious woman appears. She materializes without introduction, sits down in Thea's chair chuckling happily.

"And how are you today, my lovelies?" she wheezes.

Eden is staring with surprise but doesn't want to be rude. It's the mode in Pinnacle camp to be friendly with everyone. "We're fine. Who are you?"

"I'm Lilac Lewis. Your dedicated traveling nurse. General Starr the Magnificent sends us round to look after the health of all his people."

The woman looks as little like a lilac as possible. She's overweight yet somehow muscular, with bleached blond hair that could use a wash, wearing drab, wrinkled clothes. She pulls out a stethoscope, dangles it as she chats.

"Many folks on the move these days, you know. Don't have regular healers. We have to keep track of the wanderers, watch out for diseases, you know."

"That's very kind of you."

Eden wipes food from her daughter's hair and face, gives her a sprinkling of nuts to pick at. Mira rewards them with angelic smiles and symphonic sounds like, "Ma-ma Wa-woo ma-foo."

"How adorable!!" shouts Lilac Lewis.

Such enthusiasm seems out of place. Unease begins to creep around the edges of Eden's complacency. After all, she has never seen this person before. Why would a nurse, if she is a nurse, single them out? Wouldn't camp gossip have announced her presence?

She says primly, "We're quite healthy. You don't need to spend time on us."

Lilac Lewis responds to her stiff tone with a peremptory, "Let's see," and heaves herself up to prod Mira with the stethoscope, all the while grinning joyfully into the baby's face. Eden does not like this handling of her child, but Mira's having a wonderful time, alternately chewing on a nut and shrieking with glee. This show goes on and on until Eden can no longer bear it. She grabs Mira up into her arms, and glares at Lilac with outright animosity.

"Oh my," says Lilac Lewis without any note of apology. "Aren't we defensive!"

Mira whimpers at the sudden move but snuggles close. Eden draws strength from her warmth.

"Shall I listen to *your* chest?" the woman incredibly asks.

"Please leave us alone," Eden responds.

"Just doing my job," Lilac Lewis retorts, packs up her stethoscope, stands, fat hands on hips. "You do have a healthy baby there. Congratulations. When was she born, about a year ago I'm guessing." When Eden is silent, she adds, "Well, I'll be off to see to the other children, hoping for a little more gratitude."

During this farewell announcement, their now very healthy dog comes sauntering around the corner, having been to visit his canine friends in the camp. He stops short at the sight of the unknown woman, growls suggestively. Eden says, "Now, Angel," in a tone that conveys clearly to him that she doesn't mean it. So he growls again.

Lilac Lewis loses a bit of her bravado. "Nice doggie," she tries.

Angel is having none of it now that he has Eden's permission, and he begins a cascade of serious barks, bared teeth and all. The swift exit of Lilac Lewis is quite gratifying. Eden praises Angel, gives him a treat. He settles in for a nap at her feet. Mira has started nuzzling her breast, so she opens her blouse and feeds her child, feeling the pull deep in her core, watching the busy rosy mouth, the tiny fingers kneading her flesh, peaceful.

That evening, Thea's having dinner with a client at the barracks, so Eden shares her supper with a woman from a neighboring tent and her nine year-old son. The boy is full of news about war with Canada. "The general says if we don't fight them, they'll invade," he explains importantly, "so we're going to attack any day now."

The boy's mother smiles indulgently and admonishes, "Now don't go on about that. It's only a rumor."

"No it isn't, Ma. A soldier told me."

Along with onion and mushroom omelet and corn bread, they're having fresh peas from the garden. Mira loves picking up the peas one by one to feed herself, but then she starts throwing them at the boy, who roars with glee dodging them. The two mothers intervene, close to laughter themselves, and war is forgotten for the moment.

Eden is just drifting off to sleep when Thea and her client tiptoe in. Thea's bed is on the other side of the yurt, and the men usually keep pretty quiet when told there's a baby nearby, but this one tonight is a groaner. Along with the usual rustling sheets and heavy breathing, he lets out a bunch of deep-throated cries so loud Eden fears Mira will waken. Not for the first time, she wonders how long it will be before Mira starts to ask questions about their night visitors. Following this train of thought is the inevitable dream of planning further travels, with beloved Nesto at the end, holding out his arms to them.

October 6 dawns a gorgeous day, the air finally suggesting an end to summer's burn, bright sun without oppression, fresh air without suffocation. Mira wakes with angelic smiles, takes the breast, then spoonfuls of cereal, then feeds herself grapes, plucking them up delicately with her tiny fingers. After breakfast, Eden busies herself mending some clothes, chops onions and potatoes for a stew. She sweeps at the little bare patch that's their front yard, gazing down the mountain at the rubble below now sprouting young trees and brush. New life always, she thinks happily. She takes Mira with her over to the vegetable garden, where she weeds while the child practices walking on the mossy grass, falling down and getting up over and over, with gusto.

When it's time for Mira's morning nap, Thea is still asleep, so Eden leaves them both slumbering and heads for the market tents. Angel knows the routine, leads the way, softly barking greetings. Everyone she encounters beams with relief at the weather. "Beautiful day!" echoes around her. She's not away long. They only need some bones for flavoring, some bread, eggs and butter. When she returns to the yurt, Thea is still asleep. But Mira's little crib is empty. Mira is gone.

So beautiful October 6 becomes a day of infamy, Thea waking in horror to Eden's screams. They pack everything up that they can fit on a horse's back. Without discussing it, they know they'll rush to follow the trail. They know that every moment in time from now on will be spent finding the child.

The horse picks its way delicately down the steep and narrow path. Eden is in the saddle atop all their belongings, Thea leading the horse, as the sun breaks through heavy morning mist, Angel trotting ahead jaunty with adventure. Eden knows she's exhausted but her eyes are wide open alert, with no hint of sleepiness. Her broken heart seems to fill her whole body with shards of agony. It's obvious enough that the witch named Lilac has taken her child.

Thea stumbles and Eden calls out, "I can take the reins now. You get some rest."

But Thea retorts over her shoulder, "It's not your turn yet. Take it easy."

They acquired Cora the horse with ease in exchange for their yurt. They figure they're only hours behind Lilac Lewis and her precious cargo on the way to Worcester—that is, until Lilac is able to commandeer a machine, which will not be difficult once on level ground. Mr. B is certainly not sparing any expense in kidnapping what he must believe to be his only blood heir.

But what they feared happens: at the bottom of the mountain there's a guard's shack, a barrier across the road, and two guards in full uniform standing on either side. Thea pulls up, ready to offer her charms to get passage, but in another moment she cries, "Stu!" To Eden's relief it's Thea's favorite client, a lanky, diffident youngster who has even been privileged sometimes to stay for breakfast.

Stu greats them heartily. "I knew you'd be along this morning. I even bet Jed here that you would."

The other guard laughs ruefully. He seems to already be resigned to what will happen. Stu and Thea disappear into the shack, while Jed helps Eden dismount and gives both Angel and Cora some water. Thankfully, he doesn't seem to want anything in return, lets her sit down under a tree, brings her a cup of coffee. Her breasts full of milk are starting to hurt, so as soon as she's alone, she presses much of it out into a bowl and feeds it to Angel, who happily laps it up. What will Mira be fed for breakfast? Won't she be crying desperately for her mama? Eden's tears stream unnoticed and untouched down her face. At last she does close her eyes, sleeps, wakens to Thea's gentle touch.

"Rise and shine, my dear," Thea softly says. "Stu's getting us another horse."

Sure enough, around the corner of the shack comes beaming Stu, leading a horse that has seen better days. "This is Obediah," he announces. "He's old but he's strong."

So they take some of Cora's load for the new horse, and Thea climbs aboard. Eden mounts Cora again, and they're off at a trot, with many cries of thanks to the two young guards, as the sun climbs the sky. But now they've had to change their travel plans completely.

Stu has told Thea what all the guards know—Lilac Lewis works for General Starr and is taking the baby to his major headquarters in Maine. It seems the general is doing this as a reward for Mr. B's loyalty: the child will be better protected from its mother somewhere unknown and impenetrable. Mr. B no doubt is also highly gratified believing that Eden will come running after Mira back to Worcester, into his arms.

4

Busy at her sewing machine, Eden now and then glances out the window. The valley below is intersected by a long low building surrounded with a dozen tents, the barracks for the few troops that are kept up here at the general's Castle. A vague autumn dusk fogs the farthest reaches of the valley. Beneath her fingers slides the slippery, silky fabric of the Queen Mother's new morning robe.

Eden tries to stop riveting her eyes on the tower-like structure that rises higher on the crest behind the Castle. She has learned that this is where Mira is kept, with dozens of other children. Far from being raised like a princess, as Eden had always hoped, Mira is one among many being trained as perfect citizens, or Perkits. More children arrive weekly. The resulting army of Perkits, as teens and adults, will form the base for a thousand years of Starr-inspired reign. Eden has learned all this from her assistant and guide, Midget, who was assigned to her from the first day. Thea's assigned to the kitchen, on the other side of the Castle from Eden's workplace. The two friends have not been able to talk since they arrived, only glimpsed each other at Assembly or other major gatherings.

Eden is not a prisoner. But she's simply not allowed to go anywhere without showing her pass. She spends her days at the sewing machine or bent over embroidery. In the months since she came she has not seen Mira once.

Now here comes Midget, her arms full of silky garments, the usual haul from far flung raids. Midget is not a midget, but certainly very short with little hands and feet that belie her twenty years. She recalls that as a child she never had enough to eat. She's very grateful to the general and his mother for taking her in. Her sad little face lights up whenever she gets the chance to praise them.

"Constellation Castle," Midget likes to croon, "is home of the best."

Now she announces, "Berry, you'll be thrilled to know that the queen is coming for her fitting in a few minutes." Eden no longer starts at the use of her fake name.

The small woman busies herself spreading out the new cloths on the long tables arranged behind the five other sewing machines. Only two of the other seamstresses are at work right now, the rest attending early supper at the first shift. Midget wears her standard red overalls with simple short-sleeved white blouse. Her pale hair is cropped close.

"But it's not ready," Eden objects. Then she sighs as Midget doesn't bother to answer. They both know that whether Eden is ready or not is irrelevant.

Eden gets up from her machine for a stretch, wanders to the window. She's wearing a sleeveless long vanilla-white dress she made herself, very simple and comfortable with embroidery along one seam. The building is air-conditioned against burning heat outside, but the air inside is stuffy.

The coronation will take place November tenth. General Starr is due to arrive soon. He's been busy attacking Canada and subduing small revolts. His homecoming is the subject of much talk and eager preparation. Eden allows herself to gaze up for a few moments at the tower where her child lives. For just fleeting moments she once again tries to picture Mira as she must look now, age two. How well is she walking? Running? Talking? How many teeth? How have they cut her lovely dark hair, is it still curly? Does she have fun, does anyone hug her, does she miss her mommy, does she cry for her?

In struts Dora, the general's mother, who will be crowned Queen Mother at the same time her son becomes Lord Emperor. She's medium height but large with soft fat. Her blonde hair is stiff with repeated dying, decorated with paper flowers. When Eden displays the new dress, Dora squeals with approval. She pinches Eden's arm affectionately.

"Well done, my girl, well done. You've really got the idea. I adore the woven vines along this side, can you add some little cherries in it, cheer it up some more? Oh, oh, I shall truly look magnificent! I shall, I shall!" She claps her pudgy hands.

Midget helps her arrange the new garment over her ample shape. She sways and primps in front of the mirror while Eden makes some adjustments.

"Now I want you to know," Dora announces, "that rehearsals for my birthday celebration will start soon. We're to have singing and music and dance, of course. And as a special treat, some of the Perkits will perform. They are to represent sheep. So, my dear Berry, we will need from you a few dozen little sheep's hooves for the children to wear. Can you think of anything else for their costumes?"

As Dora sways with admiration at her reflection, Eden tries to continue breathing. Her hands are trembling so she can't hold the cloth. She pretends to cough, dipping her head to hide her expression. The very thought, the very possibility, that she could see Mira soon, grasps her by the throat. She's sick at heart having to cater to these deluded and dangerous people, her hopes of escaping with Mira the only source of strength in an aching, slowly eroding patience.

Outside, grey dusk deepens over the browned valley and the Perkits' tower, where a few lights begin to flicker in the narrow windows.

Lieutenant Ross Martin is a charming, strong-shouldered man with a lush black moustache. He first appeared in the sewing room a month or so ago escorting bubbly Libby, a fellow seamstress who finds much favor among all the soldiers, dismissing her success with scornful giggles. "I bed them, then send them packing after I get some perks out of it," she crows. The lieutenant lost no time in showing his appreciation for Eden. But attractive as he is, he made no progress. Eden was absorbed adjusting with difficulty to her situation, no desire for dalliances.

Libby assured her that she wouldn't mind sharing, and reminded her that the general and his mother encourage sexual freedom in the Castle. "You need to get yourself a man soon," she warns Eden. "They want you to play the game. It excites them, I'm sorry to say. But we do have fun around here!"

From Libby she has learned that General Starr has no wife or mistress, but keeps a sheep named Chrysanthemum close by whenever he's here. He treats this sheep with great affection. She's even to be crowned Princess at his own coronation. The Castle provides love-rooms on the top floor where any couple or group can go for sex. There's no accommodation for couples to live together.

Over the ensuing weeks, Ross Martin has kept up his attentions, never pressing too hard, bringing occasional treats like cakes or flowers, always polite and entertaining. Eden has begun to enjoy his visits. Libby passes on her favors to a buoyant young captain. Ross does not give up. Eden finally confesses to herself that she longs for comforting arms and physical pleasure, Mr. B and Nesto fading into memory. Besides, other soldiers and staff have begun to court her, some way too assiduously, so she fears she'll have to choose just to get some peace. Her reluctance melts one evening while walking with Ross on the Esplanade.

They stop at a stone bench, sit looking out over the broad park with its pebbled paths and containers of flowers. Beyond, more mountains in the distance stand out sharply against the brightly setting sun

"My dear Berry," he says affectionately, taking her hand, "I enjoy your company so much. Tell me you're at least not indifferent."

Eden smiles up at him, as Berry the naïve seamstress. "You know I'm not. You also know I'm new here, I don't understand everything that goes on. It's a bit strange."

"The whole world is strange these days. I don't know what to make of it myself."

She remarks gaily, "Lots of mysteries are kind of fun, though, don't you think?"

Other couples and groups pass by them now and then, greeting them both. Their courtship is common knowledge, accepted and welcomed. He's sitting very close. The light is fading into a soft dimness. She returns the pressure of his hand, puts up her face to be kissed.

September comes to a close with little change in the vicious heat. Every once in a while a storm of unexpected contortions whips up winds so fanatical that using the cable cars is impossible. Word comes of victories at the Canadian border, and of skirmishes everywhere resulting in Starr's glories. Life in the Castle remains routine and predictable, with the Queen Mother presiding over rituals honoring the general's valiant destiny, amid awed chants of gratitude and obedience. At one assembly, when Eden catches sight of Thea, she's able to weave her way to her side. They exchange brief reassurances, Thea reporting that Angel has found refuge with one of the kitchen boys who adores him.

Thea dashes off as trumpets announce the performance of "Love's Lambs" for the Mother's birthday celebration. Onstage toddle tiny tots sporting Eden's sheep's hooves, and sure enough, there's Mira. Eden's heart contracts, she fights to breathe. Mira's hair is longer, thicker, worn in two braids with bows; she's walking so well, holding her hands up and drooping properly in imitation of an animal; she smiles a little nervously, with a full set of teeth! Adorning her sheep's paws are the little white mittens her own mother crafted.

Midget says something. Eden feels so faint, her head falls against her.

Midget, startled, cries, "What?"

Eden tries to say, "I'm fine," but only a moan results.

Meanwhile, the music has risen to a joyful pitch, the little lambs turning in circles and skipping. A director shouts reminders, but the kids are clearly already well rehearsed. Eden clenches her teeth and sits up straight.

That evening after dinner, lying in bed beside Lieutenant Martin, cooling from their exertions, stroking his shoulder absently, Eden steels her courage for the morning. He starts to snore gently, arms still locked around her. It will have to be fast, she decides. She has reluctantly realized that the biggest obstacle is Mira herself. What will she make of the mother who suddenly reappears?

The opportunity comes quickly, too quickly to make a solid plan. The next evening after supper, when she and Ross are enjoying their evening stroll on the Esplanade, Midget comes running up breathless.

"Berry! Guess what? Hello, Lieutenant, good evening to you. Berry, listen, you just got summoned to the rehearsal hall. They want you to help rehearse the children for the Nutcracker."

Without a word, Eden gives Ross a brief cheek kiss, grabs Midget's hand, and they rush off. Just as they arrive, a side door opens and in runs a gaggle of little girls. One of them is Mira.

The children are directed to line up in front of them. Their caretaker is a harried woman with a wheeze. "Over here, over here," she screeches, without clearly indicating where. Mira looks a bit disdainful, stands in one place holding hands with another little girl. Mira's braids are woven with red ribbons. Her dress and tights are rosy pink. Eden stares and stares at her. This child, her child, now three years old, is a dream to haunt her—not real, surely. But suddenly, Mira is staring back at her. With an expression far from placid, her little face is working hard to figure out her emotions. Eden quickly looks away, pretends intense interest in Midget's comments. But when she glances at Mira again, the child is still trying to figure out what she's seeing. Now Eden panics. They must not be seen to recognize each other! She turns away to blabber at Midget. It's no use. Mira has broken ranks, and runs over to pummel Eden in the stomach. "Bad mommy, bad mommy!" She's yelling through sobs.

The harried caretaker makes a beeline for Mira, shouting, "No, no, no. None of that, Wendy. Get back in your place, right now, or else. Come on, Wendy." She has grasped Mira's arm, dragging her away.

Eden reaches out to stop her. Everyone has frozen in place to watch the drama. This is it, Eden thinks wildly. Their secret is out.

But as the caretaker turns away clutching a screaming Mira, she turns back to apologize. "Very sorry. Wendy does this all the time. She starts hitting strangers she accuses of being the mother who abandoned her."

Eden finds herself collapsed into a chair barely controlling her own sobs, as Mira is pushed back into place, and everyone resumes their tasks, ignoring them both.

General Starr's exalted arrival at Constellation Castle is delayed by raging wildfires to the south. Though the fires don't seem to be headed this way, the resulting smoke and ash have darkened the sky for days, making it impossible to go outdoors without a face mask. Eden has to hold some rehearsals for The Nutcracker in the Perkits' tower, so the little ones don't risk the choking air. Already, several of the asthmatic children are under special treatment to help with their breathing.

So that afternoon Midget and Eden don masks, brave the smoke-swirling air, and huddle in a cable car for the quick trip to the tower. The setting is charming, with flower beds, a see-saw, and a swing-set. A bright red door leads into a broad hallway echoing with small voices. Among colorful children's drawings are two enormous portraits, of the general and his mother. While Starr wears a severe expression, Dora's idealized face is the essence of benign maternity.

The rehearsal space is a large classroom, with tiny tables and chairs the right size for tiny people. Long windows look out over the mountain range, the Castle spread in its flag-draped glory just below, ghostly in the smoky air. Here and there along the corridors on the way sit little children on stools with large placards hung around their necks reading, "Bad." They're slumped unmoving, pale small faces contorted with sorrow. Eden stops short at sight of them, but the caretaker wheezes, "Pay no attention to the bad ones. They need to be punished."

In the classroom the furniture has been moved to one side, the children lined up waiting for them. Mira glares at Eden, but sets her chin grimly, silent. Today all the girls are wearing grey jackets with long tails attached, and furry mouse ears. Midget passes out the mouse paws Eden has altered from sheep's hooves. The girls all practice holding their hands in imitation of mice. A lone musician plays the music on an accordion. Eden dances along, demonstrating proper marching, jumping, and turning in circles, trying at every opportunity to get near Mira. She notes with joy Mira's pretense at indifference while maneuvering closer to Eden. Several times Eden is able to reach out to touch her daughter, as if to correct her; the feel of the beloved plump warm body shoots through her like lightening. It takes monumental self-control not to seize her in embrace.

After an hour of practice, in comes a line of marching little boys. The Nutcracker's troops, ready to fight the mice. While the boys are practicing marching in sync, Eden and Mira find themselves together, Eden squatting to Mira's level, eye to eye.

Eden whispers, "I love you."

"Mommy." Mira looks confused and pained. "You went away."

"No. They took you. Don't tell anyone I'm here. OK?"

Mira nods. "I'm sad."

"Don't worry. I'll fix it," Eden promises, and risks a hug.

But the wild joy loosed by this encounter with her child collapses into horror when Eden looks around to see the jolly, beaming face of Lilac Lewis. The woman in all her blowsy magnitude lurks just inside the classroom door, glittering narrowed eyes watching. The way a cat observes a mouse just before pouncing. Instantly Eden knows she has seen everything. Will she denounce them right away?

As she and Midget are bundled into the lift for the ride home, Eden steels herself for arrest. Her only hope is that Mira won't be blamed for talking to her. But nothing happens. In a nightmarish fog she takes her place at her sewing machine, hardly able to focus on work or the swirling black curtain of ash obscuring the Perkits' tower outside the window.

When Ross comes by to meet her after supper, he doesn't seem to pick up on her anxiety. Rather, he says he hopes she won't mind sitting together inside this evening because of the choking air outside. She wants to just tell him to go away, but she must make a show of normality, and besides, his kind eyes promise solace, his embrace a moment's peace. They enjoy a glass of wine sitting side by side, then head upstairs to the love rooms as usual. Down the corridor of closed doors, behind which now and then gentle conversation or a pleasured moan, to the room Ross has reserved for the evening. It has been months now since they became lovers, and they embrace briefly, then undress each other with mounting passion but also familiar caresses. Their lovemaking is sweet and mindless.

Afterwards, when they've been lying resting still entwined for only a few minutes, Ross suddenly says very quietly, "I have something to tell you."

For a terrified moment she thinks Lilac must have chosen this way to betray her. She stiffens, tries to pull away. But Ross holds her close and pulls a blanket over their heads to muffle their voices.

"Don't worry," he says in her ear. "I'm on your side." As he tries to soothe her trembling, softly stroking her shoulder, he adds, "My name is Raoul."

Stunned, only slowly realizing that he has a French name, and that must mean…he's Canadian?

She breathes in a dry voice, "What does that mean? Ross is not your name?"

"Listen, Berry, or rather Eden. Yes, I know your name. I know everything. Let me tell you the whole story. We have time now, but after tonight we'll have to move quickly."

She nods, so he relaxes his hold on her. She moves back a bit to be able to see his face, shadowed by the blanket, but dear enough to reassure.

He begins gently. "Yes, I am Canadian. A spy. There are half a dozen of us scattered here at the Castle, mostly in the military, getting information about troop movements as best we can out to our countrymen preparing for more Starr invasions. A few of our children are prisoners as Perkits, like yours."

Eden catches a brittle breath. "You know I'm here for my daughter! Will you help me?"

"My darling Eden. Of course we will help you."

"Is that why you chose me for…"

He chuckles, kisses her neck. "You're adorable, adorable. It was my idea to court you, as soon as I saw you. Believe me, our pleasure is precious, and so are you. Now listen."

"Mighty is he!"

The crowd in the Assembly Hall shouts the tribute as General Starr strides in, closely followed by dainty Chrysanthemum sporting a necklace of flowers around her curly snowy-white neck. Just behind them sails Dora, awash in floating silken scarves, her plump face glowing reddish with pride. Triumphant music of horns and drums, cheers, yells of joy. The entourage sweeps up steps splendid with red carpet. The general and his mother take their seats on thrones. The royal sheep poses prettily by her master's side. He rests one hand lovingly and possessively on her furry head.

"Mighty is he!"

Eden, seated with Midget, joins in the frenzy as best she can. Ever since Raoul's revelations, she's had to work even harder at maintaining her disguise. "I'm a humble seamstress," she repeats to herself, "so lucky to be here serving our magnificent leader. I'm loyal and obedient, I think he's wonderful, the best thing that could ever happen to the world. I'm a humble seamstress…"

Raoul has convinced her that Lilac will probably wait to expose her until after the Coronation, when she can create the appropriate drama. With the outdoor air almost cleared, rehearsals have been scheduled here in the Castle again. She and Mira have found several occasions to be close. Mira has started asking why she can't go with Eden when she leaves. This growing insistence on the child's part is becoming dangerous. But it's almost over, Raoul assures her. Their escape is planned, any time now. Eden manages to get word to Thea, saying only, you know where we're going; Thea will of course know she means Cod Island.

The Coronation proceeds with incantations and singing; the Lord Emperor, Queen Mother, and Princess Chrysanthemum all receive lovely crowns. The pompous Starrist monks, anonymous in their identical hooded cloaks, bestow sonorous blessings with many mysterious, awe-inspiring gestures.

The first performers leap and gyrate to drums. Someone declaims a poem. Older Perkits, about age five and six, chant a eulogy to the emperor, waving miniature Starr flags to the music announcing the battle between the mice and toy soldiers. There's beautiful little Mira trotting onstage proudly, performing all the proper steps, her mouse ears a bit precariously bobbing.

To the blare of trumpets, a standing ovation honors the newly crowned royals, Dora's expression ablaze with smug exaltation. The entourage raise their glasses of elixir toasting the glory to which they all have been raised. Everyone echoes praises, sips from their glasses. Then the newly crowned Emperor too lifts his specially enameled goblet. Starr however does not touch his lips to his goblet, but instead hands it to an aide to taste first. The aide's pale bony face turns swollen and scarlet; he drops across the table fighting for breath. Starr watches him sternly. Surely he knows what's happening. Surely he has been warned. While the aide writhes in front of him, he waves away those who come to his aid. In frozen silence the whole crowd watches the man suffocate to death.

Now Eden is running. Raoul has told her to head for the kitchen, correctly predicting pandemonium. Under her fancy gown she has hidden a belt with a few belongings, but she doesn't even have a shawl, let alone a coat. She dashes into and through the kitchen, shouting, "Help, help. The Emperor needs help!" Nobody pays the least attention to her. When she gets to the back entrance, she finds the basement stairs Raoul has described. She practically falls down them in her haste, and then right in front of her is a group of monks, standing in her way. She tries to push through them, but is grasped firmly by the arm. In terror, she raises her eyes to see the grim face of Raoul, holding her fast while someone throws a heavy monk's habit around her shoulders, yanking the hood over her head. She's pulled along with them down a dark passageway, on dirt-covered flooring, only one small light showing far ahead. She twists around to query Raoul, "Where is she?" He gestures to his backpack. "Here."

Below deck, in a corner of the bow, Eden crouches with Mira as the boat heaves in the storm. They have been three days on the water now, hiding the boat by day, inching along Lake Katahdin to the farthest shore. From time to time through the screaming wind she can hear shouts of the crew calling out orders, three of whom had been spies on the staff, the other three prisoners weakened by deprivation, none of them used to sailing in such weather. Mira has exhausted herself with crying, and sleeps deeply across her mother's shoulder.

The boat kicks like a colt. Its old boards creak and groan. They'd had to abandon the telltale military craft they escaped in on the first night. The spies exchanged their fancy castle garb for the rags of refugees. Eden covered her white gown with a rough sweater. The four Canadian children and Mira shed their cute outfits for torn castoffs. The sleek boat was set adrift as soon as they'd boarded this sorry excuse for a sailboat. But because of all this, they were now indistinguishable from desperate groups everywhere on the move.

Eden gazes down on the peaceful face of her child. She needs to sleep, too, but she's hypnotized by love, by the full black lashes on silky cheeks, the frame of dark curls, the perfect ear, the curve of the tiny slender fingers, the half open cherry mouth, those wondrous new teeth, the trusting soft weight of the little body. Close beside them curled in blankets lie the three other kids, two boys and a girl. It had not been possible to rescue all the Canadian children, only these who had been isolated for naughtiness. Raoul had tried—risking their plans—but had to give up at the last minute, running to catch up, his eyes streaming tears.

Here he comes now, brave Raoul, bending his tall frame under the low roof, clad in tattered overalls too small for him. His anxious expression clears into a grin as he spots Eden.

"Cozy?" he asks, crouching beside them. "Dry enough?"

He pulls some kind of coat around her shoulders, tucking Mira inside it.

"Just fine," she whispers. "Will the boat survive?"

"We're almost there. It's dawn and we've spotted a good bit of shore. Shall I bring you some tea and bread?"

"That's ok, I can wait." She lifts her head for a kiss. "Thanks for everything, everything."

"My love." He kisses her, lingering. "We are safe. Don't worry."

Eden's comforting confidence in Raoul ends abruptly two days later. The group has abandoned the rickety boat for a farm wagon carrying goats and chickens, so that, nestled among the animals, they pose as itinerant workers. The roads are mucky with ankle-deep mud from landslides, the countryside strewn with abandoned camps and blighted crops. Daring now to travel by day and pulled by two huge, muscled farm horses, they have made good progress in spite of the mud. As they start out one early morning, the rising sun blazing the promise of a warm January day, Eden notices with shock that the sunrise is on their right.

"We're traveling due north," she says carefully. "I thought we were going south."

"South," scoffs a young officer, "*Mon Dieu*, no, no. This is the way home."

Of course! Raoul is taking her to his own country, not to Cod Island as she'd assumed. Mira squirms in her tightening grip, wiggles away to join other children farther back, murmuring, "Mama, I wanna play. *J'veux jouer*." The child is already learning French, effortlessly as toddlers do. Eden had hardly noticed.

Eden's future is being re-written in front of her face; she's helpless, caught.

Later that day while they stop for a lunch rest, Eden finally gets a chance to confront Raoul. She pulls him by the hand away from the others, they sit under a canopy of pines. He's already alarmed at the expression on her face.

"What is it?"

"Where are you taking me?" Her voice hisses with angry panic.

"My dear Eden." He tries to take her hand.

She slaps his away. "Where are we going? Answer me. You said you'd…" But she recalls they never really discussed where, only that he would help them. "How can you do this?" She finishes weakly, close to shameful tears.

"Oh, my darling dear," he wails. "I'm sorry I was not honest with you. I love you so much, I want to keep you for myself. You will be safer there, too."

"Safer where? You're just kidnapping me. I want to go to Cod Island. You know that."

"That's not the place for you. I want you near me always. My wife will not know. I will give you and Mira a lovely little cottage by the river, my precious Eden."

She stares at him, a paralyzed moment in shifting afternoon shade, scent of pine and mud, shocked into silence.

He goes on, encouraged that she now listlessly lets him take her hand. "You will meet my children, my brave sons and daughters, Gilles, Florent, Aurore, Fleur, beautiful children. We will tell them you are just a friend, you will teach them English. I have it all planned. We will be so happy."

Eden gazes at this handsome face she has so often caressed and always trusted, feeling broken with betrayal. She averts her eyes from Raoul's probing gaze.

"You've got us now," she mutters, "We're your prisoners."

"Oh, *ma cherie*," he cries softly. "You break my heart." Then he grabs her hand forcibly. "Come, your child is safe. She's waiting for you."

Mira dashes to her arms, laughing so happily it almost makes Eden turn to thank him. She peers out at the flat and snow-patched countryside, small stone houses scattered in the distance. The two horses pulling the wagon are sauntering peacefully, their huge haunches rhythmic. Marching alongside the wagon on each side are half a dozen soldiers in uniform: the bright blue Canadian uniforms she'd been taught at the Castle to fear. The vast stretch of sky over the flat landscape is mottled gray, lowering.

The days are short this time of year, so travel is slow. During the following week, their little cavalcade struggles over snow-caked roads, through shabby villages where only emaciated dogs greet them, crossing streams perilously overflowing and encumbered with huge chunks of ice, small encampments of tents and rusted vans where ragged people run after them begging for food, now and then passing other military groups, exchanging salutes and gleaning news. Starr's troops have reportedly broken through Canadian defenses at the Augusta enclave border; on the other hand, they've been driven back and routed in northern Maine.

Once when they decide to stop at a sheep farm for cheese and yogurt, a wild-haired woman runs at them screaming, "*Allez vous en! On est tous malade ici. Vous allez mourir vous aussi! C'est la peste!*"

"It's the plague," someone translates, but without elaboration in the scramble to whip up the horses and flee.

That evening Raoul orders his men to keep going, as fast as possible, not stopping until the road is so dark that even with a lantern they can't see ahead. In the following days, they take only back roads that don't pass through inhabited areas. They flee other caravans. Eden has never seen Raoul so worried. He says, "I know what *la peste* can do. Believe me, you do not want to find out. Whole towns gone, filled only with the dead."

Eden sits by the window watching the children under her care romp in freshly fallen snow. Her hands are busy sewing a shirt for Gilles. His elder brother Florent is at fourteen already training in the military. Raoul's other children are twin girls aged seven. These three are supplemented by two more boys and a little girl. The kids who escaped with them from the Castle have been returned to their parents.

She's keeping an eye on the darkening clouds; word has it another blizzard is coming. But in this part of Canada, just north of Chicoutimi, snow in March is now an exception, so it could be rain instead. This spring they've already had two false thaws, so who knows. She's hoping the chard and carrots she planted can survive the wild swings in temperature.

The hut where Eden and Mira live is one of several crafted from the remnants of an old factory. The huts line the hill above the swollen Saguenay River, which rises even further every time there's a melt. Sometimes at night the roar of cascading water startles them awake.

Crude but sturdy, the hut has three rooms, the largest one serving as kitchen and living room, at one end the wide window where she now sits. She's holding up the shirt, inspecting the seams, deciding to add a pocket, when the light suddenly darkens. Her alarm barely has time to bring her to her feet before rain bursts out in torrents. She runs to open the door for the screaming children, who stomp into the room already soaking wet. As she fusses over them and they realize they are safe, their tears turn to laughter, and the whole drama becomes a game. They crowd giggling around the wood stove, shaking water at each other. Eden towels their hair, urging quiet and calm in English words she has taught them, "Watch out!", "Be careful," "Come here," and especially "Now!" But she's smiling in spite of herself at their spirited play.

The wild wind sounds like a creature in torment, shaking the hut, rattling dishes and chairs. Outside the window all they can see is a waterfall of rain thick as a curtain, blown sideways. When the children are somewhat warm and dry, Eden summons them to sit in a circle, serves them hot tea and cookies. But before they can even finish this feast, suddenly the rain turns to drizzle, the wind whines to a sigh, and silence falls outside. Almost at once, the door flies open and Raoul's wife Claire bursts in, distraught with worry. She rushes to embrace and inspect her three children, cooing French endearments.

Through the open door Eden can see the storm damage, trees down, limbs scattered, her garden washed into mud. The river below churns violently, whipping up swells and whitecaps, muddied water yellowed. The remnants of a dock that had been hanging on are now scattered, and a small boat still attached to a post also swirls away on the torrent. As she stands on the threshold overcome with helpless dismay, suddenly across the sky appears the most extensive rainbow she's ever seen. It arches over the entire scene, in brilliant colors. The children crowd around behind her, and Claire exclaims delightedly, "It's beautiful. *Que c'est beau! C'est le bon Dieu qui nous parle!*"

"A sign from God," Eden agrees, wanting desperately to believe it.

That evening, Raoul announces he's being sent into action on the Augusta border, where General Starr's troops have penetrated and begun their march north. He has come at his usual time, just as she and Mira finish their supper, the child running to meet him with a joy that always jabs Eden's heart. This man who has rescued them, who has kidnapped them, who is protecting them and treats them so kindly, who does not listen to anything she says about leaving, has her in a grip that angers and paralyzes her. He takes her in his arms with such tenderness, such convincing vows. He cradles Mira like his own, spends serious time teaching her songs and games and reading to her, brings her little presents the child always cherishes. For months now, Eden has been in this strange, blank trance, unable to resist him or even to seriously disagree with him. He seems to her more handsome than ever, in uniform or naked before her, a manly, gentle, sensitive man. And warmly passionate, adoring even.

Here he is now, handing Mira another little doll, this one dressed in traditional French Canadian garb, down to the apron, shawl, and ribboned cap. Mira of course clutches it to her heart, snuggles on his lap when he sits down with them at the table. The news that he'll be leaving soon, facing serious danger, unleashes in Eden a flurry of conflicting feelings, from relief to foreboding.

While he reads to her daughter, Eden clears the table, washes the few dishes, trims the oil lamp and stirs up the embers in the stove. In her bedroom she turns down the covers and lights the one small candle that often illuminates their lovemaking. Her hands are shaking, at the same time her body softening in anticipation of his touch. He will be gone, he will leave them alone, she can figure out some way of escaping, surely he won't keep as tight a grip on her now?

But from the other room his loving voice brings animal characters to life for her child's delight. Eden's treasured escape means upheaval and unknown dangers for her child, who has found happiness and safety right here.

Soon Raoul will put his arms around Eden, bury his face in her neck, press her close. How will it be to lose this sense of security, this binding gratitude, this refuge? How will it be to lose him? Appalled at her distress, she abruptly pulls the curtains on the little window, shutting out the dark.

All of It

Memoir

by Kitty Beer

The world is a wonderfully exciting place
when it's not breaking our hearts.

Look, I want to love this world
As if it's the last chance
I'm ever going to get
To be alive,
And know it.
—Mary Oliver

Foreword

My life so far has covered a period of time during which the world underwent historic changes. From my birth in 1936 to the present as I write, we experienced four wide wars and countless narrower ones, the invention of nuclear weapons, a worldwide pandemic, great strides in racial and women's equality, the explosion of the global economy, the advent of the computer, and irreparable environmental destruction. My life is a mishmash of mistakes, thrills, fears, bliss, and delusion, like most lives I suppose.

My parents Samuel and Roberta, smart kids from small Midwestern towns, went through a depression and a world war before I was ten. By the time I began to develop a sense of the broader world and my place in it, the 50s arrived to throw a pall of conformity and stagnation over it. This contrast in our youths was cause for both conflict and cohesion in our family life. In Ohio, my father lost his mother at age ten from a botched surgery. His father was a judge who never married again, so grandma was the nurturer. In Michigan, my mother was the first in her family to go to college; she not only worked her way through, but put her younger brother through college as well. Both my parents were middle children, the only ones in either family to flee to the far more sophisticated east coast.

After they graduated from the University of Michigan, my parents went to England, where my father had a Rhodes Scholarship at Oxford University. Our photo album from that time shows them young and clueless as tourists in Germany, posing in front of windows draped with giant Nazi flags. Some few years later, my papa went off to war there. After that upheaval, I grew up in an enclave of privilege and stability in Cambridge, Massachusetts. Papa was a professor and Mama stayed in the kitchen. Everything was in its proper place. The outside threats were communism and the atomic bomb—for us children rather distant rumblings that did not disturb our cozy family life.

1 Childhood

The year I'm born, Franklin Roosevelt is reelected in a landslide, Hitler decrees that all boys join Hitler Youth, and Eugene O'Neill wins the Nobel Prize. It's 1936. The Great Depression is in full swing.

A first memory is air-raid practice. Papa is an air-raid warden; equipped with hooded flashlight, he patrols our neighborhood looking for any signs of light. We learn to blacken our windows at first wail of the warning siren.

Another memory: Papa and I inventing a little old dwarf who lives in the hollow of a tree near us. We're living in Belmont, Massachusetts, while he studies for his doctorate at Harvard. We have wonderful times, my father and I, when I am three and thereabouts. We often sing a chant that goes, "How much do I love you? More than tongue can tell." When he was dying, some seventy years later, I sang that to him in his hospital bed.

In 1940, my best friend comes into the world, my sister Frances. Throughout most of my life, Fran has been my rock and my comfort. We've always been there for each other. There's an image of Mama just home from the hospital, sitting on the stairs inside the front door, looking wan. My grandmother, whom we call Neenah, has come to help out for a week or so. I think Neenah's pretty, and am proud to believe that I look like her.

The sporadic, snapshot memories of early childhood coalesce into firmer shape as I turn five. The war hits home and takes my father away: he volunteers for the army, enters officer training in Virginia. Mama and we two little girls move back to Michigan to live with her mother. It's a terrible jolt for Mama, used as she has become to a much wider world.

Charlotte, Michigan is a very small and quiet town. Church suppers are the main excitement. Neenah is a "Gray Lady;" she wears a trim gray uniform and does war-related things like collect or knit socks for the boys overseas. We have a "victory garden" in the back yard, growing our own vegetables as so many Americans are encouraged to do. The movies always start with news reports; I still remember the evil-looking faces of Japanese pilots as they strafe our boys. The only men in town are over forty and married, and Charlotte is "dry," an additional trial for Mama who loved her beer even then.

We have an icebox, that is, ice must be delivered to keep it cold. When we need it, Neenah puts a big sign in the window reading "ICE." Another memory of this wartime is beggars coming to the back door. Neenah gives them such leftovers as stale toast. We have food rationing, and Mama has a little stamp book of rations she carefully keeps track of. We eat fake butter—that is lard with an orange dye that we knead into it to improve its pallid color. The toaster opens out on the sides, and we love melting the "butter" on "salt-rising bread." Papa's an army captain in the anti-aircraft forces, so Mama makes three-legged artillery guns out of celery stalks and we pretend to shoot them, ta-ta-ta-ta.

Just a few years ago, right after Papa died, Fran and I came across a letter I'd written him then, in wobbly print: *"Papa, please, please come home."* Old lady that I was, I burst into wild childish tears, experiencing the loss afresh. I still remember a letter he wrote to me from France on my seventh birthday, describing the raindrops on his tent as like the *"patter of little feet."*

He does come home on leave once in those three years, conceiving my brother Billy, born in 1943. Possibly I witness the moment of creation: I walk in on my parents having sex. They're under a sheet, father on top of mother. He turns to me furious and spits out,

"Go away!!" Very traumatic for me, but I can surely sympathize with his reaction now, in adult retrospect.

⁂

The day Papa comes home from the war for good, I wear my new peppermint striped dress. I am made to go to school, but my teacher lets me wait by the window. When I see him coming, I run to throw myself into his arms. His face is smeared with Mama's red lipstick. Joy!

We move back to Belmont for a year while Papa and Mama look for a house to buy. He's teaching and finishing up his doctorate at Harvard. It's a gloomy year in my memory, gray and cold even inside the house we're renting. Alas, Papa tries to teach me arithmetic, which I have always hated, and this does nothing to revive our old camaraderie. He's become a rather distant authoritarian. Was it the war that changed him, or the fact that I am now eight years old? Both, I guess. He never talks about the war. One terrible thing he does tell me: in the concentration camps Nazis told people they were getting showers, but there was cyanide in the water, killing them all. Scene: I am running downstairs in my bathrobe sobbing, "Did they really do that?" My parents are horrified by my distress, and never mention concentration camps again.

So now we move to 87 Lakeview Avenue in Cambridge, our family homestead for the next sixty-three years. At age ten I'm walking up the steps for the first time, thinking, what an ugly ramshackle old house, but vowing not to show my parents my disappointment. Even that young, I wished to spare them worry, sensing their post-war anxiety of making a new life after years of stress and instability.

In fact, the house is a beautiful Victorian, built in 1873, wood painted gray with green shutters and slate roof. We all come to love it very much. Our return visits after growing up are always like coming home. The kids we three had—two each—all love it too. There's a big back yard, with many tall elms all around, and the whole street is graced with mostly nineteenth-century houses. We Beers furnish it antique style, with beds and chairs and tables from Papa's father's house in Ohio. And the books! In the library, tall bookcases boast complete Dickens, Balzac, Turgenev, Conrad, beautiful old tomes delightful to hold and behold.

You walk up the front steps to the porch, enter a vestibule, then a broad hallway. On the right is the sitting room, on the left the library. The former for all family activities, the latter for guests and other serious events. All around is the lovely dark brown varnished wood, from baseboards to ceiling trim. The library is graced by my grandfather's venerable furniture, including a beautiful old rug and maroon velvet drapes. In the hall, straight in front of you climb the stairs to the second floor and five bedrooms; just past the stairs is the kitchen, high-ceilinged and grand as the rest. Mom is always here; where else would she be? Wives in the 50s are properly located in the kitchen. Later on, Mom does get part-time jobs now and then, for example as a medical assistant. (She was pre-med in college.) She's also very active in the NAACP (National Association for the

Advancement of Colored People), when black people are still called Negroes. But Mom's activities never get much respect in our house. I never question this.

We have a wonderful big back yard, where Mom gathers grapes from a vine to make jelly. Near the back steps there's a hole in the ground containing a pail where we throw all our food garbage (separated from the trash). It gets picked up and we're told "fed to the pigs." Some fifty years later recycling comes into vogue, but with nothing quite so efficient as that! Over many years we have summer dinners out there; Pop has strung paper lanterns on the clothesline, which we light with candles.

Pop reads to me every evening after dinner, mostly Dickens, some Sir Walter Scott. *Old Curiosity Shop* to *Ivanhoe*. I'm sure he skips a lot, but I don't notice, his reading style is so enthusiastic. I love those stories still, the root of my lifelong affair with books, I'm sure. Later, when Franny and Billy are old enough to join us, he reads us Sherlock Holmes mysteries. But Mama's never in this picture. She's in the kitchen cleaning up after dinner. Many years later a therapist asks me why. She tells me that my father should have insisted we all help Mom, and include her in the reading. I am amazed that this never occurred to me before. When my own children's father reads to them, I'm always there too, listening with them, family together. So I keep realizing things about my parents, to this day. We hardly ever even helped with dishes, and she never taught us girls to cook, nor let us try, as we'd "make a mess." Why? Because the kitchen was her only domain.

She's always there, in the kitchen, cooking, ironing, darning socks. She's darning a sock when she tells me I should not masturbate because if I do, I won't be able to have children. This information has little effect on me; I don't believe her.

In winter, the big old house tends to chilly, so every morning Pop is in the basement shoveling coal into the furnace. Mom packs our lunches and we're off to Russell School, five blocks away. Now I'm in the sixth grade, age twelve. (Female teachers in public schools are not allowed to be married. Massachusetts is still very Catholic.) I have a crush on a boy who smokes and wears his shirts rolled up over his biceps, a bad boy for sure. But I doubt he ever knows of my devotion.

My first boyfriend is named Billy; we ride our bikes together. In the seventh grade I fall in love with Patrice, a beautiful doe-eyed boy from France. He apparently returns my interest, but we get no further than awkward conversation.

On Sundays we take family outings. Sometimes we go walk through the Concord woods. More often we walk over to Mount Auburn Cemetery, a beautiful, landscaped arboretum treasure. We fly home-made kites; Pop fashions flutes from willow tree branches. Many decades later, mother and father are buried there, near the Willow Pond.

In sixth grade we study geography; a huge map of South America shows products by pinning tiny packets of for example coffee or coal to it, or photos of bananas. (We don't learn anything else about South America—only what the U.S. buys there.) Around now I start my lifetime of writing—the first endeavors are imitations of Dickens' style. I also start my first diaries, writing in them every day. Pop, realizing that Russell School is not exactly first rate, acquires a French tutor for me. Monsieur Schumann is allowed to park his car in our back driveway in exchange for reading *Les Fables de La Fontaine* in French with me. Pop also crafts a time chart, stretching all along the wall, with important dates. My love of history starts here. It's breathtaking to see how short a time the U.S. existed and even European kings, in comparison to cavemen or pyramids. I love these sessions with him; I guess he has given up on arithmetic! By this time I'm very serious about ballet, having started at nine, and this passion doesn't end until I'm in my forties, reluctantly, with a stress fracture. I take classes several times a week, riding the subway into Boston, by myself. Mom makes it fun to eat healthy food. I proudly report lunches of lettuce and tomato sandwiches.

The summer of '49, Franny and I spend a month at a farm in northeastern Massachusetts. It's a brilliant move for the privileged kids of Harvard academics, and I am forever grateful to my mother for choosing it. Overlooking the Merrimac River, it's a real working farm with cows (which I learn to milk by hand), pastures, crops, and a huge horse named Dolly. Fran and I learn to lure Dolly with carrots, and jump on her back for a ride. There's a B&B of sorts, the guests mostly actors. We all dine at a huge table on the porch, then turn the table into a dishwashing event, with Fran and me rinsing and drying. A lovely granny reads stories to us, most memorable is *The Water Babies*.

Thirteen. What a turbulent time! I hasten to say that my home life is always stable, my family's place in our community firm and prestigious, attentive parents, fun siblings and friends. But the hormones begin to rage; I am feisty and rude. Of course I'm convinced that I, Kitty Beer, will live a glorious life, such as my poor pedantic parents never imagined. I must have been insufferable. Scene: we kids are to take turns with the one radio we have on the second floor. It's brother Billy's turn but I want to keep it. I rage and scream. My parents shut me in my closet. I smash the closet door. I don't get the radio. The door stays smashed for months to my embarrassment, a wise reminder of my tantrum.

On another occasion, when I'm grounded, I secure my bedroom door with a chair and climb down the shutter under my window. I flee to the bus, go to my church, and have dinner with blind kids. (That's it, really.) Afterwards I climb back up the shutter and my parents know nothing about all this until I tell them in my thirties! With gusto, you can imagine.

Pop gets tenure in the Government Department at Harvard. My parents are ecstatic. I remember only the thrill of their joy, the living room somehow filled with angelic light.

By this time, when I'm in the eighth grade, it's clear that none of the other faculty children attend public school, so I am to transfer to Buckingham, the all-girls private school nearby. I'll have to repeat the eighth grade, having had no Latin, for one thing. Later, Franny comes to Buckingham and Billy goes to the private Roxbury Latin School, very challenging. I remember him, still a boy, laboring over homework at night at his desk. Result: all three of us go to Harvard.

Scene illustrating the town and gown divide: while still in public school, I've gone to spend the night at my friend Marilyn's home. She lives on the wrong side of Huron Avenue, down the hill where the triple-deckers house big Irish families. In the kitchen I see my first cockroach. Of course, I don't know what it is. "Oh," I cry cutely, "Look at that beetle!" All eyes turn to me, hard. Is it possible this strange child has never seen a roach?!

Sadder still, when I urge Marilyn to apply to the skating club where I spend many happy hours, she is not admitted. The reason according to my mother is that her father drives a bread truck.

At one point I have a cat named Lucifer, "Loose-fur" for short. Over the years I have several cats. One of them has a litter of kittens in a drawer of my dresser. Nobody minds the blood, neither my mother nor I. Mom is always cool about natural things, a valuable legacy for me, enjoying natural functions and wonders like scabs or decay or sex or animal lives as I do to this day. She teaches us respect and awe for whatever is naturally part of life. Another scene evokes Mom: we're in the kitchen, she looks out the window and spots Eleanor Roosevelt in the back yard of our neighbors, the Morgenthau family. Out she runs, right over to knock on their door, insisting on meeting the famous lady she admires. No nonsense, straight to the point. My model for feistiness!

The summer of 1950, when I'm about to turn 13, the family spends two months in London. On the boat over, Fran and I room with a dark-haired French woman who is the captain's mistress. I vividly remember her washing her private parts at the sink we all shared. We think nothing of it. For all we know, adults always do this kind of thing.

We rent a house in Chiswick Mall on the Thames River with a little boat parked at the bottom of the garden. That boat, the *Water Gipsy*, we are proudly told, was one of the many crafts large and small that transported retreating Allied troops from Dunkirk. We kids become good friends with an English family with kids our age. I remember one fun game of hide and seek, tucked invisible behind enormous silky drapes. Pop makes us read books about English history, rewarding us with trips to such treats as the Tower of London and changing of the guard at Buckingham Palace.

Fran and I play out stories with our "poppy dolls" in the garden. By this time we've collected about two dozen of these tiny dolls about three inches tall; we make clothes for them out of scraps, and glue thread to their heads for hair. Trudy and Timmy are our favorites. Most are made from sawdust, two later additions are plastic.

Scene: Mama takes Franny and me to a horse show in a huge auditorium. Because one of the participants is from Spain, the Spanish national anthem is played. Everyone around us rises in respect. Not my mother. She sits sturdily still, and orders us to do the same. "Keep your bottoms on the seat." Fascist dictator Franco is running Spain, and my valiant mother is expressing her outrage. I am acutely embarrassed: small me, cowering beneath all the giant adults obediently standing around us. I think that experience more than any other taught me to stand up for what I believe is right, to stick my neck out.

From London Pop takes me to Paris for my 13th birthday. The war barely over, the French can tell just from our clothes that we're American. I'm proud sharing the experience with my father. It makes me feel very grown up and special. In one restaurant, I remember choosing my fish for dinner from a tank. What must it have been like for him, only a few years after being there as liberator, to return in peace with his daughter?

Summers during my teen years we rent a big old house in Eastham on Cape Cod. Depot Pond is at our front door, we three kids in the water all the time. There's a kayak that I use often. By this time we've adopted Taffy, officially Fran's dog, beloved by all. We like to run out onto the dock with Taffy rushing after us, and stop short at the end while he jumps into the water and we stand there laughing at him. I often take him out in the kayak, where he sits proudly on the prow. He's a mix of Cocker Spaniel and Spitz, golden furred, with huge ears that stick straight up.

We three kids invent Asbisba Land, which nourishes many hours of play, especially in summer. We're Kissy, Finley, and Bissy, orphans of course, living in Sea Alley in the BiFraKi Isles. Our many adventures consist mainly of resisting attacks from evil Murnts. Asbisbas and Murnts each have their own very distinctive facial expressions, as do the several other peoples in that world. To this day, my sister and I often playfully call each other Finley and Kissy.

One summer Pop teaches us all to shoot a rifle. We practice hitting floating bottles in the pond. I become a really good shot, and later often win stuffed animals at fairs. Why did he feel the need to teach us such violence? Our security must have been uppermost in his mind, in a world he'd probably not yet accepted as truly safe.

When I get my period, Mom gives me Kotex, those thick cottony "napkins" we used before tampons came along. Scene: I'm carrying a bloody Kotex to show my mother that I need a fresh one. No, she says, her frugality ascendant, you have to use it longer than that. At this time I'm appropriately reading *Gone with the Wind*, where passion and a sexy handsome man rule, my hormones blazing. That summer, my budding womanhood finally finds a spark in Teddy Tibbles, a cute boy my own age who lives nearby. We actually date! I remember a cookout party on the beach, and my first kiss in the back of the car on the way home. Hallelujah shouts my heart in delight: I've discovered what it's all about.

Mom sleeps on the couch to be there when I get home from dates. My main boyfriend is Charlie, a student at Milton Academy. One time after we've been necking in his car, she accosts me with, "I know what you've been doing." Sassy as always, I reply, "Well, the neighbors don't know, so who cares?"

Buckingham is an all-girl school at this time, housed in a lovely old brick mansion. Every morning I climb over our back fence, throwing my green book bag over first, and trot about five blocks to Sparks Street. All the houses I pass are big and beautiful, and I come to believe that's how most folks live. For the most part, I find the academic work easy enough, except for Math, and I enjoy the challenge of History and English. My diary from 1952 focuses on relationships with the other girls: who's best friends, who favors whom, being thrilled to get a phone call, etc.

I am reading the likes of *Vanity Fair* and *Tale of Two Cities*. How much more educated I'm getting than the kids in sadly townie Russell School! At the same time, I start going to The Sociables, dances for private school girls and boys, grooming us for our affluent futures. My mom teaches me to dance in the kitchen, waltzing over the linoleum. Thus my messages about society continue to conflict. I'm completely at home in my intellectual and comfy upper middle class life, while my mother keeps my perspective on adventure, rebellion, and diversity, much preferring to teach me to dance herself than some swanky dance school. She works hard for years volunteering with the NAACP (National Association of Colored People), way before it was trendy to do so. (At her memorial service, they award her a plaque.)

2 Sixteen

Mom says, "It's only a year. You'll make new friends."

"I want the friends I've already got," I snarl. "I'm not going. You'll have to lock me in a trunk and take me by force."

"Please, dear. It's a great opportunity."

"I'm not going. Make me."

Somewhat in this manner my poor mother begs me to agree to come with the family for a year in Oxford, for which Pop has got a Guggenheim grant. I grimly refuse to go. In my defense, sixteen is a terrible age to remove a kid from their social environment. At last, one day when my new best friend Sally Bender is visiting our house, we come up with the answer. We're in my bedroom, and Sally's praising the chance to live in England for a year. "Why don't you come with us," I cry. Elated, we run downstairs to Mom in the kitchen with our brilliant idea. The dear woman acquiesces, thrilled to tame her daughter's ferocious resistance. Only years later do I realize what a heroic deed it was, taking on responsibility for a fourth child, a teenager at that.

Sally has blessedly come into my life in the 10th grade at Buckingham. She and I are two peas in a pod from the start. The year in England with her as part of our family works out beautifully. Also, she escapes the tension at home: the following year, her mother commits suicide. I remember Mrs. Bender well, from my visits after school, a quiet, beautiful woman with prematurely snow-white hair. Scene: I'm upstairs getting ready for school. The phone rings (we only have one of course, downstairs in the hallway), Mom when she answers it begins immediately to gasp "No!" Sitting at the top of the stairs, I start to cry, way before I could know the cause. I am excused from school that day; I walk Sally back and forth in her neighborhood, my arm around her.

Oxford University starts a year younger than U.S. colleges, so the first-year boys are seventeen, meaning Sally and I have an active social life. We attend Miss Keyes-Young's Tutorial Academy for Young Ladies, an excellent school structured on the Oxford system of tutorials in teachers' homes. We ride our bikes to every class, zooming all over town. Latin, Chaucer, Math, French, History. We read Virgil and Chaucer in the original. We do math in pounds and shillings. We study in the elegant drawing room of our house in Park Town, listening to American radio.

The house is narrow, with one or two rooms on each floor. Hence, the kitchen and dining area are in the basement, sitting room on the first floor, drawing room on the second, bedrooms on the third and fourth. Sally and I, sharing a bedroom, must go upstairs to the bathroom. No central heating, so it's freezing at night, and we have a potty handy. A slinky black cat named Ling comes with the house. He often sleeps with us and loves to pretend to catch mice under the covers. Out in front of the house is a lovely park, the houses forming a crescent around it.

It's considered somewhat vulgar to use the phone, so invitations come via the various colleges' delivery boys on bicycles. Handwritten notes, to tea or cocktails. One time we're invited to a party in Oscar Wilde's rooms in Magdalen College: little porthole-sized stained glass windows looking out on the Cherwell River, dark purple drapes and cushions. Sally and I are having a wonderful time. Our favorite outing is walking across Port Meadow by the Isis River for tea at the Trout Inn, where peacocks strut. Crossing the meadow we pick rhubarb stems to munch on, while their gigantic leaves blow us in the wind like sails. My love of Thomas Hardy's heaths starts here.

My mom, however, is miserable. The last time she was in Oxford, she was a carefree young woman in a full-blown romance. Here she is now, almost twenty years older, caring for a household and four children as well as a very busy and popular husband. This is when she starts showing the rather unstable mood swings my father always blamed on menopause, but I'm sure there was more to it. Sally and I do the dishes every night. But we have too much fun. For example, we have a dishcloth we call "Fat Rag" that we throw back and forth at each other, laughing hysterically. One night my mother throws a knife at me, though very half-heartedly. It misses and clatters to the ground. I throw a chair back. Ditto. So no one is hurt, but that gives you an idea of the tension around my mother's resentment. I can describe my own feelings best as a kind of bitter triumph.

The Park Town rental lasts for six months, then we move to High Street ("the High") for the next six. During this spring, I meet Alastair, who develops into a serious relationship. He invites me to the Commemoration Ball, his final-year celebration. We stay up all night; the formal program lists what will be served at dawn. We end up in the morning in a punt on the river. I remember running through tall grass to take a pee, in my formal gown.

On both of our school vacations, Sally and I go to France. For the first one, in January, we stay with a family in *Villiers-sur-Orge*, outside Paris. The second one, in May, is hosted by a family in Paris near the Bois de Boulogne. After a week or so we all go to their country house near Honfleur, on the Normandy coast. We're not allowed to go down to the beach, where it is feared hidden German bombs still lurk. English school vacs are longer than ours, so we learn a great deal of French, as well as having a most glorious time.

On the way home to America, early summer of 1954, we all spend a couple of weeks in Scotland. Inverness, at the Nether Loch Aber Hotel. Alastair finds a friend with a car, and both young men drive up to Scotland. The friend's name is David, so we name the car Goliath. We spend hours necking in the car, me and A. in the back, David and Sally making out just fine in the front seat.

Alastair comes to Liverpool to see me off on the ship home. It's very sad for me, and Mom is comfortingly sympathetic.

Senior year. I'm suffocating back at Buckingham, stifling and provincial after all our cosmopolitan adventures. Besides, it's time to buckle down and prepare for college. Alastair and I are writing back and forth devotedly. But I am discovering Harvard boys. As part of a group, I'm paired with a squat and ugly boy whose name I've forgotten. Fortunately this does not involve a physical relationship, so our group escapades are lots of fun. Rock and roll is just coming in, and we are taught the proper gyrations by a student from New Orleans who really knows his stuff: one hip, then the other, separately. Quite the opposite of ballet! But I take to it easily. And I love the music (still do!) The switch from crooning to the bump and grind of Elvis turns into a true revolution.

September 24, 1954. "*A month has never gone so fast: here it is almost October and two months already since I was in Scotland with Alastair. The weather was glorious today and I did many things I was supposed to do and in the afternoon took a bike ride with Sal and ended up at La Patisserie Gabrielle for café français and we stayed almost two hours playing with Monique, la petite française à cinq ans. It's so good for our French.*"

A few days later I am offered my first job, at Mt. Auburn Hospital where I've been volunteering. October 4 excerpt: "*Father Everett is my favorite patient. He's a delicate bag of bones but so sweet and I make him his gruel every night.*"

As I turn eighteen, my sister turns fourteen. Overnight it seems, she goes from awkward adolescent to beauty. "*My, Franny has changed so in 1 month! We cut her braids the day before we landed, but she was still wearing that ugly blazer and walking as though breasts were a curse. I bought her her first bra when we got back, and she began to take pride in herself, for her hair, high swept in a horsetail, really is lovely. Now since she's started Buckingham she's completed the cycle of ending childhood—in such a short time and with such wonderful results.*"

I am working hard at school and in the hospital too. "*Mrs. Perry in 301 has cancer of the rectum and I mustn't tell a soul, 'cause she doesn't know.*".... "*Not only did I see a dead person today, but I watched her die, and witnessed her last gasps while holding the tube to her nose. I was very cool and collected outwardly, but I was trembling for an hour afterwards inwardly. It was frightening, exciting, and almost enjoyable, for think of what an experience it is! Nurses rushing everywhere for it was a heart attack and sudden.*"

But lest you think I'm not having fun, here's a report from November 20: "*…it began at Quinny's where there was a rather morbid party—four bottles of wine—and Antonio drinking it by the shoe-fulls out of Susie's "slipper." Then to St. Claire's* [an ice-cream shop] *to get the former sober (he there ate ice cream with his fingers) and from there on to Adams House, Leverett House, and Kirkland House to dance and dance…*" And from December 11, continuing my escapades with Harvard students: "*… Roman dinner party…We all were in togas—about twenty of us. We reclined on cushions and ate grapes and figs and drank wine…*" Around this time I meet David, a Harvard junior. "*We went all round Fresh Pond on our bikes and stopped for a picnic lunch and lay in the grass on dead leaves. David's beard is so soft and ummm—it was *so like the times I spent with Alastair and yet there was no pain or guilt when I thought of him."*

But I'm still a high school student and my parents are vigilant. I've pretty much been driving them crazy imagining my sex life ever since I started dating. In many cases I know I'm torturing them and take pleasure in it; I fiercely need to prove they don't control me. The year 1954 finishes with the usual mix of homework, hospital job, and intense socializing. *"I've just written a short letter to Alastair telling him how beautiful the snow is tonight—it was almost to my knees as I walked home from Susie's about 11. Sal and I spent the day in the Square—we rode each other down there on the sled. I really, really miss David. I'm just a girl who needs a man always."*

After Sally's mother dies (January, 1955), my diary shows deepening thoughtfulness about life, but also a schedule that's almost reckless. That spring I add to my hectic schedule by performing in Joyce's *Finnegan's Wake* with the Poet's Theater. Susie's mother Mary Manning has adapted it, and we're doing the world premiere. Harvard professor Harry Levin is called in to explain to us what we are saying. My diaries never mention my parents at this time, except for remarks like "parents are the worst" and "over-worrying father." Now and then I make note of how grownup and beautiful Fran has become, and details like Billy getting a new leather jacket. Clearly I'm at an age when my family has faded in significance. But Mom is still cooking my meals and Pop is still paying my bills, so I seem to myself now rudely ungrateful.

In the spring of 1955 I start dating a boy named Luigi who at twenty only finished the eighth grade and has Mafia connections, as well as a lovely baby-blue convertible. I meet him while doing *Finnegan's Wake*. Luigi arrives one day by giving a ride to our stage manager who was hitchhiking. I'm still fiercely a virgin, but my poor parents imagine the worst. They've told me that I must in no way have sex until I'm married. Imagine my anger when years later I found out they lived together in college and didn't get married until Pop had completed his Rhodes Scholarship. And my mother had two abortions before having me! My kisses with the likes of Alastair, David, and Luigi are certainly passionate but I am adamant in the face of all their persuasions. I look upon my virginity as a gift I'll bestow when I'm ready. A consequence of all those Victorian novels I grew up on? My parents' gift of self-worth, too.

Once when I go to a fancy coming out event (I scorn to come out—I'm my mother's daughter), I get fed up with the pretensions, go into the kitchen to sit on a counter in my elegant gown, chat with the help, and phone Luigi to come get me. Which he does. I climb over the side of his convertible despite my gown, and off we go into the democratic sunset.

In 1955 Rosa Parks is arrested for refusing to give up her seat on the bus to a white. Adlai Stevenson runs for president. Around this time we get a car and Mom learns to drive and Pop starts wearing a wedding ring, instead of the ring his war battalion men made for him from a German plane. It seems he does not value her and the new ring is the result, we kids deduce, of therapy (hers not his).

I graduate from Buckingham in May. In June my Harvard boyfriend invites me to his senior dinner. I get his fellow student, David Halberstam (yes later the famous reporter) a date with my friend Mimi.

I decide to use my job money to go visit Alastair the following summer, and also travel to Italy. While working at the hospital, I watched the terror of an elderly Italian woman, who knew no English, as she got a skin graft. She was completely conscious, but nobody explained to her what was happening. I felt so helpless unable to help her, I determined then and there to learn Italian. When signing up for my first courses at Harvard, I am thrilled that I can take Italian, and I do. As a result, when I get to Italy, I can already converse somewhat.

3 Harvard

My freshman year isn't the wrench it usually is for students, as I have already been dating and hanging out with Harvard students for over a year. Traditions like coffee in "the Bick" (Hayes Bickford cafeteria) are already old hat for me. Also, I'm still living at home. (Fran had to live at home her first two years at Harvard, too. We both still resent this, as our brother was allowed to live in a dorm from the beginning.) Taking severe warnings from Pop to heart, I buckle down and study hard. However, though he has cautioned me against extracurricular activities, I succumb to persuasion by the student director (whom I already know), and join the cast for *The Tempest*. I'm a nymph with lots of dancing and a few lines. At one point I run through the audience to the stage and throw my legs around the waist of a young man, falling backwards. I love how easy that is for me, and the gasps I get.

I meet my first husband the spring of my freshman year. Gary Campbell is a junior from Asheville, North Carolina, with a blonde moustache and touch of a gentle southern drawl. He wastes no time in relieving me of my virginity. I am eager. We accomplish this in his bunk bed in Leverett House, obeying the "parietal rules" of that time, meaning females have to leave boys' rooms by 4 p.m. Many times I am running down the stairs just in time to check out, still combing my hair. We spend all our time together. Gary takes excellent lecture notes, which I share; our studies are not neglected. He sees me home to Lakeview Avenue via my bike: we take turns with it, leaving it at intervals for the one who's walking to pick up. It's a magical spring.

Fortunately, I still have a great adventure ahead before settling into the monogamous life. Plans are already in place for me to return to Alastair. I have earned my passage, am booked on the *Nova Scotia*, a tanker that takes limited passengers. Here I am on the deck in Boston Harbor, looking down at Gary and my sister Fran waving goodbye. I share a stateroom with three old ladies, who when I tell them about Alastair, comment breathlessly on my having a paramour on both sides of the ocean.

There are six Canadian nurses on board, about my age. We have merry times with the crew, frowned upon by the officers. I remember a makeshift band on deck at night with the explosion of stars seen only at high sea. One sailor shakes an empty beer can with pebbles in it, another strums a thin rope strung along a tree branch, there's a harmonica, and we dance. At one point all of us girls hide in the bathroom from a prowling officer.

In London I meet up with Alastair. It's very romantic but you can imagine that after all my sexual experience, I am not the naïve wide-eyed girl of two years ago. We take off for Italy. I've told my parents that I'm going to take classes in Perugia, which I have no intention of doing. Why do they let me go? I will speculate about that forever.

So here I am in Italy with Alastair. We still have not had sex, and we never will. The first night we take a room together, I ask him to get me a glass of water from the pitcher on the table. He replies he has used it all up washing his feet. I burst into tears.

We've chosen Livorno arbitrarily by looking at a map—it's on the ocean, that seems nice. The next day we go out separately looking for a place to stay. But I've already decided to get one for myself only. And I do.

Poor Alastair. When we parted that morning to look for a room, it was understood we would live together. But I go around knocking on doors and fairly quickly find a place for myself, in the home of Gina and Salvatore Saviozzi in via San Jacopo.

Meeting Alastair back at the hotel and announcing my find, he is deeply distressed. This was not his plan! It's all downhill for Alastair from then on. I have my meals with the Saviozzis, and go to the beach every day where I quickly make friends. Everyone is fascinated by the pretty young American (I am called *Caterina l'Americana*). The girls finger my bathing suit, which is made of some mysterious synthetic material. The boys sing to me, my living Romeo radios. I am paired by everyone's consent with Innocenzo, a soccer star known affectionately as Piffero. He is, admittedly, gorgeous. I get a stunning tan. Poor Alastair is quickly superseded, and leaves town a very sad man.

I share my little room with a couple dozen canaries. Signor Saviozzi takes me for fun rides on his Vespa. On Sundays we have meat: always pigeon, served with the head still on. Tasty, though, after all the pasta the rest of the week. Evenings we often take a *passegiata*, strolling arm in arm along the major boulevard. Sometimes we watch TV in a nearby café; everyone's favorite is a comedy show. Once when I buy fried anchovies on the street and get sick, Gina feeds me a variety of concoctions from bottles—a green one works, who knows what it is! Their son comes home for a short visit, a small man who has been a jockey. He tells a story about when he was working in England and shows off his English by pronouncing proudly, "It's fucking cold." He has no idea he's cursing, and I don't enlighten him.

Piffero and I double date with Constanza and Paolo, but she's not allowed to go out at night without a chaperone. One day, when it's dark, Piffero takes me on a bus ride out to distant rocks by the sea, where we are very sexual but stop short of going all the way. I tell him I'm still a virgin and he believes me.

My friend Sally Kuhn from Cambridge and Radcliffe comes to visit me. So in another week, we two are off to Rome. Sal had met a boy named Pino on the train from Germany, so we meet up with him and his friend Roberto.

Rome, August 10, 1956
We've just been out with Pino and Roberto. We had dinner, then much walking and a few baci. They're terribly nice. This morning they showed us the Pantheon, many excavations of ancient Rome, and the place where Mussolini asked the Italians if they wanted war. They're Fascists as all the young men are.

One of our funniest adventures is when we get on an empty bus and I sit at the wheel and Sal sits in the ticket-takers booth. People who start boarding the bus are astonished. Eventually, the real driver appears and chases us off. After that, *I took my shoes off and began dancing madly down the boulevard. We gathered an army of fascinated Italians: a soldier, two sailors, 5 motorcycles, and 3 cars—all escorting us as we pranced along. Finally I put on my shoes and Sal took out her knife (switchblade) and we became dignified. We escaped into the Excelsior Hotel and had two glasses of ice-water and went home.*

In another week, we're off to Venice. The dreamlike trance of Livorno continues. The sun, the trattorias under vine-covered trellises, the wine, the delicious pasta, the warm and vivacious Italians, the beauty all around.

Upon request, my father has sent me extra money. And Sally's father has sent us money specifically for a place called Harry's Bar, where we go, of course. It has swinging doors like the saloons in Westerns. We visit the Biennale where Soviet art is rather a joke, all glowing youths working ecstatically. (Sally's father is professor of Fine Arts at Harvard. During World War II, he was one of the Monuments Men who saved stolen artwork from the Nazis.)

At Harry's Bar we meet some boys Sal knows from the ship; we go to a few other bars with them, and a party, where from a balcony we watch the fiesta—a parade of lighted barges. The last barge has a full orchestra on it. *Then in the dawn we strolled across San Marco and had scrambled eggs. We were on our way back when we ran into Bruno for about the third time, and this time he bought us drinks.* Bruno is a spectacularly muscled male prostitute. With one of us on each arm, he tours us all around town, with from time to time enamored little men begging to serve him. We arrive back at our hotel so late, they've locked the door. Somehow Bruno gets us in. About sixty years later when I query her in an email, Sal responds, "Have image of him scaling a wall and going into a window but may be a hallucination."

In late August I return to Southampton to take the ship home. Who should greet me at the dock but old Alastair! He's grown a beard and is so anxious to please me. Oh dear. By then he's entirely off my radar, and I make short shrift of him. On the way home I have little yearning for Gary either. A young Irishman named Mike, who's going to Canada to make a new life, becomes my honey for the voyage.

Sophomore year at Harvard. My favorite course is *The Iliad*, taught by Prof. John Finley, who dances with the microphone cord as he blazons the tremendous feats of Achilles and Hector, pacing the stage of grand Sanders Theater, all polished wood and stained glass. Everybody goes to "the Bick" for coffee between classes, and one day the beat poet Gregory Corso shows up wearing a gorilla mask. I've never laughed so hard in my life.

I give in to Gary's relentless pursuit and am back dating him regularly. When Pop takes me to lunch, he asks if we're getting married. I say no—I've never thought of it—but when I tell Gary this, he says, "why did you say no?" As simple as that. Soon we are engaged; we buy a cheap ring at Woolworth's. Gary's a senior and so it all moves quickly. In December, 1957 we are man and wife. I am barely 21 years old.

Do you detect a note of regret? Well, I was so young, and not mature for my age either, romantic as hell, deluded by a protected girlhood. The bright side is, this marriage brings me my two precious children, delight of my life.

My mother doesn't lift a finger to help with the wedding. Not out of malice, I guess, but more out of shock and confusion. Pop arranges for a reception at the Faculty Club, and I myself order and address the invitations. We're married in the Congregational Church, go to Rockport for our honeymoon. Mind you, it's the middle of the winter, just before Christmas. I wear my old flannel nightie, not imagining anything else. We practice with my brand new contraceptive diaphragm, which the state of Massachusetts finally permits me, now that I am a safely married woman!

4 New York

We newlyweds settle in a cheap apartment on 109th Street, near Amsterdam Avenue. I experience cockroaches for the first time, horrified and flabbergasted. We have no phone, and budget very carefully even the dimes it takes to go out and make a phone call. Gary's in grad school at Columbia, with some teaching to help make ends meet. (His father pays the tuition.) The summer of '58 I work in a settlement house (community center) on Avenue A, in charge of kids age 5-7. We all take a bus to Jones Beach once a week.

I'm enrolled at Barnard College, "as a Radcliffe student," meaning my credits go to my Harvard degree. This arrangement only lasts for the semester, finishing up my junior year. Then I will need to take all my senior credits back at Harvard, via summer school. Until then, I take a job at nearby St. Luke's Hospital, interviewing poor patients to determine their level of payment. A couple of times Gary comes by my office window, at basement level, and throws in a yellow rose.

Yes, we're having fun. A group of friends from Harvard move to New York about the same time, including Dave Soeiro, John Tangeman, and Athans Boulukos. I'm often the only girl in our escapades. Several times we dare as a group to go to Harlem, to hear the jazz at Small's Paradise.

Gary and I practice parenting with a blue parakeet named Quetzalcoatl, and later a handsome gray cat named Crispin. We lose Quetzal because he's allowed to fly around the apartment, and one day we leave the window open a tiny bit. He's gone when we come home. There are trees outside and we like to think he's out there singing his freedom. I don't get pregnant on purpose, but when I do, we are excited to create a child. It's like one more grand adventure, and surely proves we are grown up at last.

Duncan Andrew Campbell is born in New York Hospital on September 27, 1960. I trained in "natural childbirth," so I am awake the whole time. My long hair is collected into one braid for the ordeal. Of course it hurts like hell, but Gary is allowed to be there for most of it, massaging my aches, and my memory of the event is of breathless pride. My baby, 8 ½ pounds! Right afterwards I order a big dinner of steak and mashed potatoes.

My mother is out of the picture, sad to say. She has a nervous breakdown when I'm about seven months pregnant. I go to visit her in the mental hospital, and she feigns a kick at my stomach! I'm not afraid of her at all, but I'm not sorry for her either. I think my uppermost emotion is scorn, followed by hurt. I know she loves me, but that hardly matters. She has a fierce aggression towards me, which my sister has always called jealousy. But she's often loving, too, and truly caring, a hearty, warm, rich soul that got lost somehow. My adolescence and sexual development just drove her crazy.

Running the house and having babies seems to be Mom's closely guarded realm, so I must not grow up and thereby threaten her only source of power and prestige.

So, Mom does not come to help out with the new baby, and I certainly don't want her to. But my sister does. Beautiful Fran, age 20, strawberry blond hair to her waist, a Harvard senior. She brings sunshine and laughter to us sleep-deprived, starving new parents. The first thing she does is bake us a chocolate cake. Gary and I eat it all in one fell swoop.

I am nursing little Dundy, at all hours of the night of course.

We're now living on 111th Street, an easy walk for Gary to Columbia. He's an instructor while studying for his PhD. He has chosen as his thesis topic Shakespeare's *Othello*, fascinated by the theme of sexual jealousy. Nothing ever comes of that thesis project, however. For a while he's rated as up-and-coming in academia, but he falls out of favor, and before Dundy is three, has to find a new job. Our New York years are fun as well as a maturing experience. We hire babysitters and go out on the town with our friends, and to the theater, etc.

That November, 1960, I am thrilled to go vote for Jack Kennedy. My parents have always touted voting as a supreme right, duty, and satisfaction. Around this time my father, who is chairman of the national ADA (Americans for Democratic Action), introduces me to Martin Luther King. Gary obligingly stays home to babysit, while Pop and I attend a gala Democrat dinner. I am mesmerized by King, his cosmic charisma; shaking his large warm hand is electric. What an icon! Larger than life, almost mythical.

To finish my Harvard degree, I must take three courses in summer school, two summers in a row. Mom has rented us an apartment down the street. (It's no secret that she doesn't want us living with her.) Gary does valiant duty taking care of Dundy, and I sweat through the months studying like crazy. Officially, I am graded harder than regular summer school students. Rightly so—I am earning the most valued degree in the world. Eventually, the following year, I write a thesis on Henry James' *Portrait of a Lady*; I'm rewarded with a *cum laude* degree.

5 Montreal

For Gary's next teaching venture we choose McGill University in Montreal because, still in our mid-twenties, we long for further adventure. Canada seems exotic enough; we become "landed immigrants."

Here I am on the plane from Boston to Montreal. Dundy's a hefty two year old who walks all over my lap. He's wearing his travel outfit, a brown corduroy jacket and matching broad-brimmed hat. Gary has rented an apartment on Benny Avenue, a good twenty-minute bus ride to the center of town. It's convenient to a supermarket and a park, but rather windblown and banal. Here's where we live for the next five years.

Gary has a good job at McGill, based on the assumption that he's finishing his dissertation and thereby acquiring his doctorate. Which never happens. His thesis topic continues to be Shakespeare's *Othello*—but it never gets off the ground. We enjoy the other folks in the English Department. And we discover the vibrant party life through a café downtown on rue St. Denis. Go there on a Saturday night and you'll get the word where the party is. Our closest friends are Irving and Coucon, an English and French couple full of fun and life.

Our first babysitters come from a pool of elderly ladies, whom we send home in taxis (we don't have a car). Then we discover the Ferguson twins, teenagers who live down the street. One of them is always available and Duncan enjoys them. One Halloween Gary makes a knight costume for Duncan, cardboard helmet and sword painted silver.

Winter is phenomenal in Montreal. The snow comes in November, covers the park benches, and never recedes until April. It snows all the time. But the city plows constantly, loading trucks with snow to haul out of town. They even plow the sidewalks. The subway is not yet built, but the buses run unhindered. When you go to a special event, you wear your warm boots, and carry your dress-up shoes in a little tote bag.

The second year in Montreal, I get a half-time job as secretary in the Spanish Department. After that, I teach freshman English at Sir George Williams University (which later becomes Concordia). At three, Dundy enrolls in a *maternelle*, all in French. Every morning a *monsieur* picks him and other kiddies up in a van.

At some point I return to ballet classes. And I'm writing when I can. I win a Canadian short story contest in 1964, and it's read over the CBC radio. Then I get a story published in *The Montrealer*, a real coup. I become close friends with Lloyd, an American who works at McGill's publishing house. I go to French theater productions with Coucon. Gary and I go to demonstrations against the Vietnam War. This is probably when our FBI dossier is begun. (I acquire it years later under the Freedom of Information Act.) Sometimes the demos are mixed with those of French Canadians protesting English domination. "*Le Vietnam aux Vietnamiens! Le Québec aux Québécois!*"

❧❧

I'm pregnant again! Amelia Katherine Campbell is born August 4, 1965 in Queen's Hospital. During labor I have two sweet midwives holding my hands on either side. She's six and a half pounds. At home, Gary does all the post-birth work, from cooking to laundry. (Fran's in Paris with new husband Bart.) I nurse our Amelia for a couple of months. I'm still nursing her when I start German classes at the Goethe Institute. For we have decided Gary will take a job in Germany, at the University of Munich.

6 Munich

We move to Munich for two years in the fall of 1966. Duncan is turning six, and Amelia, one. We travel by ship so we can take all our stuff, including linens. Gary and I have chosen this rather daring exploit in the name of adventure. But also, McGill is making noises about his not yet having a doctorate, and we realize he'll have to look for a new job soon. The University of Munich is happy to have this Harvard-educated American as a *Gastdozent* (guest lecturer), teaching Shakespeare to young Germans, who generally love the Bard.

Via my brother Bill, who makes the contact at a party in Paris, we've rented an apartment in Neuhausen Gern, just a short trolley ride from the city center. At Tizianstrasse 19, you enter a little gate and walk up a long drive lined with flourishing rose bushes. Our landlady, Frau Braun, lives on the first two floors and our little family on the top floor—where the walls slant down, *unter dem Dach*. We settle in gratefully after the long trip. We'd spent a few days in Paris, where I had land sickness; that's when after a sea voyage you still feel the water undulating beneath you. And Milly has the flu. We take her to the American Hospital in Neuilly. The doctor proclaims we're all exhausted, but just fine.

Settled into our cute Munich apartment, we're warmly welcomed by Gary's university colleagues. Duncan starts first grade at the International School, and I go grocery shopping every day toting little Milly in her stroller. Butcher, baker, grocer. Beer is delivered to our door, and a *Kartoffelmann* (with a wheelbarrow of potatoes) strolls down the street singing his wares.

The washing machine in the basement has a boil capacity, great for Milly's diapers. Eventually, with huffy annoyance, she learns to pee in her little potty.

I'm taking German classes evenings at the Berlitz School, where I find fun pals, especially Willy Nibbrig, who's Dutch. She's here in Munich living with her fiancé Gerd Jan. We all go out for beer after class, including the teacher. Later on, I take classes at the *Auslander Schule* at the University, learning to read and write properly, which Berlitz does not bother with. Berlitz is great for teaching immediate communication, but not educated German.

One evening after Berlitz class, I'm hurrying home from the trolley stop, starting up our long driveway, when a man grabs me from behind. He's big, looming over me. Pushing me towards the wall, he says, *"Nicht schreien oder ich schiesse."* ("Don't scream or I'll shoot.") Somehow I reply, in German, "I don't speak German. My husband is looking out the window." But still he's pushing me. Somehow I don't believe he has a gun, get the strength to inhale deeply, and let out a gigantic scream. At that, he drops me and runs away, feigning a chuckle. This experience is very traumatic, and is still with me whenever I walk down a dimly-lit street at night.

I report this to the police, but they say I must come to the station to make a complaint. I refuse in fury, telling them that in the U.S. the police would rush to the woman's house to take the information. Which is true, and I still think their attitude was shocking.

Gary and I make friends widely and easily. The Vietnam War is raging, so we join a protest demonstration, as we had in Montreal. But here in Munich, the demo is at night. We form long lines linking arms, at the end of each line someone carrying a huge lighted torch. We run from street corner to street corner. At every intersection we all kneel down together and chant, *"Burger kommt aus dem Balkon, unterstütz den Vietcong!"* I recall we lit our cigarettes at the torches.

Our parents visit us at various times. Pop and Mom come for *Fasching*, a Mardi Gras that lasts the whole month of January, with many parties, everyone in costume. After that comes *Starkbierzeit*, "strong beer time" in February, when they scrape the bottom of the barrels and the drink is especially strong. Gary's parents come, buying us a car that we all then travel in for a week. This is the car that we take back to the U.S. with us on the ship. Its name is Moby (because it's white), "without the dick" as we gleefully proclaim.

With our new car we expand our side trips. That summer we rent a place on the lake shore in Annecy, France. I remember swans swimming and preening. One day Milly drinks a cleaning fluid,

Monsieur Propre (Mr. Clean), and she and I are rushed to the doctor by our landlady, in a gorgeous Mercedes with polished teak dashboard. Fortunately, she only needs an antidote.

We decide to spend New Year's Eve in Vienna. It's not a long drive from Munich, but on the way it starts to snow heavily, so we pull off the road to spend the night in a little village called Traun. (The German word for dream is Traum.) We find a cozy B&B, eat a cozy meal, and put the kids to sleep. Then we go into the bathroom and make love. Another sweet memory of this Vienna trip: New Year's Eve, as we have dinner in a restaurant, a man is playing the zither. This is the instrument that provides the gorgeous background music to my favorite movie, *The Third Man*. I ask him to play that theme and he does! I'm thrilled.

The second winter we and the kids head for Berlin. What an experience! To reach West Berlin we have to drive through a great swath of East Germany, under Soviet control at the time. Officials usher us into a garage, close the doors on both sides—creepy—and affix a special license plate to our car. One day with the kids we take the subway to East Berlin (in retrospect a risky thing to do!). That Soviet part of the city is a different world, stark and poor; in front of one monument soldiers are marching in goosestep like the Nazis.

Duncan plays an Eskimo in a *Fasching* parade, Milly learns to shout, "Nein, nein!" at the other kids in the sandbox, I teach English at the *Sprachenschule*, we enjoy *Oktoberfest*, Gary and I go to many parties, opera, and plays. Our babysitter is Frau Thielicke who lives next door. Frau T—nicknamed Tika by the children—asks us urgently why we Americans didn't stop Hitler's re-arming. *"Um Gottes willen, warum?"* She likes to tell the story of how she and her friends walked long distances just to avoid passing a national monument where they were all obliged to give the Heil Hitler salute.

Our two years in Munich are fun, but towards the end, of course we are concerned about what's next. I type many application letters for Gary to sign. At last we get a bite, from Hobart College in upstate New York.

7 Geneva, New York

So, in the fall of 1968 our little ill-fated family moves to shoddy Geneva. It's a provincial backwater in the Finger Lakes district, where the downtown area has been abandoned to decay. Poor Duncan, who at the age of eight has never seen a football, goes to the benighted elementary school. I can only guess at the adjustments he has to make, and the teasing he no doubt endures.

This dreadful place is the scene of much turmoil and the disintegration of our marriage. The group of young faculty and their wives we hang out with is rife with flirtations and hanky panky. Several of the husbands take up with female students, and eventually so does Gary.

Meanwhile, as the Vietnam war still rages, we both join students and faculty to demonstrate and protest it. In many ways, we have a semblance of normalcy. Milly goes to a cozy preschool down the street; I audit a course in *Beowulf*.

The second year I enroll at Cornell for my master's degree, which Pop pays for. Cornell is in Ithaca, only about an hour's drive from Geneva, so I'm able to get to classes several times a week. My old Harvard tutor Edgar Rosenberg, a professor in the Cornell English Department, has arranged for me to skip the usual exam required for grad school. I love my courses and the whole learning experience, from discussions around a seminar table to deep research in the library. Ithaca is a whole world of difference from Geneva, cosmopolitan and intellectual. My focus is the American 19th century—after seven years living in other countries, I'm eager to learn more about my own.

Before I get my driver's license, I take the bus to Ithaca. Gary drives me to the bus station. He's supposed to be working on his thesis, but he isn't. At Christmas time when we visit my parents, he refuses to watch the kids so I can study. My mother does that instead, while I work hard in Widener Library writing papers. I remember getting great satisfaction from a comparison of Cooper with Chateaubriand. As my academic life prospers, Gary's stagnates; the tension between us grows. One night I've locked myself in the bathroom with the kids while Gary rampages around the apartment. He throws some of my clothes out into the snow.

My diary of the time, October 1968 to January 1970, tells many daily details—I learn to drive, Dundy has his tonsils out, I study hard at Cornell which is in upheaval over student anti-war protests, my family visits for Thanksgiving and we go to Cambridge for Christmas. Fran visits a few times, the kids and I visit her in Toronto, we vacation in Nantucket for two weeks, Dundy starts 4th grade, Milly celebrates her 4th birthday. Entry for October 9, 1969: *"We're still in emotional upheaval and peace won't be solidly with us for some time."* November 4: *"Another beautiful sunny fresh all colored month outside; bitter and tense, deep disillusion inside, with all the hypocrisy has gone also all the trust and if not hope too, hope has lost its meaning."*

Other horribly grim scenes come to mind. It's very hard to find words for this whole nightmare time. Scene: I am knocking on the door of an apartment down the street where I know Gary is staying. Someone has warned me not to come here("Kitty, don't go there.") But I'm in a frenzy—when I find the door locked, I break the glass panel and reach in to unlock it. Gary appears in his underpants. I barrel into the bedroom and find his blonde student in the bed. I grab her arm and spit, "I hope your husband does this to you some day," then I run out and home and start packing a suitcase. My friend Asta drives me and the kids to the airport. My parents take us in.

Now in Cambridge, spring of 1970, Duncan has to attend yet another new school. I take Milly to a preschool for half a day on my bike every morning. I'm getting much needed rest. A woman neighbor my age takes me running regularly, getting me back in shape. My parents are wonderfully supportive, bless them.

Within a few months Gary comes to visit and tries hard to reconcile. I refuse to return to Geneva, so he agrees to find an apartment in Ithaca. I have called Hobart to report the student's behavior, so his fling is over. Meanwhile, I have a few flirtations of my own, delighted to find I am still cute when not depressed and exhausted! One of my boyfriends is about 20, with a motorbike, a real flower-child type, with long flowing hair.

So now we're living in Ithaca, fall of 1970. On Cornell Street in a half house which unfortunately is owned and run by a vicious witch. A saving grace is that a few doors down lives the Clavel family, who become close friends for the three of us. Duncan starts school at Belle Sherman, just five blocks away. He has a dear teacher, Mrs. Shannon, with whom I keep in touch as our family life deteriorates again. Gary is commuting to Hobart in a carpool, and I am finishing up my master's at Cornell. But Gary starts beating me up again. (The hitting started in Geneva.) I call the police, who walk him around the block. (That's how the authorities handled domestic violence in the old days.) I go to teach a class with bruises all over my face.

Gary has to leave Hobart, no thesis having materialized, so he gets a job in Montreal in their junior college system. He moves back to Montreal; I don't. This is supposed to be temporary until we work things out, and that's what poor Duncan believes. But, in fact, the marriage is over.

For me, this means glorious liberation. The end of such tension means a peaceful home, and I don't realize how hard the separation is on the kids. At this time, everyone is getting divorced, it's no big deal. Isn't it better not to suffer from warring parents? Yes, but. They will always miss their father. He visits often, and I put them on the bus to Montreal sometimes. Thus ends our terrible family ordeal.

8 Ithaca, New York

I live in Ithaca for the next twenty years. It's a beautiful little city on Cayuga Lake, with a vibrant car-free downtown, dominated by Cornell University with its international energy and diversity. It's a perfect place for kids to grow up—clean and safe and cosmopolitan, with excellent public schools. You can be in the countryside within minutes, from woodland to gorges and waterfalls.

Our dreadful landlady, Mrs. Rosica, torments us for the year we live on Cornell Street. For example, when I tape pictures the kids have drawn in the windows, she reaches in and tears them down. Our comfort is the Clavel family—the mother, Ann, is my best friend, and Duncan is pals with their son Pierre. After that, we move to Dryden Road, the first floor of a rambling old house, with a big front porch and a yard at the back. The kids can easily walk to Belle Sherman School. I am finishing my degree and also teaching a freshman class. My course is part of the budding women's studies program; some of the books had been out of print for decades. Gary and I have a separation agreement, so I have the funds to live on. He tries to renege at first, but I get a Montreal lawyer and threaten to tell his department chair, so his plan is short-lived.

My social life is great. My grad school colleagues are good company, especially Meg and Dolores. I join a group called "Ithaca Singles Thing," which has parties all the time, and meet plenty of interesting men. One teaches German at Syracuse University, another studies astrophysics at Cornell. I continue my new workout of running, keeping in shape. I start classes at Ithaca Ballet, joining a Saturday group of women close to my age; we often go out for coffee afterwards.

I pass my orals and get my master's. I join a group of Cornell women jockeying with the administration to form the first "Female Studies" program. We have many fraught meetings, and have to fight hard, but we do prevail. This is among the very first programs that become "Women's Studies" everywhere.

About this time, my sister and brother are establishing their academic careers. In Toronto Fran's a professor at York University; Bill's a professor at Brooklyn College. Soon they are starting their wonderful familes, two spectacular kids each. Jessice, Denis, Nicole, Joshua. Our family ties are strong.

My first job after getting the degree is in the Cornell Administration building, taking notes and reporting on meetings. I arrange for Milly to go to a friend's house after school, for which I pay the mom, and pick her up on my way home from work every day. Duncan is old enough to go home by himself; he's eleven now and very responsible. Sometimes he even babysits his sister for a couple of hours while I go to a movie. He starts to play ice hockey, getting up at 5 in the morning to take turns with his team at the rink.

For me, everything's better without Gary. Ithaca is a small, peaceful city with plenty of upscale activities, thanks to Cornell. Plus, the public schools are excellent. Settled on Dryden Road, we have the first floor of a rambling house with a big secluded front porch, and share a yard. Belle Sherman school is only minutes away.

But I don't really know how the children adapt. They seem fine, continue doing well in school. Dunc rides his bike to DeWitt Junior High. He helps pay for his bike with a paper route and selling the *New York Times*. He's an enthusiastic member of the Junior United Nations. Plays sports, too, of course. He loves lacrosse, joins a group learning scuba diving in the lake, and makes the cross-country running team. At fifteen, as he sets out with his school for a visit to the U.N. in New York City, I feel wildly sad at his growing up and away:

Poem to Duncan 1976

THERE WILL BE NO BIRDS

There will be no birds singing
The morning my son leaves
Home.
I practiced a little just now,
Seeing him off on a two day
Absence. Taller than me,
At fifteen so near a man.
He had his best clothes on.

It was dark—at 6:35—
As he went.
Carrying a suitcase.

When it happens for real
Will I be able to contain
These tears?

Meanwhile, I'm dating all I want, making friends, enjoying my job, reveling in the kids' new lives. But at one of the singles dances I meet Max Mattes, and my fate is sealed. He's very tall and athletic, a bit of a goof in a cute way. At Cornell as a student he was a basketball star. I am smitten and so is he. He's still married but heading for divorce and trying to get custody of his two daughters, ages four and five. Scene: in the park at the edge of Cayuga Lake I arrive with six year old Milly to meet up with him and Kathleen and Myfanwy. It's a chilly fall day, overcast. The playground is deserted except for the five of us. Like a Bergman movie, fraught with significance. For many months extending into years, we spend all our time together as a family. Milly, just a year older than Kathleen, easily adapts to her new sisters.

I help Max get full custody, which is not difficult because his wife is a notorious alcoholic. He builds a rough house on a hill in the country. We all spend time there watching him dig the foundation with a rented bulldozer, pour the concrete, and raise the walls. I help nail in sheetrock. When Milly and I stay overnight, Duncan sometimes joins us, but as often stays home, often with his pal Kenny. Max and I take many long walks in the woods.

I get another job, at a chicken farm outside town, running their newspaper. I negotiate a lower salary in exchange for working 9 to 3, so I can be home for the kids after school. At one point I go with our team to an international conference of chicken farmers in New Orleans. I translate for a French company there, which is great fun. One delegate invites me out on the town, and N'Orleans' sexy ways include a show of nearly nude guys dancing on a bar.

In 1973 I have stomach pains that lead the doctors to operate. Eventually it's revealed that the pains were caused by bruises from a fall and the surgery was unnecessary, but meanwhile I almost die from an infection from the procedure. Pus is pouring out of the slice in my stomach. I'm in the hospital for a month. My mother, bless her, comes for weeks to take over, and even Gary comes to help out for a few days. Max does a great job of reassuring and stabilizing the kids.

After I get home, I quickly recover, but I lose my job. A co-worker comes one day to visit and informs me I'm fired. Now begins a creative time on unemployment, writing a children's book for Milly. At that time all the children's stories had boys as the main characters, so I write one with a little girl as the hero. It's titled *Amelia's Adventures in the Land of Dreams*. One afternoon as I'm writing, Milly comes in with her friend Manette and I ask them to invent me a villain. They immediately concoct a snow monster, which I incorporate into the story with creepy drama. I make a copy of the finished book for each of our three girls, and they read it over and over.

When the Mattes family stays with us overnight, I always sing each little girl a song after they are tucked in bed. Favorites are *My Bonny Lies over the Ocean*, *I Been Workin' on the Railroad*, and *Pussywillow Down by the Brook* (which my Mama taught me). Max and I take some great trips together, including Puerto Rico and Bermuda. Max builds each of the girls a dollhouse.

Best friends Valerie Grey, Susan Reisbord, Ann Clavel.

In 1976 Max and I buy a house together, only blocks from Belle Sherman School. Dunc is now in junior high, but he can easily ride his bike there. I get a job at Cornell's Johnson Museum as Membership Coordinator. My desk looks out over the lake, a gorgeous view. My duties range from writing press releases to organizing the film series. In 1978 Max and I get married.

It's the second marriage for both of us, and we both bring two kids to it. So our activities together from the beginning often include all six of us. But we do take some very romantic trips by ourselves, to Florida and St. Croix, New York and San Francisco. We have a lot in common, and the sex is good, too. We both have full custody, and we become a cohesive family.

Max is building up his business, making good money creating and installing communications systems for large institutions like hospitals. I accompany him to conferences, staying for free in his room and enjoying the parties and attention. Some of the trips are a real treat, for example to Italy and Mexico. We are able to afford buying a cottage on the lake, which we rent out in winter and enjoy in summer.

Duncan starts George Washington University in 1978. Max and I drive him down to D.C., and I'm in tears on the way home, missing him already. He makes Dean's List, and the next year transfers to Cornell. Milly leaves for Syracuse University in 1983. She's getting her BFA in acting, her passion ever since she played Oscar the Grouch in elementary school. I drive our little red car "Ruby" back and forth quite often to visit or fetch her.

Poem for Milly
on the occasion of her High School Graduation. June 25, 1983

Wasn't it only yesterday
I held you to nurse at
My breast, felt
The trusting curl of
Your minute hand?
Surely it was only yesterday that
You first said mama, took
Your first step into my proud arms; pushed about
Your wicker doll carriage,
Mastered your first two-wheel bike.
Only yesterday you said,
"Read me Pinocchio,
Sing me the pussy willow song."
You sold lemonade sitting at
A cardboard box,
And you washed the dishes
Standing on a chair.

My angel, light of my life,
Beloved daughter,
Yesterday has gone, suddenly.
The child has become a woman,
The rose has bloomed.
You are going now;
You are taking part of me with you.
But when your sweet golden sunshine
No longer warms me day by day,
I'll still have you in my heart.

Milly spends one semester at S. U.'s London branch, after which Max and I go to stay with her in her London apartment for a couple of weeks. During that time she goes to visit Duncan in Italy. The next year Kathy starts at the community college and Myfanwy starts two years in private school. Duncan has moved to Italy in 1986—he went just for the summer but met an Italian girl he followed to Italy and decided to stay. He takes a formal leave of absence from Cornell, which because his grades are good, they are happy to grant.

In 1981 I write a booklet, "In Your Hands, A Citizen's Guide to the Arms Race." I get a great illustrator, and the book is published by a young man with access to the high school printer. We all work for free: we call ourselves Parents for Peace. It is reviewed in *Library Journal*, and as a result I get orders from as far away as Australia—charging all of $3 a copy. These are the worldwide urgently active years of the "call to end the arms race," while the U.S. and Soviet Union are building up their nukes at a crazed pace.

Once while accompanying Max to a business conference in D.C., I secure an interview at the Pentagon as a reporter for *The Ithaca Times*. Here I am being escorted down long, very wide, starkly lit corridors, sitting around a large oval table with nuclear spokesmen. One takes out a recorder, places it on the table. I do the same. My tape is vital later when they try to dispute what I write.

My mom dies in 1987. Packing for the airport, my knees don't work—I have to walk around with bent legs. At 87 Lakeview, Pop, Fran, Billy and I are at the kitchen table with a typewriter writing her obituary. We deliver it by hand to *The Boston Globe*. Death is such a nightmare and outrage always, but to lose a mother is to lose your sense of life. Where am I to put all this love I feel for her? It dangles in the wind around me, rootless. Before we bury her, Pop has her brought home, her casket there in the library, home once more. When we have a memorial service for her a year later, the NAACP presents her with a plaque of gratitude. A friend of hers tells me she was not made to be a faculty wife, but better suited to a bohemian life in Greenwich Village. In any case, she was a free spirit somehow daunted. Poor Mom.

The clouds begin to loom over our marriage in the mid 80s. Our sex life falters, with Max less and less interested. He likes to race his sailboat every Sunday during the summer and, bored with all that competition, I instead play tennis with a British friend. I start therapy with Dr. Komar. I start a friendship with a Greek grad student named Thanassis. He's teaching me Greek and I love having dinner at his place. He's writing his thesis on nuclear capabilities in Europe, so I help him sometimes with his English prose, before he has to return to Greece for his military service.

Meanwhile, with the arms race slowed, my concern with nuclear destruction has evolved, as with many people, into an awareness of environmental disaster. It's a natural shift from "nuclear winter" to global warming. I join the Society of Environmental Journalists, publishing articles on such emerging subjects as municipal composting, integrated pest management, and the bovine growth hormone (BGH). At one point I'm interviewing by phone small farmers in Wisconsin and Vermont impacted by Monsanto's push to force them to use the hormone in milk production.

On Earth Day, April 1990, I'm in New York City, fully engaged. It's a heady time for those of us flinging ourselves into the climate emergency. Central Park is flooded with enthusiastic crowds listening to speakers. Times Square is closed to traffic, throngs cheering as we're addressed among others by a group of Inuits who'd canoed down the Hudson.

Now my marriage is really faltering. Max becomes more and more distant. In the spring of '91 through summer and fall he's going away almost every weekend to "look for boats." I am suspicious enough to hire a detective. On one occasion when I'm in New York, I find through the yellow pages a detective agency. I am ushered into a small room all furnished in plush white. When I tell the kind man interviewing me what I'm up against, he says, "This will be easy."

The detective instructs me to let him know as soon as Max announces another trip supposedly to find a new boat. I have taken to rooting through his wallet when he's in the shower, and find a reference to a hotel in New York City, which I convey to the detective. Then I wait. At one in the morning, the call comes from the agency: Max is staying at the New York hotel and has gone out, carrying a travel bag, to a notorious gay area, the meat-packing district of Greenwich Village. They report he's wearing a wig of long black hair. I'm paralyzed with shock. At the same time, there's relief. Now I can be truly free of him.

Confronted with the detective's report, Max is like a zombie. But my lawyer says I have to go on living with him until a formal separation agreement is in place. This takes six months, a very strange time, needless to say.

I am comforted by my friendship with Vivek, a beautiful young Indian graduate student at Cornell. He's only twenty-five versus my fifty-four, but that's no problem. We have great times together, walks and dinners. Vivek is a wonderful, spritely comfort in otherwise deeply dark times. I also learn to meditate, a tremendous relief from the stress. I belong to a group that meets often, learning various methods, along with all the chakras and their colors.

Finally, in the spring of 1992, I leave. What joy! Scene: the kitchen in Irving Place, saying goodbye to Max. I've sent my furniture on its way to Cambridge; the car is packed, including my plants. Max walks away from me, and I say, "You've turned your back on me for the last time." Then I call to my dog Jeff and I'm out the door. Jeffie and I travel happily to our new home. I have rented a wonderful apartment not far from Harvard Square, the first floor of a big house, with the sweet family who owns it living upstairs.

While waiting a few days for my furniture to arrive, I stay at my old homestead, 87 Lakeview Ave. Pop and Jane (his new wife) are still in Washington for the winter. I sit in the back yard gazing at the huge trees and stately houses all around, murmuring "enclave of comfort and privilege." I feel both safe and adventurous, myself again at last.

Of course at first I have frequent bouts of fear and insecurity. But I know that if I had stayed with Max I would have become a bitter old lady fast. I am a newborn soul instead.

9 New World

My life comes alive again. I touch base with some old friends from many years past, primarily Sally Wulff, my best friend from high school. But my main social contacts at first come from the Unitarian Church in Harvard Square. I join a health club, and often go to aerobics class. I also join a very active environmental group, Sustainable Cambridge Coalition, engaged in many projects from city recycling efforts to making Central Square pedestrian-friendly, and end up in charge of their newsletter. We have frequent exciting and productive meetings in City Hall. I get an assignment from Harvard to write a brochure outlining all the courses relevant to its new environmental studies major. I get an assignment from *Harvard Magazine* to write a feature article on the new major. Thanks to my lawyer, I'm receiving a reasonable amount of money every month from Max, while the interminable process of divorce grinds on.

My new therapist is a sweet lady whom I meet with at her house. She informs me that the experience of discovering Max's secret life has been traumatic. "You have been traumatized." It's a comfort to accept what a staggering blow it has been.

At church, five of us form a women's group. One introduces me to a singles group which has dances almost every weekend, mostly in churches. I carpool with Christina and Laura, meet suitable dates. Also, I'm devoted to the aerobics classes at my health club. I join the Boston Local of the National Writers Union. My therapist says, "You have become yourself."

My journal of 2/3/93: *"I have made a voyage like crossing the Andes or riding the rapids. Here I am, me and myself!"*

During this time I am job hunting, involving research such as info interviews because I'm not in a hurry. I start working at the Hospitality Program, based in the Episcopal Diocese in Boston. I easily commute on the Red Line from Central Square, crossing the Charles River, always beautiful. At first the job is half time, but then they offer me full time which I can't refuse. I get a sitter for my beloved dog Jeffie, a high school student who comes every day around two to walk and entertain him. When I get home, it's a love fest, though he does allow me to spend ten minutes meditating, still a welcome stress relief.

I have to take several very stressful trips back to Ithaca, requested by my lawyer in the divorce process. One of those times when Ann picks me up at the bus station and we drive through all the too familiar places, I'm in tears. "I was so unhappy here."

An Ithaca friend, Eppie Boze, has moved to Cambridge too, only a few blocks away, and we have many merry times. Jeff and I often saunter over to her place. I meet Helen Snively, a close friend to this day, who also lives nearby. She has frequent potlucks, where I meet other comrades like Myra and Alison. We all go to the contra dances, for a while almost every weekend. I am dating as much as I want: Moody, Jack, Bob, etc. Starting the summer of '93, I spend two weeks in August at a cottage in Wellfleet, continuing this fabulous tradition for years to come.

Duncan visits from Italy twice, before coming home for good. For much of his time there he was in demand to teach English; for example, while in Turin he taught English to Fiat executives. But he and Laura finally broke up after almost ten years together. Pop lets him stay at 87 Lakeview while he and Jane are in D.C. (every winter), and he gets a good job at Huron Drug Store. Pop and Dunc often come over to join me for dinner at the nearby Dolphin Restaurant.

Milly and I visit each other often. My favorite times to go to New York are November and March. Graduated from Syracuse University, she has a nice apartment on East 82nd Street. She finds an agent and starts getting cast, while mostly waitressing and pet sitting. She and her roommate have a business called Yuppy Puppy, which is quite lucrative. Eventually, her acting career takes off, with roles both onstage and in film.

My brother Bill is diagnosed with brain cancer. Fran and I visit him as he grows weaker; his valiant wife Rosie oversees hospice, keeping him at home until the end. My father kneels at the coffin, face pressed against it, lets out a long groan. His mother and father, his brother, his wife, and now his son. The only time I ever see swans flying is while in Long Island for Billy's funeral. The sight of these heavy gorgeous birds on the wing, is stunning, unforgettable. The pain of Billy's going is still with us.

10 Haskell Street

After five years, the divorce is finalized. I don't have enough money to buy a house in Cambridge, where everyone wants to live. I should be looking in Somerville or Arlington. But I've got used to overcoming obstacles. I'm so tough, I just keep looking in Cambridge. Of course I have moments of fear or panic. I remember sitting on the couch sobbing, "It's hard and scary, God. It's hard and scary."

So that spring I get tenacious with my real estate broker, ambushing her in her office Saturday mornings when the for-sale listings first come out. For weeks she arrives and finds me waiting, having already perused the new offerings. And voila! On one such morning I've found a condo (half a house) in North Cambridge with two bedrooms and a huge yard. The price is attractive, only $180,000, because the folks renting it are in a feud with the owners and resist renovations and showings. I ask Pop for the additional $20,000 I will need, and he says yes.

17 Haskell Street, near Davis and Porter Squares, complete with gorgeous huge back yard and deck, robin's egg blue with a white picket fence, no less. It's perfect, a dream come true. Bob, my boyfriend of the moment, refers to "Kitty's shining house."

I give POA to my real estate lawyer and go to the Cape for two weeks while she buys the house for me. For years thereafter I return to that glorious old cottage overlooking Wellfleet Bay. Wellfleet becomes my most spiritual place of renewal, and to this day I can't imagine a summer without it.

At first I'm so worried about changing jobs that I don't unpack all the boxes, fearing I will have to sell the house for want of money. But after a short-lived job at the Appalachian Mountain Club, I find the perfect job directing publications at the Episcopal Divinity School. It's in Harvard Square and I often walk home from there. One of my boyfriends at that time is Moody, a Texan who wears cowboy boots.

Pop seems to grow more distant. I see him less and less. Now it's mostly me visiting him and Jane. She's good for him, but very possessive; she and I don't like each other, though we're friendly enough on the surface. Her family adores him, which is great for his very large and hungry ego, but I feel they are replacing me in his heart. I lost my playful papa in 1942 when he went away to war, and I lose him again in 1997.

My precious daughter gets married in October. Beautiful wedding in Central Park by a pond. I am so happy for her, but at the same time feel I'm losing her. She's not my little girl any more. At her wedding: her father Gary and his sister Rocki, my step-daughter Kathleen, my old friends Dave Soeiro, Sally Wulff, Sally Kuhn, Eppie Boze, and Pop and Jane and Tony's parents Alan and Barbara Arkin. Dancing with Gary a moving experience—it's as if our bodies remember all that intimacy!

So that year 1997 is remarkably intense. Eight major stress points: finally getting divorced, changing my name; losing my job, starting another; buying a house, moving; child getting married. In addition, the increasing distance from my father. My wonderful therapist Fatima tells me to think of all this as opportunities, not stresses—as "part of life." For relaxation I continue with meditating, and of course aerobics that always refreshes me.

Duncan is helping me a lot, even after he moves to 87 Lakeview and gets a good job. Every Sunday he comes for dinner and makes his spectacular authentic Italian pasta. I'm also having fun going to the singles dances with Christina and Laura many weekends. I'm doing aerobics all the time. My new therapist is invaluable, as is the women's group she facilitates for us. My UU church is an essential rock almost right from the beginning. My dog Jeffie is an indescribable comfort, so devoted, loyal, and fun.

So 1998 presents a brighter and more stable prospect. On January 22 I write, "When I was young I used to wonder how some old people could be so happy. Now I know *why:* We love *all* of life, not just our own."

My therapist graduates me: "You're fine."

I agree. *"I feel as if I'm really starting to have a normal life."*

About the Author

Photo by Amelia Campbell

Kitty Beer grew up in New England and raised her two children in Canada, Germany, and upstate New York. She holds a B.A. from Harvard University, and her M.A. from Cornell University.

Beer's stories and articles, including her work as an environmental journalist, have appeared in print and online in the U.S. and Canada. The story "Mrs. Professor Bostwick" was nominated for the 2021 Pushcart Prize. Beer's series of novels about climate change, titled *Resilience: A Trilogy of Climate Chaos*, reflects an emphasis on the courage of overcoming disaster. The novels in the trilogy are *What Love Can't Do* (2006), *Human Scale* (2010) and *The Hampshire Project* (2017).

Beer is an active member of the Harvard Institute for Learning in Retirement, where she studies a wide variety of subjects. She's a member of the Unitarian Church, the National Writers Union and the Society of Environmental Journalists. She has traveled extensively in Europe, living mostly in London, Paris, and Munich. She speaks French and German and conversational Italian. She is loving and tolerant, but likes to speak truth to power.

www.ingramcontent.com/pod-product-compliance
Lightning Source LLC
Chambersburg PA
CBHW030518080526
44586CB00011B/240